Contents

PART THREE: MAKING THE WORLD A BETTER PLACE

PART FOUR: LOOKING IN THE MIRROR

AMERICA'S OTHER ARMY

THE U.S. FOREIGN SERVICE AND 21ST CENTURY DIPLOMACY

NICHOLAS KRALEV

Also by Nicholas Kralev:

Decoding Air Travel: A Guide to Saving on Airfare and Flying in Luxury

Copyright © 2012 by Nicholas Kralev

Editors: Darrell Delamaide and Markus Nottelmann
Consultant: Barbara Slavin
Cover design by Jennifer Fleischmann
Author photo by Mary Calvert

ISBN-10: 1466446560
ISBN-13: 978-1466446564

First edition: September 2012

Foreword

Why Should We Care About Diplomacy?

The evening news bulletin on Bulgarian National Radio began with a familiar item: Another meeting of the Politburo of the Communist Party's Central Committee. Then the announcer uttered a sentence that left Bulgarians stunned: The country's dictator of 35 years, Todor Zhivkov, had been "relieved of his duties."

It was November 10, 1989. I was only 15 but understood that what had happened was not just a simple personnel change in the government of the Soviet Union's most trusted satellite. Within minutes – though a day late – I learned about the fall of the Berlin Wall. Those events changed my life more fundamentally than anything else I have experienced before or since.

Up to that point, I wanted to be a theater director, but now the theater was in the streets. At daily demonstrations and processions, hundreds of thousands of people expressed themselves freely for the first time in their lives. Not everything was joyful – empty store shelves and snaking lines became a common occurrence. Hoping to help others understand these momentous events, I became a journalist and published my first news story at 18. A year later, while a university student, I became a reporter for the Bulgarian National Television evening news.

As a TV reporter, I had my first encounters with American diplomats at the U.S. Embassy in Bulgaria. From them, and through my studies, I began learning about the role American diplomacy had played in ending the Cold War – and how it was helping the former communist countries of Central and Eastern Europe to transition to democracy and market economy. Eventually, my interest in diplomacy and international affairs led me to the Kennedy School of Government at Harvard, and to being a correspondent for the *Financial Times* and the *Washington Times*.

However, after a couple of years of covering the U.S. State Department and traveling around the world with the secretary of state, I realized that those opportunities provided only momentary and somewhat superficial glimpses into what diplomacy is about. Below the surface, I wanted to know what it is really like to be an American diplomat in the 21st century, especially in a post-September 11 world. What do those people do every day in hundreds of embassies and consulates, when they do not host visiting dignitaries or participate in high-stakes negotiations? On a human level, how does the Foreign Service lifestyle affect its members and their families?

With these questions in mind, in 2003, I set out to write a series of articles about the Foreign Service in the *Washington Times*. As I started visiting overseas posts and talking to dozens of the service's members, more questions arose: How does the work of American diplomats fit into the big picture of U.S. foreign policy? How exactly does it serve the national interest? Do they have sufficient resources to carry out their mission? What kind of skills is the State Department looking for when selecting America's diplomats? How does it train them?

This book is an attempt to answer these questions. It is the product of nine years of research, five round-the-world trips and several shorter ones, visits to over 50 embassies and consulates, and interviews with some 600 diplomats.

The paramount question that guided me throughout this effort was this: Why should we care about diplomacy? I was looking for a more pragmatic and relatable answer than the well-known saying, "When diplomacy fails, war follows." Hopefully, the book will provide such an answer, but let me just say this right at the outset: American diplomacy has a real and lasting impact on millions of people across the globe every day. I have seen that impact with my own eyes. In fact, I have been a beneficiary of it – it set me off on a journey that resulted in my moving to the United States, becoming an American citizen and spending a decade traveling with Madeleine Albright, Colin Powell, Condoleezza Rice and Hillary Clinton.

Moreover, U.S. diplomacy affects the everyday lives of Americans, including their safety and security, their ability to travel and communicate with people in other countries, their employment and overall prosperity. Yet, it is astonishing how little we know about our diplomats, and about their skills and work. I thought I knew more than most people – but those old perceptions went out the window during my very first research trip.

So forget everything you think you know about diplomacy, and enjoy the book!

PART ONE

DIPLOMACY'S SEARCH
FOR IDENTITY

Chapter 1

What Does the Foreign Service Do?

Cameron Munter's mobile phone rang at 3 a.m. Sleep was the last thing on his mind, so he answered the call. "We hear there has been a helicopter crash. Was it one of yours?" the high-ranking Pakistani official asked. Munter could not answer the question – not because he was uninformed, but because he was sworn to secrecy, at least for another few hours.

It was May 2, 2011, and Munter had just watched a live video feed of the raid that killed the world's most notorious terrorist, Osama bin Laden, just 30 miles from where Munter was in Islamabad. But he was not allowed to say a word about it even to the Pakistani government – as had been the case for months – until the official announcement by President Barack Obama in Washington. Keeping the secret had been easy compared to Munter's next challenge: repairing the already tense U.S.-Pakistani relationship, which had been further damaged about three months earlier, when an undercover CIA contractor fatally shot two Pakistanis, claiming self-defense.[1] In the days after bin Laden's death, it fell on Munter and his colleagues to explain to the Pakistani government why it had been kept in the dark about a foreign military operation on its own territory.

Three years earlier, Munter had helped behind the scenes to engineer the election loss of former Serbian Prime Minister Vojislav Koštunica, after evidence emerged that he had approved an attack that burned down a part of the U.S. Embassy in Belgrade, following Washington's recognition of Kosovo's independence from Serbia. And two years before that, Munter had led a team that taught Iraqi provincial authorities how to govern effectively, and trained local judges how to conduct trials and other court proceedings – amid frequent shootings, roadside bombs and rockets. He is an American diplomat.

About the time Munter worked to evacuate that attacked embassy in Belgrade in February 2008, Yuri Kim was in North Korea. She accompanied the New York Philharmonic during a rare concert tour in the communist country. In fact, Kim had helped negotiate the unprecedented visit, which Washington hoped would improve Pyongyang's cooperation in efforts to dismantle its nuclear weapons program. She was involved in those efforts as well. In 2012, now in Turkey, Kim tried to persuade the country to use its influence with neighboring Syria to end the Damascus regime's violent crackdown on anti-government protesters. She, too, is an American diplomat.

Also in 2012, in another one of Turkey's neighbors, Iraq, David Lindwall worked on deals to sell U.S. military aircraft and other equipment worth billions of dollars to the government in Baghdad. A few years earlier, on the other side of the world, Lindwall had participated in successful efforts to reform Guatemala's previously corrupt child-adoption system, which many Americans use, and to improve child nutrition. In Haiti in 2010, he managed the search for missing U.S. citizens after the country's devastating earthquake and helped the local government recover from the disaster. Lindwall's house collapsed from the seismic shock, and he escaped what would have been certain death had he been there at the time. He is also an American diplomat.

After another earthquake, in Japan, a year later, Marc Wall also helped the evacuation of Americans, but his main job was to expand business opportunities for U.S. companies in the world's third-largest economy. In the mid-2000s in Chad, Wall worked with the U.S. military to establish a counterterrorism program in the African country. He also reached out to rebels in Sudan's Darfur region, which neighbors Chad, as part of international efforts to end the violent conflict there. He, too, is an American diplomat.

Just as Wall got ready to leave Chad for Washington in 2007, Anjalina Sen was there already, issuing American passports. Within months, she was in China, issuing U.S. entry visas. Two years later, Sen arrived in Thailand, where she worked to secure protection for refugees from across East Asia, and to resettle some of them in the United States. She is an American diplomat.

Gavin Sundwall's first time in a Panamanian jail was in 1998. Two Satanist killers sat across from him – one staring at Sundwall with menacingly piercing green eyes, as if sizing him up for execution. Fortunately for Sundwall, he was just visiting the criminals, who were U.S. citizens, to make sure they were being treated humanely, and to relay any messages to their families back home. In early 2012, now in Kabul, Sundwall helped put out major public relations fires after U.S. service members burned copies of the Quran, the holy book of Islam, and another soldier killed 16 Afghan civilians, mostly women and children, in cold blood. Sundwall is also an American diplomat.

Defining the mission

How can these six people all be diplomats? How can teaching effective governance, participating in nuclear negotiations, organizing a cultural event, reforming a child-adoption system, selling weapons, recovering from a natural disaster, promoting U.S. business, setting up a counterterrorism program, issuing passports and visas, resettling refugees, visiting prisoners, and fixing public relations problems be part of the same profession?

Welcome to the U.S. Foreign Service.

If you are confused just by reading this, imagine if you had to perform all – or even a few – of the above-mentioned duties. And keep in mind that this list is only a partial representation. Because of the growing demands on their profession, America's diplomats have to take on an ever-wider variety of tasks during their careers, whatever their specialty may be. But exactly what purpose do all these activities serve? Is there a direct link between them and specific U.S. interests to justify spending tens of billions of dollars each year to carry them out?

Let's first establish what the U.S. interests are. There is a document that does just that – the National Security Strategy – and every American president issues at least one version of it, based on his or her administration's policy priorities. The latest version was published by the Obama White House in 2010.[2] It identifies three core national interests: the security of the United States, the country's prosperity, and the values it stands for (human rights, democracy and equality). These interests are so fundamental that there is usually political agreement on them, regardless of which party is in power. The current strategy also says that the international system is vital for achieving the U.S. interests.

Another guiding document, the first-ever Quadrennial Diplomacy and Development Review (QDDR) issued by Secretary of State Hillary Clinton also in 2010, elaborates on the importance of the international system.[3] It says that, in order to ensure the security of the United States, the entire world has to be secure and stable, because today's threats, such as terrorism, transnational crime, climate change and pandemic disease, are "global, interconnected, and beyond the power of any one state to resolve."

"We cannot expect to be protected by our geographic position, which historically has been such an advantage for America – I think September 11 demonstrated that conclusively," Clinton told me in June 2012. "In order to maximize the chances that we will enjoy security and tranquility here at home, we have to be in effect the chairman of the board of the world – to try to get friends and allies to work with us, to mitigate problems, to bring about solutions that neutralize or prevent non-state actors, as well as rogue states, from taking actions that put the lives and property of our people and our friends and allies at risk."

The QDDR also links America's prosperity to global economic growth, due to the interdependence of national economies and the openness of world markets. "Shocks and economic disruptions in other countries can and do have profound consequences for the U.S. economy and the American people, including job losses and declining standards of living," the document says.

To sum up, for the United States to be truly secure and prosperous, the whole world has to be secure and prosperous – and that is "the world we seek," according to the National Security Strategy. At the same time, the White House recognizes "the world as it is" and acknowledges that the U.S. government must deal with it. What tools does Washington have to work toward these goals? Certainly, the best military on the planet, but mainly as a safeguard of peace and stability, rather than an agent of change, because armed conflict is hardly the first choice of responsible statecraft. There is another option, much less costly in terms of both financial and human resources – that's right, it's called diplomacy.

So this is the dual mission of the U.S. Foreign Service: *It deals with the world as it is and tries to reshape it into a more secure and prosperous place, so the United States can be secure and prosperous.* "We are not out here just because it's intellectually stimulating, but because we serve U.S. interests," James Zumwalt, a career diplomat since 1981, told me in 2011 in Tokyo, where he was deputy chief of mission. The chief of mission is, of course, the ambassador.

Determining the strategy and tactics

The two parts of the Foreign Service's mission are parallel, and many diplomats work on both at the same time. Clearly, the mission is very complex and ambitious, but let's bring these lofty phrases down to earth and see what they really mean. How do American diplomats deal with the world as it is? In other words, what is their strategy for accomplishing the first part of their mission?

The beginning of the answer is in the classic definition of diplomacy. As the QDDR points out, "the word *diplomat* comes from *diploma* – an instrument of formal accreditation issued by a government to envoys officially designated to represent another nation." Depending on which edition of the Oxford English Dictionary you open, you will find diplomacy described, perhaps with slightly different wording, as the management of a country's affairs with other states by representatives living abroad.

This is the first of four strategies, each of which naturally has its own tactics. In the case of managing bilateral relations, the tactics include negotiating treaties and other agreements – on trade, arms control, children's issues, criminal matters – as well as monitoring developments in the host country to make sure U.S. interests are not being hurt by legislation or other actions, and trying to neutralize those actions if they do harm the United States. American diplomats also explain U.S. policies to their host government, and the host country's policies and positions to policymakers in Washington.

While managing official relations is mostly done behind the scenes, the next two strategies that also fall in the category of traditional diplomacy could not be more public. The first is the representational role of the Foreign Service before the government and people of another country – at various events, in the media and elsewhere. The second is assisting American citizens abroad by issuing them temporary passports, registering their newborn children or helping them out of danger, which we will discuss in Chapter 7.

Finally, the Foreign Service works with other countries on transnational issues, such as terrorism, weapons of mass destruction, energy, the environment, human rights, and many others. This is where the so-called multilateral diplomacy comes into play. It is managed by international organizations like the United Nations and the North Atlantic Treaty Organization (NATO), where the United States is also represented permanently.

So to review, the four strategies to accomplish the first part of the Foreign Service's dual mission – dealing with the world as it is – are: *managing relations with other countries; publicly representing the United States and its people; assisting American citizens abroad; and addressing transnational issues.* We will look at the tactics of each strategy – or function of traditional diplomacy – in detail in Part Two.

Now let's look at the second part of the mission. No doubt, making the world more secure and prosperous is an enormous undertaking, and the strategy Washington has chosen to tackle it is equally daunting: *It seeks to ensure good governance in as much of the world as possible.* What does that mean? Good governance exists when a country's government is accountable to its people and takes care of them by providing essential services, respecting human rights, guaranteeing safety and security, and building a functioning economy. The absence of these conditions, U.S. officials say, creates a cycle of poverty and violence – it disenfranchises citizens who may turn to terrorism and other criminal activities, and produces internal instability that could easily provoke a regional conflict and harm U.S. interests.

This is why the QDDR says that one of the things American diplomats do is try to "make life better" for people around the world.

"Many of the problems we face in keeping America safe and prosperous do have their origins in the living conditions of people in other countries," said Anne-Marie Slaughter, who headed the QDDR process as Clinton's first director of policy planning at the State Department. "Whether it's alienation, violent extremism, disease, poverty or environmental degradation that ultimately drags down countries, it hurts global security and the world economy as a whole, and it certainly reduces U.S. markets. All of those are issues that can't really be resolved by traditional diplomacy," said Slaughter, who is now a professor of politics and international affairs at Princeton University.

Whether you agree or disagree that American diplomats should try to improve the lives of people in faraway countries, there is a consensus on this among Democratic and Republican administrations.

"More peaceful, prosperous and democratic countries are not only good for the people living in them, but also good for the United States and our global goals," Clinton said. "There is no doubt that, where people feel that their aspirations can be addressed through their political and economic systems, and where they have accountable governments, they are more likely to be partners in helping us solve problems."

The National Security Strategy puts it this way: "Proactively investing in stronger societies and human welfare is far more effective and efficient than responding after state collapse."

Condoleezza Rice, secretary of state in the George W. Bush administration, fully agreed with the Obama administration's argument. "Ungoverned and poorly governed countries and spaces that can't act as responsible sovereigns end up giving their territory over to terrorists, drug traffickers and human traffickers. And those are then dangerous places from which a lot of transnational threats emerge," Rice told me, citing Afghanistan as a prime example of a failed state that provided safe haven to those who attacked the United States on September 11, 2001. "Nobody thought that we'd have to worry about the fifth-poorest country in the world, an ungoverned territory or a failed state. But that's not a matter of largesse and compassion – it's a matter of security." When Rice was in office from 2005 until 2009, she labeled the work of reshaping the world *transformational diplomacy.*

So what are the tactics of this strategy? How does the Foreign Service try to bring about good governance and make people's lives better – the function of transformational diplomacy?

The first tactic is teaching and guidance, and the second is financial assistance. The areas they cover include organizing free elections, building and reforming democratic institutions, infrastructure, education and health care systems, creating independent media – and running specific programs, some of which I mentioned when introducing the six diplomats at the beginning of the chapter.

I hope it is now clear why those officers have helped foreign countries to improve child nutrition and adoption, recover from natural disasters, resettle refugees and learn how to fight terrorism. We will discuss these tactics in detail in Chapter 8, but it is worth noting the importance of development work in making the world more secure and prosperous. Those efforts are spearheaded by the U.S. Agency for International Development (USAID), which is a key part of the Foreign Service.

What about the third core U.S. interest outlined in the National Security Strategy – the signature American values of human rights, democracy and equality? Where do they fit in? As we saw, the U.S. seeks a world in which countries are led by responsible and accountable governments. That essentially means democratically elected governments that afford their citizens human rights, respect, dignity and equality.

But more than that, U.S. diplomats say they are guided by these fundamental values in everything they do, including when they deal with the world as it is. Sometimes, standing up for those values may collide with short-term U.S. national security interests in places like China and the Middle East, which requires a very careful balancing act.

Modest resources for diplomacy

To accomplish its ambitious mission, the U.S. Foreign Service requires truly global reach on a permanent basis, as well as an exceptional workforce backed by sufficient funding, the trust of the country's political leadership and the confidence of the American people. We will see if and to what extent U.S. diplomats enjoy trust and confidence later in the book, so let's now focus on their resources and area of operation.

When it comes to global reach, the United States is unsurpassed. Currently, it has diplomatic relations with 190 countries. The United Nations has 193 members, so the U.S. is missing only three: Cuba, Iran and North Korea. There are 275 U.S. embassies, consulates and other permanent missions around the world, 95 of which are located outside of national capitals, according to a March 2012 fact sheet from the State Department, which is the Foreign Service's home agency in Washington. "We are so enmeshed in so many ways in the rest of the world, and American citizens are everywhere, that I think our reach will be global for some time to come," said Marc Wall, the former ambassador to Chad mentioned at the beginning of the chapter, whom I met in 2011 at the embassy in Tokyo, where he was the counselor for economic affairs.

Now let's look at the human and financial resources provided to American diplomacy. According to the same fact sheet, the U.S. has 7,920 diplomats, whose official designation is *Foreign Service officers*. Let's be more inclusive and add the Foreign Service technical and support staff – the *specialists*, as opposed to the already-mentioned *generalists*. That figure is 5,710, which brings the total number of Foreign Service members to 13,630. Why not be even more liberal and include the 10,631 Civil Service employees the State Department has across the U.S.? Finally, let's not forget the 44,764 foreign nationals working at U.S. missions abroad and officially known as locally engaged staff.

So the State Department, the federal agency charged with carrying out the country's foreign policy – dealing with an increasingly complex and dangerous world, and making it more secure and prosperous – has a grand total of 69,025 employees at its disposal. Any idea how many people serve in the U.S. Armed Forces? According to Pentagon data, as of December 31, 2011, the active-duty military personnel are 1.4 million.[4] If we add civilian employees, the number exceeds 2 million.[5]

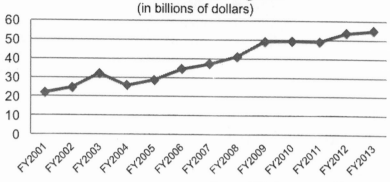

Total Budget for Department of State and Other International Programs
(in billions of dollars)

Source: U.S. Government Printing Office

The budget figures tell a similar story. For the 2012 fiscal year, the so-called discretionary budget authority for the State Department and other international programs, including development and foreign aid, totaled $53 billion, according to White House data.[6] That is not much more than the military's medical expenses.[7] The total 2012 discretionary budget authority for the Department of Defense was $646 billion.[8] A fiscal year for the federal government runs from October 1 to September 30.

As little as $53 billion may be compared to $646 billion, it is still a lot of money – it exceeds the annual gross domestic product (GDP) of more than 100 countries, according to the International Monetary Fund.[9] So is it being spent wisely? U.S. diplomats say they always strive for that, and we will see if their efforts are successful later in the book. But in general, they insist the American people are getting a great return on their investment. With effective diplomatic and development work, "we avert the need to commit overwhelming military resources" to address foreign challenges, and "we reduce the burdens on American taxpayers," the QDDR says.

It adds that sustainable U.S. leadership in the world "requires the restoration of our own strengths and capacities at home" – "a dynamic economy that generates jobs, reforming our health care and education systems, rebuilding our physical infrastructure, and tackling our government's deficit and debt."

Anne-Marie Slaughter said the government has "to be able to explain to someone who doesn't have access to good food and good health care in the United States why their tax dollars should be going to health care or education halfway around the world." In addition, "we know that, unless we fix our own problems, our influence is reduced," she said. "There is no question that people are less likely to look to us when our economy is not growing very fast, our health care is incredibly expensive and complicated, and our education system needs reform. So we must fix our problems at home, because it does affect what our diplomats do. But there are many countries in which we still look like a paradise in comparison, and a tremendous part of the world where they are still very grateful and eager for our assistance."

The difficulty of building a fan base

It is not just the Foreign Service that deems the funding for diplomacy and development insufficient. Many political appointees from both parties who have held national security posts – inside and outside the State Department – have decried the limited resources. Perhaps the most prominent was former Defense Secretary Robert Gates, a Republican who served in both the Bush and Obama administrations from 2006 until 2011. He surprised many in Washington when he called on Congress to increase the State Department budget significantly – "blasphemy" for some at the Pentagon, as he put it.

"What is clear to me is that there is a need for a dramatic increase in spending on the civilian instruments of national security – diplomacy, strategic communications, foreign assistance, civic action, and economic reconstruction and development," Gates said in a speech at Kansas State University in 2007. "We must focus our energies beyond the guns and steel of the military, beyond just our brave soldiers, sailors, Marines and airmen. We must also focus our energies on the other elements of national power that will be so crucial in the coming years." He also noted that, when former Chairman of the Joint Chiefs of Staff Admiral Michael Mullen was chief of Naval Operations in the middle of the last decade, he said he would give part of his budget to the State Department "in a heartbeat," provided the money was spent wisely.[10]

In another speech, at the Center for Strategic and International Studies in Washington in 2008, Gates acknowledged that "getting the additional resources and authorities for soft power is not an easy sell politically," because it "simply does not have the built-in domestic constituency of defense programs." For example, "the F-22 aircraft is produced by companies in 44 states – that's 88 senators," he said in reference to the two U.S. senators representing each state.[11]

Things have improved since Gates' speeches – at the time, there were about 6,600 Foreign Service officers, and the State Department budget was $36 billion, as cited by the secretary. However, the current levels are still not nearly enough to fill all vacant positions around the world, allow employees to take short-term assignments at other government agencies, which benefits both sides, and to permit a regular training flow that is vital for maintaining a skilled and effective workforce, diplomats said. They also pointed out that, with well over 2 million people in the U.S. Armed Forces and a large national network supporting them and their families, chances are that most Americans know someone connected to the military in some way. At the same time, the vast majority of the country's population has never met anyone working in diplomacy – after all, the work of the Foreign Service takes place outside the United States.

Building a fan base remains one of the Foreign Service's most formidable challenges. As we saw, this is not about being liked or popular, but about having enough resources and backing for carrying out a mission of supreme importance to the country. After a decade of studying the issue and talking to hundreds of people about it, my conclusion is that the Foreign Service is unable to form a meaningful support base because of a lack of knowledge and understanding about what it does among all parts of American society, including to some extent on Capitol Hill.

There are two reasons for that: one external and one internal. First, to most people, diplomacy is just not that interesting. When I broach the subject with ordinary Americans, I often hear, "Soldiers fight and diplomats talk." Everyone seems to know what fighting means, but how exciting can talk be? Another comment I get is, "It must be fascinating to be a diplomat." But those who say that usually refer to what they perceive as a glamorous lifestyle and rubbing shoulders with powerful people – and meeting with foreign officials and writing cables to Washington are hardly adventures one can tell thrilling stories about. Of course, diplomats do much more than talk and hold meetings, but one has to be interested in learning about that to appreciate it.

The second reason for the lack of understanding actually lies with the Foreign Service. It is really bad at promoting itself – and that has little to do with being shy or modest, and lot to do with not being able to articulate what diplomats do in specific human terms, and how it relates directly to concrete national interests. I have been around the Foreign Service and dealt with government bureaucracies for more than a decade, but even I cringe when diplomats tell me that what they do is "defend U.S. interests" or "serve the American people" or "advance a positive agenda." What on earth does that mean? How can most human beings relate to such vague and abstract phrases to describe one's profession? Even something slightly more specific like "engaging with foreign audiences" is not entirely clear. Some people think it means sipping fancy drinks at extravagant cocktail parties. And how about "Diplomacy is about communication"? Well, so is marriage.

Some Foreign Service officers attributed their limited ability to promote their work to the Smith-Mundt Act of 1948, a Cold War-era law that bans the State Department from propagandizing Americans through information intended for foreign publics. Obviously, explaining the nuts and bolts of what they do and why it serves U.S. interests was never part of the "propaganda" that foreigners might have been exposed to. Moreover, in the 21st century, anything the department puts on any website can be accessed by U.S. citizens. A bill to "modernize" the law was introduced in Congress in 2012, seeking "to authorize the domestic dissemination of information and material about the United States intended primarily for foreign audiences, and for other purposes."[12]

Excuses aside, let's look at an example of a taxpayer-funded program the State Department calls "specific." In May 2012, it announced $1.5 million for a joint project with the Organization for Economic Cooperation and Development (OECD) to improve governance and civil society in the Middle East. A department press release said this: "Specific activities include assisting the governments of Jordan, Libya, Morocco and Tunisia in reviewing and assessing institutions, policies and practices supporting the implementation of open government principles at both central and local levels, as well as improving coordination between government and national civil society."[13] Such a description may be specific for the bureaucracy, but it is hardly so for the public. How about something like this: "Concrete activities include abolishing government media censorship efforts, creating an ombudsman office and establishing an anti-corruption commission"?

There is no question that simplifying and generalizing is very difficult when it comes to explaining the Foreign Service. American diplomacy in the 21st century is complicated and diverse – probably more diverse than any other profession. As one mid-level officer, Cynthia Haley, put it, "I've negotiated with foreign ministers, but I've also watched people's luggage, and I've walked a visitor's dog – that's the range we are talking about." As hard as it may be, educating Americans about diplomacy and the Foreign Service is just too important to be ignored, because the work of U.S. diplomats affects people's lives in the U.S. and around the world every single day.

More importantly, a better understanding of what the Foreign Service does, and why it is vital to American national interests, will likely improve the resources for diplomacy and development, said Hillary Clinton. "Everybody who does understand it, like Bob Gates, supports greater resources, because they have seen firsthand what a difference these professionals, with their various areas of expertise, can make in furthering American values, interests and security," Clinton said. Even though many members of Congress have a keen interest in diplomacy and appreciate the work of the Foreign Service, there are still funding challenges, said Jack Lew, chief of staff in the Obama White House and former deputy secretary of state for management and resources. Lew co-chaired the QDDR process with Anne-Marie Slaughter. "What we've tried to do in this administration is make a case that we have national security needs that come in multiple colors, and they all have to be considered part of our national security budget. I think that argument is catching on, but it's always going to be hard," said Lew, who was also director of the Office of Management and Budget in both the Obama and Clinton administrations.

The humanizing of diplomacy

One way to make diplomacy more interesting and accessible is to try not to simplify it, but to humanize it – and the fact that it touches so many people, even though they may not realize that, is a good start. There are actually three categories of beneficiaries of the humanizing of American diplomacy that has occurred in recent years: U.S. citizens, foreign publics and the Foreign Service members.

Obviously, diplomacy has always been done by humans, but for decades it was an almost exclusive club of mostly white male elites who dealt with foreign countries' elites, mainly their governments. That is no longer the case. The Foreign Service is still very selective, because it naturally wants the most qualified candidates – to quote Yuri Kim, whom we met at the beginning of the chapter, "We aspire to be elite, though not elitist." But today any U.S. citizen between the ages of 21 and 60 who passes a written and oral exam can become a diplomat, even without a college degree. While the service still has a long way to go, now it looks more and more like America – in terms of ethnicity, gender, religion, educational and professional background, and even country of birth – as we will see in the next chapter.

In addition to being an exclusive club, diplomacy has long been viewed as a profession practiced in a stratosphere of officialdom, far out of the reach of "real people," and with little regard for their opinions, aspirations and desires.

That has changed dramatically since 2001. "One of the biggest shifts from the 20th to the 21st century is that keeping America safe and prosperous is no longer just about maintaining certain relations with other governments," said Anne-Marie Slaughter. "We need to connect with the people of those countries, but also to connect them to Americans and to each other." In many parts of the world, citizens are not nearly as well organized and socially linked to others as in Western democracies. Where they are at least somewhat connected, the Foreign Service works with non-governmental and other civil-society groups, think tanks, professional organizations, universities and other academic institutions. And where a functioning civil society does not exist, U.S. diplomats help to create it.

"Diplomacy is not only about government to government anymore, but also human to human," said Victoria Nuland, State Department spokesperson under Hillary Clinton and a former ambassador to NATO. "What we try to do, and get other countries to do, is empower people. American diplomacy is increasingly done from the bottom up. We recognize that, with the craving for democracy and freedom of expression, with the Internet and social media, countries are changing as much from the bottom up as they are from the top down. So we need to know those people and be connected to them."

How does the Foreign Service empower ordinary people? Sometimes it gives them grants to start organizations, implement community projects or hold events – or just advises them how to do those things. And sometimes it simply seeks their views on the situation in their country. Michael Fitzpatrick, currently deputy chief of mission in Lima, Peru, whom I met in 2003 at the U.S. Embassy in Brussels, said that many of his private contacts in African and other developing countries have told him, "You are the first person who has asked me what I think. Even my own government doesn't care." Having "worked on political issues on five continents, I continue to be taken by the similarity of reactions from many people all around the world," he said.

The Foreign Service has been engaging with foreign publics for decades through cultural events, exchange programs and the media. But that function used to be separate from the substantive diplomacy and was carried out only by designated public affairs officers. Today, it is called public diplomacy and is being integrated in everything the Foreign Service does – in fact, the service cannot truly fulfill its mission without it. The State Department has become a global leader in using social media and the Internet in general for foreign policy purposes, and Clinton has encouraged further innovation in communicating directly with people in other countries.

Public diplomacy, which we will discuss in detail in Chapter 6, is now supposed to be everyone's business, including officers working in political, economic and consular affairs. It is also a major part of the job of ambassadors, as well as senior State Department officials in Washington, both at home and during their foreign travels. Longtime political and economic officers say that reporting, analysis and meeting with government officials used to be their main daily duties. In recent years, however, they have had to broaden their horizons, get out of their offices more often, reach out to private groups and even individual citizens, give media interviews and public speeches, and participate in various other events.

It is ironic that the Foreign Service has had to become more open and friendly to private citizens in foreign countries just as U.S. embassies have tightened their security, which hardly makes them welcoming – some actually look more like fortresses. At the same time, as the QDDR points out, "very real threats to our people have over the years required us to limit the movements of our personnel. This has restricted their ability to work, particularly in those very dangerous places where their operations on the ground may be most urgently needed." Under Clinton, the State Department has been trying to find the right balance between managing the risks and allowing diplomats "the flexibility they need to complete mission objectives within a country and to establish new platforms for outreach beyond the embassy and capital," as we will see in Chapter 12.

Foreign publics are not the only beneficiaries of the Foreign Service's attempts to make diplomacy more open and inclusive. The State Department has reached out to U.S. businesses, nongovernmental organizations, the academic and scientific communities, the cultural and entertainment sector, and even private Americans. "We will embrace new partnerships" that can help U.S. diplomats "promote open governments around the world that are accountable and participatory," the QDDR says. In other words, while current efforts are just baby steps given their huge potential, the State Department is trying to empower not only people in other countries, but Americans as well. For companies, foundations and other nonprofits interested in helping to build business capacity, improve access to finance, enhance science research capabilities or expand educational opportunities in developing countries, there is an office at the State Department called the Global Partnership Initiative.[14]

The last aspect to the humanizing of diplomacy that has emerged in recent years has to do with making the huge State Department bureaucracy friendlier, more accessible and transparent to employees. There are still big problems to be addressed, as we will see in Chapters 11 and 12, but important strides have been made in taking care of the employees and their families. The department has expanded the previously almost non-existent training for mid-level and senior officers and increased employment opportunities for the spouses of Foreign Service members. It has also recognized the partners of gay diplomats, with most benefits offered to heterosexual spouses, including diplomatic passports – except foreign same-sex partners, who are not allowed to become U.S. citizens, because the federal government does not recognize same-sex marriage.

Challenging diplomats' identity

Kerry O'Connor and John Nylin's first day as Foreign Service officers was September 10, 2001 – on that Monday, they began their orientation class, known as A-100, at the Foreign Service Institute outside Washington. They both had left good private-sector jobs and taken significant pay cuts, but they wanted to serve their country and see the world.

What happened the next day altered any expectations O'Connor and Nylin had about their new line of work. It was clear the game had changed – what that meant remained to be seen, but it had certainly become more dangerous. If a terrorist group hiding in Afghanistan could kill nearly 3,000 people on the U.S. mainland, American interests around the world, primarily diplomatic missions, were obvious targets more than ever before. But that did not scare away the 104th A-100 class – or any other U.S. diplomats, for that matter. "On September 12, everybody showed up to work," Nylin recalled in 2011 at the embassy in Tokyo, where he worked on economic and trade policy. "We all stuck with it."

There are few professions that have changed as much as diplomacy has because of the terrorist attacks in New York and Washington. The shift has been so big that diplomats have had to acquire skills and perform duties that were never expected of them before, and were not even associated with diplomacy. "That challenged our identity," said Michael Hammer, currently assistant secretary of state for public affairs and a Foreign Service officer since 1988. "We knew what we came in to do, but all of a sudden we were asked to do something different."

We already discussed some of those differences, and we will outline the rest shortly, but let's first look at the big picture in a historical context. Here is how the Obama National Security Strategy describes the Foreign Service's current duties: "Our diplomacy and development capabilities must help prevent conflict, spur economic growth, strengthen weak and failing states, lift people out of poverty, combat climate change and epidemic disease, and strengthen institutions of democratic governance." The reason for these demanding tasks, as we saw, is the Foreign Service's mission of making the world more secure and prosperous.

Now let's review two National Security Strategies from immediately before September 11, beginning with the 1990 document issued by President George H. W. Bush, the first after the end of the Cold War.[15] For decades before the fall of the Berlin Wall in 1989, U.S. foreign policy had been defined by containment of the communist threat, and the mission of diplomacy had been to help prevent countries from adopting a communist system and to avoid war with the Soviet Union. With the old threat gone, American foreign policy spent the next decade looking for a new focus, and so did the Foreign Service.

The Bush strategy listed as an objective "a stable and secure world, fostering political freedom, human rights and democratic institutions." But it did not link that directly to the internal security of the United States, and it certainly did not charge the Foreign Service with transforming the world. In fact, it said that "our first priority in foreign policy remains solidarity with our allies and friends." Why? Because "we have been blessed with large oceans east and west, and friendly neighbors north and south," but "many of our closest friends and allies" are not so lucky. What a different time, was it not? The 1990 document did not connect U.S. prosperity with economic growth abroad, either. It described "promoting market-oriented structural reforms in Eastern Europe and the developing world, or aiding refugees and disaster victims" simply as a "humanitarian goal," and said that Americans have a "responsibility" to "do our part."

Similar statements could be found in the 1996 National Security Strategy issued by President Bill Clinton.[16] It cited efforts to "promote democracy and human rights," as well as "alleviate human suffering and pave the way for progress toward establishing democratic regimes," but it provided no direct link to the core U.S. national interests of security and prosperity. In fact, as Madeleine Albright told me toward the end of her tenure as Clinton's secretary of state in 2000, "there are humanitarian interests that rise to the level of national interests." That was the justification for Washington's intervention to end the conflicts in Bosnia and Kosovo during the 1990s.

The 1996 Clinton strategy begins to recognize many of the emerging transnational threats I mentioned earlier, as well as the need to "pursue our goals through an enlarged circle" that includes "private and nongovernmental groups." Actually, it listed so many challenges, professed so many interests and called for so much involvement around the world that there could be no mistake about it: the demands on the Foreign Service were about to grow tremendously. The problem was that, as the United States extended its global reach diplomatically, the resources for diplomacy decreased significantly. Budgets were slashed and hiring in the service slowed down and eventually stopped completely.

Unlike the core national interests, America's new global engagement did not enjoy bipartisan support in Washington. Many Republican members of Congress openly opposed and even derided it. The late Warren Christopher, Albright's predecessor in the Clinton administration, told me in 2004 that those congressmen boasted about how little they knew about foreign policy, "and then proceeded to cut our funding. A number of them proudly indicated they had never had a passport and didn't want to have one."

Against that backdrop, U.S. diplomats had to adapt to new realities and learn new skills of nurturing democracies and helping to end genocide and ethnic cleansing. Still, what became known as nation-building was fairly limited at the end of the last century. Most of the Foreign Service still practiced traditional diplomacy on a government-to-government level, even when helping countries in Eastern Europe during their transition from totalitarian regimes to democracy and market economy. So while the new demands of the 1990s challenged diplomats' identity, it was September 11 that marked the start of an identity crisis in the Foreign Service.

'Shock to the system'

When George W. Bush was elected president at the end of 2000, U.S. diplomats were not quite sure how their work might change. During the campaign, Bush had promised a "humble" foreign policy and criticized the Clinton administration's appetite for active international engagement. "If we don't stop extending our troops all around the world in nation-building missions, then we are going to have a serious problem coming down the road. And I'm going to prevent that," Bush said during a debate with his Democratic opponent Al Gore, Clinton's vice president.[17]

I spoke extensively during the campaign with Condoleezza Rice, who was Bush's chief foreign policy adviser at the time. She complained that the Clinton administration had inserted itself in too many places and was too involved in the internal affairs of foreign countries, including Russia. "Let's get out of Russian domestic politics," she told me. "Let's get back to the state-to-state great-power relationship in which we deal with the issues." Does not sound anything like transformational diplomacy, does it?

Bush's appointment of Colin Powell, a widely respected retired Army general and former chairman of the Joint Chiefs of Staff, as secretary of state gave the Foreign Service hope that the new president might want an active foreign policy after all. In reality, "it was a new administration with very strong personalities and no real foreign policy," Powell told me after leaving office in 2005. "A lot of time had to be spent creating something." Many diplomats sensed the lack of direction and continued doing what they had done until then.

After September 11, 2001, it became clear that military and other unilateral action – not diplomacy – was the White House's preferred method for dealing with the aftermath of the attacks. Still, maintaining relations with nearly 200 countries takes a lot of time and effort, so U.S. diplomats had no shortage of work. In fact, they had to learn a new skill: how to sell deeply unpopular policies to skeptical – even hostile – foreign governments and publics. That became especially difficult when Bush decided to invade Iraq in 2003, but Foreign Service officers around the world did their best to explain Washington's point of view. Only three of them resigned over the Iraq war. The bigger problem I discovered while visiting dozens of embassies in 2003 and 2004 was that many officers were not quite sure how what they did every day fit into the big picture. Some even said that they felt the White House did not fully appreciate their work, though that perception all but disappeared during Bush's second term.

"It has become increasingly difficult for American diplomats to sell our view of how the world should work, because many countries see us as the biggest challenge," a mid-level officer in Africa told me in 2003. "The world wants us to lead, but also to compromise. You can't organize 200 countries unilaterally. The more we move away from collaborative efforts, the harder it is for the world to follow. They don't just want to salute."

The United States being seen as an impediment to peace and stability was a huge surprise to the Foreign Service. Like the heavy new demands on diplomacy in the 1990s, that realization and what many diplomats described as the "militarization of foreign policy" challenged their identity.

By the end of Bush's first term, it was clear that Iraq would not be stabilized by military means alone, so the Pentagon handed responsibility for the country's reconstruction over to the State Department. Suddenly, hundreds of diplomats were needed to serve at the embassy in Baghdad every year.

When Condoleezza Rice became secretary of state in 2005, the administration created joint civilian-military expeditionary forces called Provincial Reconstruction Teams and tasked them with stabilizing Iraq province by province. Hundreds more Foreign Service members had to staff those units. Without almost any training, they were thrown into a war zone – protected by the military, but without weapons themselves – and asked to do things they had never done in their lives. We will discuss what is known as *expeditionary diplomacy* in detail in Chapter 9, but it required nothing short of building a functioning society almost from scratch. That included creating a political process – sometimes even preventing rival groups from killing each other – and an economy, as well a judicial, education and health care systems. U.S. diplomats had to deal with urban planning, infrastructure, paving roads and securing electricity and water.

Such reconstruction teams actually originated in Afghanistan, and many of their principles were embedded in permanent U.S. missions in poor and weak countries in Africa, South Asia and elsewhere. As a result, thousands of Foreign Service members have already participated in this kind of transformational diplomacy. It will be difficult for the rest to avoid it, because work in hardship posts is now a requirement for promotion to the senior Foreign Service.

"The Iraq war was a shock to the system," said Michael Hammer. "We hadn't worked in war zones and done things like infrastructure and local governance, which we had not come in trained and expected to do. You have to go back to the Vietnam generation to find people who did things like that, and it wasn't quite the same. But now, if we have to do nation-building again or pass certain skills on to foreign governments, we know how to do it. We've come out a stronger Foreign Service as a result."

Rice said that diplomacy is a "different business" today from what it was just a few years ago. American diplomats must be "prepared to go to hard places and really get involved in people's lives," she said. She recalled that her views were very different before 2001, but "September 11 changed all that," because a failed state – Afghanistan – had harbored Osama bin Laden and his al-Qaida group while they were plotting to attack the United States.

"When I became secretary, I felt that the Foreign Service mostly existed in the halls of foreign ministries and did its work mostly with foreign governments," Rice told me in early 2012. "Modern diplomacy is much less about writing reporting cables and much more the diplomacy of deed – whether it's being out helping to pave the way for USAID to do its work in the Guatemalan highlands, or in AIDS clinics in Botswana, or working with the military in Kabul and Baghdad in a very seamless way. I was really surprised that we had as many people serving in Germany, with just over 80 million people, as we had in India, with a population of more than a billion. In fact, there were two Foreign Services – one that served in Vienna, Berlin and Paris, and another one that served in Nigeria, Guatemala and Iraq."

Cameron Munter, who, as you probably figured out at the beginning of the chapter, was the ambassador to Pakistan during the bin Laden raid, agreed with Rice about the two Foreign Services, admitting that he used to belong to the first one. "I had never been more than an hour's flight from Berlin in my entire career until I went to Iraq in 2006," said Munter, whom I first met in Warsaw in 2004 and later visited in Prague and Islamabad. Although many diplomats said they do not expect to make a habit of serving in war zones, that type of work will continue to be required in other places. "The world is full of hot spots, and we are still going to need to deal with those situations and operate in those kinds of environments," said Marc Wall. Munter noted that the Foreign Service had done pieces of transformational diplomacy "on an ad hoc basis" in the past. "Faced with an opportunity, we'd gone out and done this," he said. "Well, we are not going to wait for opportunities anymore – this will be what we do."

Chapter 2

Who Are America's Diplomats?

When Cameron Munter joined the Foreign Service in 1985, most U.S. diplomats looked like him – about 80 percent were men, with nearly 73 percent white male, according to the Association for Diplomatic Studies and Training, an independent nonprofit.[1] It had been only 13 years since female diplomats were allowed to marry, and security checkpoints were a rarity at U.S. embassies. Before entering the service, Munter had taught history at the University of California at Los Angeles – history, political science and international relations were the most common specialties among his colleagues.

By the time Shane Siegel received a conditional employment offer from the State Department in 2009, a lot had changed. Women represented nearly 40 percent of the service, and the department was actively recruiting minorities. It had lifted the ban on HIV-positive candidates a year earlier. But, as Siegel discovered, at least one frontier remained to be conquered: He was denied medical clearance, because he was a diabetic. It took two years for the rules to change, and the department now permits individual assessment, instead of automatic disqualification.[2] It requires that applicants be able and fit to serve anywhere in the world, including in the toughest hardship posts. "I'm not going to let my diabetes hinder my career in any way," Siegel said over lunch, having self-administered his regular dose of insulin before he started eating. Siegel, who had managed a bar in Rome and worked as an analyst for an Italian investment bank, started his A-100 orientation class in January 2012.

Caleb Goddard was in that same class. He joined the Foreign Service after 16 years in financial journalism. "I was tired of being an observer and wanted to be more of an actor in state affairs," he said at the Foreign Service Institute, where I attended some of the sessions of the 165th A-100 class. Among Siegel and Goddard's col-leagues were lawyers, teachers, business executives, a musician, a neuroscientist, a professional poker player, a paraglider and a Taekwondo black-belt-holder. The age range in the class was be-tween 24 and 55, according to the institute.

As in most recent A-100 classes, there were also war veterans. Theresa Meyer was one of them. A retired Air Force colonel, she was in the very first class of the United States Air Force Academy to in-clude female cadets in 1976. "I really wanted to take an oath of office and serve again, though in a different capacity," she said. Todd McGee's nine-year service in the Navy included a yearlong tour in Afghanistan, where he "accomplished much more not by fighting, but by talking to the Afghans." He soon learned that he could have a job in which he could talk to foreigners for a living.

Sumreen Mirza's path to the Foreign Service began not in Af-ghanistan, but across the border in Pakistan, her parents' homeland. She was an intern at a non-governmental organization in the south-ern port city of Karachi in June 2002, when the U.S. Consulate was attacked in a massive explosion that killed 15 Pakistanis.[3] Mirza's proximity to the terrorist act and the torn-down consulate wall had an unexpected effect: It encouraged her to consider a diplomatic ca-reer. "I thought I could make a difference on the other side of that wall," she told me in 2012 in Baghdad, where she worked as a politi-cal officer covering Iraqi domestic politics. "I had a background in urban planning and environmental engineering, and worked for the Army Corps of Engineers."

Hans Wechsel's background was even more removed from for-eign affairs before he joined the service in 1999. After earning an undergraduate degree in secondary education, he had managed res-taurants in Montana and Oregon, and done seasonal work as a tour guide at Yellowstone National Park. "What a great system for some-one like me, where you can, based on merit and ability, get into a career like this," he said when I first met him in Brussels in 2003. As we will see in Chapter 8, Wechsel went on to direct the Arabian Pen-insula office of the Middle East Partnership Initiative, a major State Department program aimed at creating and strengthening civil soci-ety in a region vital to global stability.[4]

For Traci Goins, diplomacy is a third career. A registered nurse from South Carolina, she was in the health insurance business in the late 1990s, but her company downsized her office at the beginning of the new millennium. Although "they raised my salary and re-duced my responsibilities, I was very unhappy," Goins told me in 2011 in Singapore, where she worked as a consular officer, a mandatory requirement for all new diplomats. "That's when I decided to go to law school, like every other middle-aged idiot who has no idea what they want to do next. I'm really glad I did it. I can't believe they don't teach more basic legal education in high school." After graduation, she got a job at a Philadelphia law firm. "I enjoyed it, and it was a lot of money," but two years later, "I started to get tired, and I had absolutely no personal life," she recalled. As it happened, a friend mentioned the Foreign Service, and Goins was intrigued. "I thought this was perfect. Every couple of years, you get to reinvent yourself and get new bosses and new coworkers. How exciting is that! So I took the Foreign Service exam and got through the first time."

Jimmy Mauldin, a former freight-carrier labor and sales manager from Alabama, also learned about the diplomatic corps by accident. "I was in Ghana as a missionary working as a hospital administrator, and I'd never heard about the Foreign Service until one of the doctors told me about it," Mauldin said in 2012 in Islamabad, where he was an economic officer, having joined the service at the same time as Mirza seven years earlier. "I've come a long way being where I'm now from the peanut fields of southern Alabama," he added.

Clayton Bond can relate to coming a long way, though on a very different level. Black and gay, he belongs to a very small minority, but his mere presence in the diplomatic ranks is a victory of sorts. When his now-spouse, Ted Osius, became a Foreign Service officer in 1989, those found out to be gay were often expelled from the service – that did not change until 1994.[5] Bond, who grew up in Detroit and holds master's degrees from both Harvard and Oxford, was in the same A-100 class as Kerry O'Connor and John Nylin, whom we met in Chapter 1, starting on September 10, 2001.

Exclusive club no longer

To a certain extent, the demographic changes in the Foreign Service have occurred naturally, as the U.S. has become more diverse, and minorities' rights have improved. But those changes are also the result of a deliberate effort prompted by the service's transformational mission and global reach. The expanded engagement with foreign publics, civil society, the private sector and individual citizens is much more effective when those audiences interact with a more humanized U.S. diplomacy that is representative of the American people, State Department officials said. In addition, the new mission requires a wider variety of skills and depth of knowledge than those needed in traditional diplomacy, they said. Because many older people with extensive professional experience, rather than recent college graduates, have joined the Foreign Service in the last decade, the term "junior officer" was replaced with "entry-level officer."

The State Department began a serious push to increase diversity in the service during Colin Powell's tenure in 2001, and those efforts continued under Condoleezza Rice and Hillary Clinton. But despite the good intentions and determination to have a diplomatic corps that truly reflects the nation, the actual progress has been limited. According to an April 2012 fact sheet provided by the department, 83.4 percent of Foreign Service officers are white, 7 percent are Asian-Americans, 5 percent are black and 3.8 percent are Hispanic. In comparison, according to the 2010 census results, 72.4 percent of Americans are white, 12.6 percent are black and 5 percent are Asian. Hispanics were reported to be 16.3 percent, but they may belong to any race, which is why the total number exceeds 100 percent.[6]

The department focuses seriously on attracting minorities, said Jeffrey Levine, director of recruitment, examination and employment from 2010 until he became ambassador to Estonia in the summer of 2012. Then it is up to the candidates to pass the written and oral exams, as there are no special privileges for minorities. Clayton Bond, who worked in the recruitment office in 2005 and 2006, said that high-caliber minority job seekers who would make good diplomats often choose more traditional and better-paying professions like law and medicine. "Our challenge was to show them that our work is no less important and rewarding," he said. Several department officials noted that some applicants may be turned off by the relatively long selection and entrance process – even though it has been shortened, it can still exceed two years.

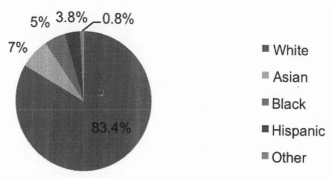

Foreign Service Ethnic Breakdown

5% 3.8% 0.8%
7%
- White
- Asian
- Black
- Hispanic
- Other
83.4%

Source: U.S. Department of State

Overall, diversity is growing, but it will take time for the entire Foreign Service to look like the A-100 classes of the last decade, officials said. Naomi Walcott, a Japanese-American with a nonprofit background in domestic violence and child-abuse issues, was pleasantly surprised by her A-100 class in 2005 – Sumreen Mirza and Jimmy Mauldin were in that same class. "It was very diverse in every possible meaning of the word: age, religion, ethnic and educational background, and I was delighted," Walcott said in 2011 at the embassy in Tokyo, where she was an economic officer. However, another surprise followed when she first arrived at post in 2008. "I was one of very few female officers here. I went through a bit of an existential crisis of wondering if this job was really for me, and whether there was a place for me in this organization. I started talking to other women and men at the mission and other parts of the Foreign Service, asking if it's normal. It wasn't that way at my last post in Honduras, and it turns out it's not really normal in the service. That started a good conversation, and it encouraged me to seek a variety of mentors."

Whatever the challenges, the U.S. Foreign Service is more diverse than other countries' diplomatic corps, which tend to attract mostly people with expertise and background in international affairs, said many American diplomats. "I have a New York City guy in the consular section who was a parole officer on Staten Island before coming here," John Dickson told me in 2003 at the embassy in Mexico City, where he was deputy chief of mission. "I dare you to find another diplomatic service in the world that has a former parole officer."

Serving their country is by far the most cited reason for joining the Foreign Service by American diplomats, though a desire to travel and see the world, as well as financial security, are often mentioned as well. "First and foremost, we are patriots," said Michael Hammer, the assistant secretary of state for public affairs. "We come in because we want to serve the country. We want to advance American interests. What we don't necessarily know when we come in is how we are going to do that."

In spite of all the information new officers gather from the State Department website, existing literature and the many blogs of serving diplomats that have appeared in recent years, none of the newcomers knows exactly what to expect. What they do depends on their specific future assignments in a highly unpredictable career path, and we know from Chapter 1 how different those can be. More broadly, I have found that the only people who truly know what an embassy does every day are those who have worked in an embassy.

Skills old and new

For U.S. diplomacy to succeed in its mission, it needs a workforce that has more than dedication and a desire to serve – it must possess the right knowledge and skills. In Chapter 1, we outlined the functions of traditional and transformational diplomacy, as well as the Foreign Service's duties linked to them, so now let's look at the skill sets required to fulfill those duties.

In traditional diplomacy, what are the skills necessary to manage relations with foreign states, which is usually done by political and economic officers? For decades, those officers had to be good observers and writers, because they mainly monitored developments in their host country and reported them back to Washington in long cables, as we will see in Chapter 4. With the advent of the 24-hour news cycle and instant global communications in the 1990s, the need for factual reporting diminished and the focus on analysis increased. In addition, the best officers use the reporting channels to issue calls for action – when they see opportunities for the U.S. to do something, or threats that Washington needs to address.

The best of the best officers do not stop there. They roll up their sleeves and take the actions they advocate, because they have a solid understanding of U.S. policy priorities and know their boundaries. In 2011, Kristie Kenney, the ambassador to Thailand, requested permission from Washington to help the Southeast Asian country recover from devastating floods that had almost paralyzed it. But Kenney, a former ambassador to the Philippines and Ecuador, and her team did not passively wait to be told what to do. "We put together a flood relief package in literally 24 hours," she told me in Bangkok a few months later. "I even got on the phone with Marine commanders in Okinawa, U.S. Pacific Command, and our commercial guys."

In Chapter 4, we will see how Hans Wechsel, the former restaurant manager, succeeded in overturning a Belgian law that could have been used to legitimize the arrest of senior U.S. officials.

Political and economic officers' other main duty is engagement with their host government, which used to consist mostly of delivering démarches – documents requesting certain actions from that government or just stating U.S. positions – and other formal interactions with the Foreign Ministry.

That is not sufficient anymore, and what is necessary is advocacy of both political and business interests, said Thomas Countryman, who was the political counselor at the embassy in Rome when I first met him in 2004 and became assistant secretary of state for international security and nonproliferation in 2011. "You have to spend a lot of time advocating your positions all over the host government, the parliament, and even the non-governmental community. There are many analysts at think tanks who publish articles in the media and have influence on government decisions. You also have to engage the media and do TV interviews, preferably in the local language – even networks that may not like U.S. policies would be happy to have someone from the U.S. Embassy on their programs." Countryman said he did many of these things when trying to secure Italian support for the war in Iraq, though he wished his Italian had been better so he could have given more TV interviews.

To sum up, traditional diplomacy practiced in the 21st century requires excellence in the following skills: *writing; analysis; negotiations; advocacy; and communication.*

These skills do not only apply to political and economic officers. There are three other career tracks in the Foreign Service, also known as cones: consular, management and public diplomacy. They all require some reporting and obviously good communication skills. Consular officers must also be good analysts of the situation in their host country and the personal circumstances of visa applicants in order to make the best decisions. Management officers have to be good negotiators, because they need support from local authorities for various embassy buildings and operations. More importantly, American diplomats often take assignments in cones different from their own, and some even formally switch tracks in the middle of their career.

Now let's look at the skills required by transformational diplomacy. The above-mentioned ones are clearly necessary here as well, but the mission of reshaping the world and improving people's lives calls for "agents of change," as Victoria Nuland, the State Department spokesperson, put it. What does that mean? American diplomats have learned that, in order to help other countries build democratic institutions, improve infrastructure or reform their economy, just pushing those governments to act is not enough. What is often needed is for the U.S. Embassy in a particular country to train and advise the government and any non-governmental stakeholders involved, and even to propose and oversee specific projects. As I noted in Chapter 1, Marc Wall and his team did some of that in Chad when he was ambassador there. In Chapter 8, we will discuss the major role the embassies in Chile and Guatemala played in implementing judicial and child-adoption reforms, respectively.

So what kind of skills does a diplomat need to accomplish such non-traditional tasks?

First, "a broad understanding of government, politics, economics and science, and the ability to apply that in everyday judgments and decisions," said Francis Ricciardone, currently ambassador to Turkey and a former ambassador to Egypt and the Philippines, where I first met him in 2003.

Second, one must be a quick study, capable of becoming almost an instant expert in a new field. "I remember coming out of Taiwan several years ago to a job in Washington and seeing notices advertising positions of new envoys for biotechnology and conflict minerals," said Marc Wall. "I had no idea what either of those was about. I ended up with a job in the Africa bureau a couple years later, where I was basically responsible for conflict minerals and biotechnology. So we constantly have to take on new issues and learn about new areas as priorities change."

Third, "we need to be entrepreneurial, figure things out and find opportunities that lie beyond the daily threats and distractions," Ricciardone said. For decades, U.S. diplomats in the Middle East were used to "working with kings, sultans and presidents for life," Nuland said. "But they didn't know much about the people in those countries. They didn't know how to promote democracy or manage economic support funds. Then we had the revolutions in Tunisia, Libya, Egypt and Syria. So those officers have had to change and learn new skills, because we need transformational folks." While risk-aversion has long been part of the Foreign Service culture, it has had to give way to creativity and innovation, especially in hardship posts, as we will see in Chapter 9.

To review, the skill sets required by transformational diplomacy are: *broad knowledge and understanding of how a country works; ability to quickly acquire basic expertise in a new field; and entrepreneurship and innovation.* As I noted earlier, there are no clear boundaries between the skills applicable to traditional and transformational diplomacy. Innovation is certainly helpful in dealing with the world as it is, but it is crucial in the ambitious efforts of making the world more secure and prosperous.

Making things happen

The mantra in the Foreign Service today is that it has become more operational, which encapsulates the shift from passive reporting and analysis to active engagement and societal changes. In plain English, an American diplomat must be capable of *making things happen.* That could mean something as significant as persuading a foreign government to support a U.S.-sponsored resolution at the United Nations, helping a country modernize its infrastructure in order to increase its oil production, or preventing a discrimination law from being passed in a foreign parliament. It could also be something seemingly less important, such as securing a better building for a new embassy, organizing a media event, or improving the interview process for visa applicants.

"You have to find wherever the ball is rolling on the field, and with a sense of vision and strategy, move it down the field," said William Burns, a Foreign Service officer since 1982 and former ambassador to Russia and Jordan who became Hillary Clinton's deputy in 2011. "While we can't escape from the nuts and bolts of traditional diplomacy, what's most important today is getting concrete things done."

There is something else that all diplomats must have: the ability to work for both Democratic and Republican administrations, and to implement policies regardless of whether they agree with them or not. Victoria Nuland is one of the best examples of Foreign Service officers who have been entrusted with high-level positions by administrations of both parties. During the George W. Bush administration, Nuland was an adviser to Vice President Dick Cheney and, as mentioned in Chapter 1, ambassador to NATO. Hillary Clinton's decision to appoint her chief State Department spokesperson in 2011 surprised many, but Nuland had been valued by Democrats before – in the Clinton administration, she was chief of staff to Deputy Secretary of State Strobe Talbott.

So how can the same person champion the policies of Bush and Cheney, and a few years later do the same with Obama and Clinton's policies? "My fundamental starting point is that everybody in these top jobs, whether Cheney or Clinton, has a single common thread, which is that they love their country, and fundamentally what they want is to do what's best for America," Nuland said. "Then you have to be willing to politely challenge assumptions that you think are wrong. However, once you've made your case, and if they choose to move forward in a different direction, your job is to implement what they chose to do, or to say that you can't and you'd like to be somewhere else."

Shortly after September 11, 2001, the Bush administration launched a unilateral attack on Taliban-ruled Afghanistan, which harbored al-Qaida. Nuland, who was deputy chief of the U.S. Mission to NATO in Brussels, and her boss, Ambassador Nicholas Burns, thought that getting other countries to join the U.S. operation would bring long-term benefits in the global fight against terrorism. But the powers in Washington were not interested. "We spent four or five months saying to the White House, 'We get it, you don't want allies at the front of the spear, but they can help hold the spear, and here's how.' They ignored us, ignored us, ignored us, and then finally started saying, 'All right, we'll do some of this.' We felt that we opened their eyes to the possibility of getting the allies on board." Eventually, dozens of countries joined the international forces in Afghanistan.

Another important ingredient of a good diplomat is flexibility – in terms of both geography and type of work. After all, the Foreign Service lifestyle of moving around every three years or less is not for everyone, as we will see in Chapter 12. There is no longer "one definition" of a diplomat, because you could be "negotiating a treaty in Geneva," or "slogging through a maize field in Latin America trying to improve crop yields," or be "embedded with a military unit in Afghanistan reaching out to local tribal elders," Clinton said. Kristie Kenney, the ambassador to Thailand who joined the service in 1980, said that such diversity often marks the experiences of a single officer. "You have to expect all of that in a career," she noted.

Selecting future diplomats

It has become evident by now that professional versatility is highly prized in the Foreign Service – in fact, it seems that a U.S. diplomat is expected to be "Jack of all trades," which risks being a master of none. All those different skills are no doubt needed in the service, so is there an alternative? The most obvious one is to hire people who are already experts in a particular area, but State Department officials say that makes little sense, because it is often impossible to predict where certain expertise may be needed and for how long.

"We need people who are as good at getting things done on the ground overseas as they are in the Situation Room at the White House, driving the policy debate," said Bill Burns, the deputy secretary of state. "That's not a common combination, but it's what we need to aim for."

Jeffrey Levine, the former recruitment and examination director, said the department looks for "basic skills" and the "broadest applicant pool," noting that "there is no one path or group of experiences that will lead you to the Foreign Service." The only officially required qualifications are outlined in 13 general "dimensions," which include "composure, cultural adaptability, objectivity and integrity, planning and organizing," among others, he said. Although "in theory, every officer should be competitive for every job, realistically that won't happen – people start to specialize," both in geographic regions and subject matters, and of course they have their formal career track, Levine said. In addition, officers take into consideration their families' needs and promotion opportunities when bidding on jobs. "What really happens is you have self-selection," he added. He also pointed out that diplomats do not always have to do everything themselves, as long as they know where to find people who can. "You don't have to know how to build a clinic yourself, but you should know who in the government can do that," he said.

The entrance process is extremely competitive. In 2011, 20,474 people took the written exam, officially known as the Foreign Service Officer Test (FSOT), but only 547 were eventually hired, Levine said. There are separate exams for specialists. Registering for the four-hour written test is done on the department's website, and it is offered in many U.S. cities and embassies around the world three times a year, in five-day windows. It is a standardized multiple-choice test with questions about history, politics, economics, geography, popular culture and other areas, and also includes an essay. Levine said the test has not changed fundamentally in more than a decade, though the specific questions are different every time.

"It's such a random mix of information that the best thing you can do is read *The Economist*, *The New York Times*, watch the TV show 'Jeopardy' and do crossword puzzles just to loosen up your brain," said Shane Siegel, whom we met at the beginning of the chapter.

Those who pass the written exam move on to the second of three steps, the so-called Qualifications Evaluation Panel (QEP), where candidates' résumés and answers to questions about their experience are reviewed by the Foreign Service Board of Examiners.

The board also conducts the last stage of the process, the Foreign Service Oral Assessment (FSOA), which is offered three times a year, in Washington and two other U.S. cities. It consists of a group exercise based on a case study of a fictitious foreign country where the U.S. Embassy must deal with a certain situation, as well as an individual interview and a case-management exercise, in which each candidate must write a memo to a superior recommending a course of action. Both Siegel and Traci Goins said they had practiced in informal groups on Skype with fellow candidates they met in the large online community of aspiring diplomats.

No one has discovered the universal recipe for success on the oral exam. Christopher Quade, a mid-level officer I met in Tokyo, said he was the only first-time candidate in his six-member group in 1999, and the experienced applicants tried to give him tips, but he was the only one to pass. Matthew Ference, who was the public affairs officer at the consulate in Erbil, in northern Iraq, when I met him in early 2012, attributed his first-try success in 2003 to being relaxed and trying not to care too much. He had already been accepted to two graduate programs, so he "didn't study for the exams or expect to pass, which reduced the pressure immeasurably," he said. "I didn't grow up dreaming of being a diplomat, so I approached the written and oral exams like any other test – great if I passed, but not the end of the world if I failed."

As we saw with Siegel's diabetes problem, exam success or even a conditional employment offer does not mean you will definitely become a Foreign Service officer. Your name is put on a register, and you have 18 months to receive an actual job offer – that depends not on you, but on whether a position in your chosen career track becomes available – assuming you get security and medical clearances. If it does not, you drop off the register and have to go through the entire exam process again. Caleb Goddard, whom we also met at the beginning of the chapter, received his job offer just four days before his conditional employment was scheduled to expire in December 2011. He had already passed the written test again three months earlier, but at least he was spared another oral exam. Jeffrey Levine said the department warns applicants never to "give up another opportunity on the chance that this will work out."

'Each hire is a $5 million investment'

It is Foreign Service candidates' sweat and tears that remain on exam-room floors, but they are not the only ones with a very high stake in the outcome of the entrance process. The consequences are even bigger for the State Department, because accepting the wrong applicant but rejecting the right one directly affects the service's ability to fulfill its difficult mission. So the importance of designing the best possible examination and selection system, and appointing the most qualified officers to the Board of Examiners, cannot be overstated. Given how general the 13 "dimensions" are, and how subjective the oral assessment can be, one can hardly be absolutely sure that the people joining the Foreign Service will become superb diplomats.

Several longtime officers expressed doubt in the qualifications of some Board of Examiners members, particularly older ones – including retirees – who may have 20th century definitions of a good diplomat. Those officers spoke of a "cultural gap" between "old-school" colleagues and the younger generation. "How much training do those guys have in evaluating people? I'm not sure it's enough," said Edward Stafford, who joined the service in 1991 and was the political-military counselor in Ankara, the Turkish capital, when I met him in early 2012. "They probably have a wealth of experiences, but have they been properly shaped so they can judge the people in the room doing these exercises?"

Levine sought to alleviate Stafford's concerns. "We are very proud of the process," he said. "We have not seen a process that we believe exceeds ours. Through feedback from industrial psychologists, we believe we are using every modern method to assess candidates. Each hire represents a $5 million investment on average in terms of wages, benefits, training and retirement, so we are making the best possible efforts to get it right."

The "basic skills" the State Department tests for and the diversity of the "broad pool," to use Levine's words, logically necessitate substantial training to prepare incoming diplomats for their formidable mission. For decades, however, the department did not value training and provided no professional development beyond learning on the job and foreign language instruction. That has changed in the last decade, but diplomats continue to be thrown into little-known territory without the proper skills or training, as we will see in Chapter 9. To be fair, given the rapidly changing global environment and the specificity of different tasks, classroom learning is not always the most effective solution, so it is essential that diplomats work on self-improvement, many of them say.

Although new Foreign Service officers are unlikely to hold very important policy-making positions at the start of their careers, the demands of transformational diplomacy provide many of them with opportunities to prove themselves not too long after joining. Dozens of service veterans and several political appointees like Anne-Marie Slaughter said most of the officers who have entered in recent years are exceptionally talented and eager to "get their hands dirty in on-the-ground jobs in tough places," as Slaughter put it. "They don't want to work with paper," said Victoria Nuland. "They want to work with people."

Richard Boucher, a former State Department spokesman who ended his 32-year Foreign Service career in 2009 as assistant secretary of state for South and Central Asian affairs, said that new officers "will get a chance to show what they can do in the first five years."

That was exactly what happened to Cameron Munter back in September 1989, his fourth year in the service, when he was the Czechoslovakia desk officer at the State Department. Shirley Temple had just become ambassador to the communist country and was determined to end an 11-year freeze of high-level relations by urging Secretary of State James Baker to meet with Czechoslovak Foreign Minister Jaromir Johannes during the opening session of the U.N. General Assembly in New York. "Even though I didn't know the Berlin Wall would fall in two months, I thought it was a terrible idea," Munter recalled. "But Temple managed to persuade Baker to do it, and I was given the job of announcing it to the Czechoslovak Embassy in Washington. Imagine me in a cab up Connecticut Avenue, steaming."

During the ride, Munter remembered that a prominent Czechoslovak dissident, Zdenek Urbánek, was banned by his government from visiting the U.S. on a fellowship he had received. The young diplomat saw a rare opportunity to make a difference. "The cab dropped me off at the embassy, I walked in and told my contact, 'I have a deal for you: If you give Urbánek an exit visa, we'll give you a meeting with Baker.' He immediately said, 'Deal.' So Johannes met with Baker in late September, and Urbánek arrived in the U.S. in October, weeks before the wall fell."

Learning from the best

Thomas Pickering's first job in the Foreign Service in 1959 was in the State Department's employment division, "answering letters of people who wanted to work for the department." It was not the most prestigious foreign policy position, but he was happy to have a steady income. "I had one child and another one on the way, so I needed work," he said.

Even though Pickering did not think he "had a particular flair for interpersonal relations," he became one of the most admired and effective U.S. diplomats of the 20th century. He earned the trust of both Republican and Democratic presidents and members of Congress, as well as foreign leaders.

In the 1970s, the late King Hussein of Jordan called him "the best American ambassador I've ever dealt with." A decade later, when the powerful Republican Senator Jesse Helms demanded Pickering's removal as ambassador to El Salvador, accusing him of manipulating elections there, President Ronald Reagan not only backed Pickering but promoted him a year later to the high-profile and important ambassadorial post in Israel.[7] In 1989, his nomination by President George H. W. Bush as ambassador to the United Nations was approved by the Senate in a 99-to-0 vote.[8] Having also served as ambassador to Nigeria, India and Russia, Pickering retired in 2001 as undersecretary of state for political affairs in the Clinton administration, the highest career position – and third-ranking overall – at the State Department.

Bill Burns, the deputy secretary of state, said there is no current or former Foreign Service officer he admires more than Pickering. "Tom is as principled, big-hearted and modest as he is skillful and professionally accomplished," Burns said. "Encyclopedic in his grasp of issues, whether nuclear throw-weights or the widgets in the embassy boiler room; a superb advocate of American interests and values; an unsurpassed problem-solver and negotiator; and a tireless champion of his colleagues and embassy communities."

Of the currently serving U.S. diplomats – though he is likely to retire after Hillary Clinton steps down in 2013 – Burns is widely considered one of the best. However, his career "didn't exactly get off to a rocket-propelled start," he said. In 1983, with a war raging between Iran and Iraq, he volunteered to drive a truck with communications equipment across the desert from his first post in Amman, Jordan, to Baghdad. But as soon as he reached the Iraqi border, he was arrested and held for two days, before being escorted to the capital by police. Not only did losing the truck not hurt his career, but he quickly rose to the top.

At 32, he was charged with running the Middle East office at the National Security Council in 1988 by Colin Powell, who was President Reagan's national security adviser. Burns returned to Jordan as ambassador 10 years later, in an appointment by President Clinton. It was no surprise that, when Powell became secretary of state in 2001, he chose Burns to be assistant secretary for Near East affairs. In 2005, President George W. Bush named him ambassador to Russia, and three years later, Condoleezza Rice promoted him to undersecretary for political affairs. Just before Rice left office in 2009, she said that there is no "better repository of skill and dignity and integrity and honor" than Burns. "Bill is absolutely the finest example of a Foreign Service officer that I've ever met," she said, praising his "extraordinary patience," as well as his "sense of optimism and equanimity."[9]

When Hillary Clinton became secretary of state, she broke with the tradition of replacing top officials from the previous administration and kept Burns as undersecretary. "He immediately lived up to his stellar reputation as a seasoned diplomat, and I have valued his insight and judgment every day," she said in 2009. "He personifies the very best of our Foreign Service and is a model of dedication to our country." In 2011, she made him deputy secretary of state, typically a political position that very few career diplomats have held in the country's history.

Republicans had equally flattering things to say about Burns. "What makes Bill so special is that he is calm, unflappable, informed, with an absolute steel core," said Richard Armitage, who was deputy secretary of state under Colin Powell. "He is a man of principle who will not bow to expediency." James Baker, the former secretary of state, called Burns a "top-notch public servant" who "speaks truth to power in an understated way." He is "not ideological, calls it like he sees it, and everybody has confidence in him," Baker said. "I don't know anyone who thinks ill of him, and if you look at the results of his work, you will know why."

Both Pickering and Burns have the rank of *career ambassador*, the highest in the Foreign Service. According to the State Department's Office of the Historian, only 53 officers have received it since it was first conferred in 1956, the year Burns was born.[10]

In addition to him, the other currently serving holders of the title are Nancy Powell, ambassador to India; Anne Patterson, ambassador to Egypt; Earl Anthony Wayne, ambassador to Mexico; as well as the recently retired ambassador to Iraq, James Jeffrey, and to Afghanistan, Ryan Crocker. In fact, having received exceptional accolades from both Democrats and Republicans while he was in Iraq during the Bush administration, Crocker was called back from retirement to go to Kabul in 2011. When President Bush awarded him the Presidential Medal of Freedom two years earlier, he called him America's Lawrence of Arabia. "He has repeatedly taken on the most challenging assignments," Bush said of Crocker. "The man has never run from danger."[11]

The tricky concept of political ambassadorships

There are dozens of photographs in Charles Rivkin's office – on the walls, tables and his own desk. He is shown with President Obama, Hillary Clinton, Senate Foreign Relations Committee Chairman John Kerry and other recognizable faces. But the photos dearest to him are those of his father, William Rivkin, who passed away in 1967, when Charles was a 5-year-old boy. "I never really knew him, but these pictures have been an inspiration for me my entire life," he said.

William Rivkin was President John Kennedy's ambassador to Luxembourg, and President Lyndon Johnson's ambassador to Senegal and Gambia. However, he was not a career diplomat – rather, he was a political appointee. A lawyer who befriended Kennedy while working on his 1960 election campaign, Rivkin became one of the most dedicated and respected political ambassadors in U.S. history, eager to take on assignments not only in plush European posts but also in poverty-stricken Africa. In fact, the Foreign Service thinks of him almost as one of its own to this day. A year after his death, his family established an annual award in his name. It is still given to a career diplomat for constructive dissent – the State Department has a "dissent channel" that goes to the secretary of state's staff – by the American Foreign Service Association, the diplomats' union.

Charles Rivkin grew up among political royalty. "Bobby Kennedy sent me a telegram when I was born" in 1962, he said in reference to the former president's brother Robert. "And here is a picture of me at the 1968 Democratic National Convention, with Vice President Hubert Humphrey, who wrote a note on a napkin to get me out of school." Humphrey was Rivkin's godfather.

Although Rivkin chose a career in business, rising to the very top at two entertainment companies and making many powerful friends in Hollywood, he eventually found a professional path to his father's legacy. In 2004, he worked on John Kerry's presidential campaign and was the California finance co-chair of Obama's 2008 campaign. "I joined the campaign before anybody believed that Obama was possible," he said. A year later, he was named ambassador to Paris, where I met him in early 2012.

"The day I'm confirmed by the U.S. Senate, it doesn't make a bit of difference whether I'm political or career, Democrat or Republican," he said. "I have the same responsibilities to the president, the Congress and the American people. This is not a place to have fun and parties, but to get things done with one of our oldest allies. It's not only a duty, it's also a gift."

Rivkin is a political ambassador of the rarest kind. He has a direct line to the White House, he is very well plugged-in when it comes to political and social developments in France, he is highly respected in Paris, he does extensive public and media outreach, he knows how to run an organization with 1,000 employees, who give him high marks – and he speaks the language of his host country, which many Americans wrongly assume is the case with all ambassadors. During my visit, I accompanied him to a conference in Parliament, where he gave a speech in fluent French. He learned it while studying and working in France in his youth, but he still takes lessons to erase any hint of a non-native speaker. A 2012 report by the State Department's Office of the Inspector-General called Rivkin a "dynamic and visionary" ambassador who "has fostered excellent morale among both American and locally employed staff."[12]

In the last half-century, about a third of all ambassadorships have been given to political appointees, which is unique in the world and has caused some controversy in the Foreign Service. Career diplomats have expressed amazement that many people think diplomacy does not require any special skills and can be done by anyone. "Why is ours the only profession where it's considered acceptable to appoint someone without any experience?" said Steven Kashkett, consul-general in Tijuana, Mexico, and former vice president of the American Foreign Service Association. "Would you appoint someone to head a hospital without medical experience?"

Rivkin cited three main areas where political appointees have an advantage over career diplomats. First, "they have a relationship with the White House." Second, they tend to bring innovation and are more willing to challenge the bureaucracy and "fight institutional lethargy," because they are not afraid of wrecking their careers. Third, they usually have extensive management and leadership experience.

That is certainly a description of the perfect political ambassador, and it applies to Rivkin and others, such as Clark (Sandy) Randt, President George W. Bush's ambassador to China for whom both Colin Powell and Condoleezza Rice had high praise. President "Hu Jintao once told me that Sandy knew more Chinese people than Hu Jintao did," Rice said of Randt, who is a fluent Mandarin speaker. However, most political ambassadors do not speak the language of their host country. Many do not have a direct line to the White House, either, and even if they do, they rarely use it. While those with executive business background are usually good managers, there are academics, lawyers and others who are not. As for innovation, that of course depends on the individual.

Among the political ambassadors considered successful, though not perfect, in recent years, are Tom Schieffer, whom Bush sent to Australia and then Japan, and Howard Baker, Schieffer's predecessor in Tokyo. Neither of them spoke Japanese. Schieffer had long business and management experience and was a close friend of Bush's. Baker, a former Senate majority leader and chief of staff to President Reagan, had superb understanding of how Washington works, which is one of the main deficiencies of the Foreign Service, whose work takes place mainly overseas.

Cameron Munter also praised William Cabaniss, a businessman from Alabama and one of Bush's ambassadors to the Czech Republic. "He had good connections in Washington, he was not an ideologue, and he understood the business and public affairs world in a way most Foreign Service officers don't," said Munter, who was Cabaniss' deputy in Prague. An effective deputy chief of mission can often compensate for a political ambassador's lack of diplomatic or government experience. Other Bush ambassadors, however, "didn't work out, and we had to fire them," Powell said without naming names.

Obama's appointments have also been a mixed bag, career diplomats said. In addition to Rivkin, John Roos in Tokyo, Gary Locke in Beijing and Michael McFaul in Moscow are often cited as some of the best. But at least a couple of others have had to leave prematurely.

Cynthia Stroum, a former investor in start-up companies, was one of them. She was forced to resign as ambassador to Luxembourg in early 2011 after just 11 months in the job, following a scathing report of her tenure by the Office of the Inspector-General.[13] "Most employees describe the ambassador as aggressive, bullying, hostile and intimidating, which has resulted in an extremely difficult, unhappy and uncertain work environment," the report said. "The bulk of the mission's internal problems are linked to her leadership deficiencies, the most damaging of which is an abusive management style." Things got so bad that "most of the senior staff, including two deputy chiefs of mission and two section chiefs, have either curtailed or volunteered for service in Kabul and Baghdad."

Many ambassadors indulge in renovations of their residences, but Stroum apparently crossed a line. "Too many of the limited resources of this embassy have been allocated to issues related to her personal support," the report said. In the summer of 2010, several staff members "spent several days locating and purchasing an umbrella" for Stroum's new patio, the document added.

Another 2011 inspector-general report criticized Douglas Kmiec, ambassador to Malta at the time, for neglecting his overall duties and engaging in "outside activities [that] have detracted from his attention to core mission goals."[14] Kmiec, a law professor and former legal adviser in the Reagan White House, spent most of his time promoting his Roman Catholic faith, mainly by writing various articles and speaking about religion, as well as issues such as abortion.

Many people outside the State Department are surprised that new ambassadors – both career and political – get only two weeks of training at the Foreign Service Institute, which has no plans to extend the course, said its director, Ruth Whiteside. "The expectation is that they will be doing individual consultations on their particular post, have briefings at various agencies and other preparations," she said. "These are appointments made by the president of the United States. There is no higher power. Our job is to give them the maximum chance for success." Charles Rivkin said the formal preparation process was not sufficient for the standards he set himself, and he "interviewed dozens of former ambassadors, took a lot of notes and learned a lot."

Most Foreign Service officers do not question the value of political ambassadors, some of whom have put to shame career chiefs of mission. What they wish for is that the White House made selections based on nominees' skills and experience, which is in fact required by the Foreign Service Act of 1980.[15]

"The American people wouldn't use a toothpaste that has not been certified by the government or drive over a bridge that wasn't built according to the highest standards," said Ronald Neumann, president of the American Academy of Diplomacy and a retired career ambassador. "Why do people think that anyone can do foreign policy?" Neumann's late father, Robert Neumann, was a three-time political ambassador under Democratic and Republican administrations. Political appointees, of course, occupy other posts at the State Department, such as undersecretaries and assistant secretaries, though each secretary of state tries to have a balance between political and career officials in those positions.

Public perceptions and misperceptions

Colin Powell listened with growing but controlled anger. "It's bullshit," he fired back. "That's quotable." It was 2004, and we were sitting in the small inner office of the secretary of state on the seventh floor of the State Department, talking about some of the perceptions about the Foreign Service in Washington – particularly among his fellow Republicans.

For years, some of them have accused diplomats of being more interested in appeasing foreign governments than defending U.S. interests. With a Republican administration in office at the time, former House Speaker Newt Gingrich had written in *Foreign Policy Magazine* that the Foreign Service was "out of sync" with President Bush's policies and was deliberately undermining them.[16] "We can no longer accept a culture that props up dictators, coddles the corrupt and ignores secret police forces," Gingrich wrote in an article with the title "Rogue State Department," and a sidebar "Foreign Dis-service."[17] Another conservative, Christian Coalition founder Pat Robertson, said around the same time, "Maybe we need a very small nuke thrown off on Foggy Bottom to shake things up like Newt Gin-grich wants to do."[18] "Foggy Bottom" is often used as a substitute for "State Department" and refers to the agency's neighborhood.

That was what made the usually calm and composed Powell drop the diplomatic etiquette and resort to using a barnyard expletive. Gingrich's statements were interpreted by some in Washington as a personal attack against Powell for his perceived lack of enthusiasm for the Iraq war, which we will discuss in the next chapter. Still, the broader accusations stood on their own, Powell said. "There is al-ways a bias in Washington against the State Department, and when you have a very conservative Republican administration, it's worse," he told me in another conversation after leaving office. "The percep-tion is that diplomats are bad – they want to talk people into things, while soldiers fight or get ready to fight."

That perception was evident as recently as the 2012 Republican primaries, when then-candidate Rick Perry, the Texas governor, ex-pressed doubt that "the State Department serves us well." In a Fox News interview, he said, "I'm talking about the career diplomats and the secretary of state, who all too often may not be making decisions or giving advice to the administration that's in this country's best interest."[19]

In reality, the State Department does not have a foreign policy – it carries out the president's policy, no matter who he or she is, and to which party he or she belongs, U.S. diplomats said. If the depart-ment "propped up dictators," as Gingrich claimed, it did it because that was what the president at the time wanted.

Six former secretaries of state from both parties and six former Republican political ambassadors agreed, with James Baker calling suggestions to the contrary "patronizing" and an "insult" to the pres-ident. "He is not going to sit there and let the State Department un-dermine his agenda," Baker said.

Howard Baker, the former ambassador to Japan, disagreed with Gingrich "emphatically," saying that "the Foreign Service is loyal and dedicated and serves the president well." George Herbert Walk-er III, a former political ambassador to Hungary and first cousin of President George H. W. Bush, said the Foreign Service officers who worked for him were "team-players" and "very serious" about their jobs. "Everything I've asked for all of a sudden has appeared – it's amazing," Walker told me in Budapest in 2003.

Eliot Cohen, a Republican who was the State Department counselor under Condoleezza Rice, said he was "quite taken" by the "dedication, hard work and intelligence" of the Foreign Service. "I was impressed by the professionalism and discipline, and in some cases self-sacrifice," said Cohen, a longtime Johns Hopkins University professor. "There were some people who were downright heroic."

As they tried to explain the perception that the Foreign Service is less loyal than the military and other parts of the government, several diplomats said their role in policy deliberations may be misunderstood. They are aware of the criticism that they get too close to their host countries and end up advocating their interests. They said, however, that conveying other countries' positions to Washington does not mean they support those positions. Even if they offer advice that is ultimately rejected, they still implement whatever the policy decision is, they insisted.

"You signed up to represent the United States, not yourself. Even if you don't like the policy, you still carry it out," said Stephen McFarland, whom I met in 2003 in Venezuela, where he was deputy chief of mission, and visited again in 2010 when he was ambassador to Guatemala. "But you owe it to yourself and the Foreign Service to make your views known and to express them in the right way."

Henry Hyde, the late Republican congressman from Illinois and former chairman of the House International Relations Committee, agreed that the input of the Foreign Service should be encouraged, because "when you make foreign policy, you need people who can interface with other countries." But he said that sometimes policymakers have the right to question a diplomat's instincts. "People trained as diplomats always think that things can be negotiated, and usually they are right – but not everything," Hyde told me in 2004. "They want to keep relationships with foreign governments serene. They have to be reminded who they work for and what their mission is, although the right kind of people don't need too much reminding."

By now, the most common perception of diplomats as tea-sippers in striped pants has, hopefully, been debunked. Another perception – that the Foreign Service is out of touch with Washington – still holds largely true, though significant progress has been made in the last decade toward a better understanding of the interagency process through training and short-term assignments at other agencies. No organization is perfect, and some older officers are quite resistant to change, while others will give you five reasons why something cannot be done, instead of applying some creativity and doing it. There are also many problems with the bureaucracy, as we will see in Chapter 11.

Overall, however, "we have an excellent Foreign Service," Rice said. Whatever issues one might have with U.S. diplomats, "contact with the Foreign Service turns out to change people's minds." That was certainly the case with the president she served, she said. "Members of the Foreign Service bring valor and professionalism to their work every single day," Bush said at the State Department in 2009. "I have relied on your expertise, your advice, and your good judgment."[20] The critics "don't spend enough time with the Foreign Service," Rice told me. "When members of Congress and their staff go overseas and meet our diplomats, they are very impressed."

The Foreign Service-Civil Service division

Kerry O'Connor, one of the members of the A-100 class that started on September 11, 2001, from Chapter 1, loved her first tour as a political officer in Ghana, where she helped to democratize the police and combat child labor and trafficking. In fact, she loved it so much that she did not want to leave. She felt the same way when her next tour in Morocco came to an end. "Every time I left my post, you had to pry my keyboard out of my hands," she said. "I invested too deeply. But you have to understand that you have to go. I determined that I'm a type of person who likes to dig deep on a project."

Something else was happening at the time. "I was going through hard times in my marriage, and I didn't have my friends or a close group of people to talk to," said O'Connor, whose former husband is also a Foreign Service officer. "Would counseling have saved my marriage? Maybe, maybe not. I didn't have access to it, so I will never know." After her first two overseas tours, she took an assignment in Washington. She was relieved to go home every night and "have a life" again. "I can see my good friends and talk to a counselor or a life coach, or I can take up rock-climbing – all kinds of things I can't do in the Foreign Service lifestyle."

So for both professional and personal reasons, O'Connor converted to the Civil Service at the State Department in 2011. Since 2009, she has been running the department's Sounding Board, an online forum for employees to discuss issues that concern them, which Hillary Clinton started soon after taking office. It has made a big difference in solving problems and introducing innovation, as we will see in Chapter 11. Civil servants often perform the same duties as Foreign Service officers, but they are hired for specific domestic positions, and if they want to apply for a better job, they have to compete with candidates from outside the department.

The Civil Service's role in American diplomacy is a charged and controversial issue. Civil servants see themselves as the State Department's institutional memory, and a vital support system for the Foreign Service in Washington, where diplomats usually return for two-year assignments between overseas tours.

Political appointees often empathize with what they see as the Civil Service's limited career opportunities and talk about of a "caste-based system," to use the characterization of Eliot Cohen, the former counselor under Rice, "where Foreign Service officers are on top and the civil servants are down below." Anne-Marie Slaughter said it is "striking" that the Civil Service has no "career trajectory" and high-level positions to aspire to. "You have many talented people who become experts in everything from the Middle East to arms control to international economics, and there is no clear path for them to rise," she said. Several political appointees called for more excursion overseas tours for civil servants and said the current very strict rules for permanently converting from the Civil to the Foreign Service should be eased.

The American Foreign Service Association (AFSA), the diplomats' union, has a different perspective. "A strong, professional career Foreign Service is fundamental to an effective American diplomacy," said Susan Johnson, the organization's president. "Allowing lateral entry by civil servants and others to take good Foreign Service jobs without accepting any of the concomitant sacrifices demoralizes and undermines the career service. The Foreign Service has a personnel system modeled on that of the military, with entry by examination, competitive annual evaluations, an up-or-out process and mandatory retirement at 65," which do not exist in the Civil Service, she said.

In 2000, the incoming ambassador to Peru, John Hamilton, wanted Roberta Jacobson, a civil servant since 1986, to be his deputy. "I didn't think that could be done, but the director-general of the Foreign Service assigned me as a limited non-career appointment," Jacobson said. Even though she had passed the Foreign Service exam years earlier, she had chosen to stay in the Civil Service, because living abroad and moving around would have forced her husband to sacrifice his career, she said. When her Peru assignment was made, however, "AFSA mounted a campaign to get me out of there," arguing that deputy chief of mission is the highest post most senior Foreign Service officers will ever occupy, and it should not be given away to civil servants, Jacobson said.

Johnson said that AFSA's "opposition to that appointment was not personal, but on the grounds that the assignment violated the rules and undermined the integrity of the Foreign Service." The Foreign Service Grievance Board sided with AFSA, ruling that Jacobson "had to leave Lima within a year, but Madeleine Albright overruled that decision on foreign policy grounds and allowed me to stay for two years," Jacobson recalled. "I was surprised by the anger and hostility I got from people in the Foreign Service who didn't know me. But I didn't set out to break the rules or change the system – I just loved the work and accepted every job I was asked to take." In 2011, Clinton appointed Jacobson assistant secretary of state for Western Hemisphere affairs.

While being protective of Foreign Service positions, over the years AFSA has agreed to some temporary overseas opportunities for the Civil Service. Historically, those have been jobs that could not be filled by the Foreign Service, often at not very attractive posts. However, a new program has designated certain positions in developed countries like Denmark that will be available to civil servants for a couple of years and will then revert back to the Foreign Service, Johnson said.

"Civil servants watch their Foreign Service colleagues go out to be political officers, consular chiefs, deputy chiefs of mission, and they think 'Well, there is nothing in this for me'. We are trying to help them out and get them overseas," said Nancy Powell, the ambassador to India who was previously director-general of the Foreign Service. "Maybe it's a three-month tour of duty, maybe it's a chance to go for two years." In addition, "civil servants are going to leadership positions like country desk officers, office directors and deputy assistant secretaries," Powell said. "I still hear about assistant secretaries who won't allow a civil servant to take a particular job, but that's being broken down."

Several current and former diplomats said that those civil servants who want to work abroad and wish for a better career trajectory can always join the Foreign Service. William Harrop, a former ambassador to Israel who retired after 39 years in the Foreign Service, said it is not fair to his colleagues, who accept the obligations and sacrifices of the Foreign Service lifestyle as well as the benefits, to have some of their positions go to people who have not made such commitments. Harrop also said that having worked in Washington for years does not necessarily make a civil servant qualified for an overseas assignment.

"Could one of the several thousand professional, deserving Civil Service officers in the Pentagon be assigned to command a U.S. Marine Corps battalion in Afghanistan? What would the Marine Corps think of that proposal?" said Harrop, who chairs the Foreign Affairs Museum Council, a nonprofit that works with the State Department to create the U.S. Diplomacy Center, a museum of American diplomacy and a hub for educational outreach. "In academia, there are brilliant scholars who lack a record of teaching experience and who have not committed to the arduous study required to earn a doctorate. To eliminate discrimination, should they be considered for tenure?"

Johnson said the problems of the Foreign Service-Civil Service division are too big to fix with any programs. "The Civil Service rank-in-position system is an anachronism badly in need of serious reform," because it does not "integrate or work well with the Foreign Service rank-in-person rotational system," she said. "There are very few positions that are so specialized in nature that they should be non-rotational, such as in the Office of the Legal Adviser or in the Office of the Historian."

However, Johnson conceded that sweeping reforms are not likely anytime soon and suggested "exploring developing more rotational tracks for the Civil Service" in Washington. "Assigning civil servants to more and more Foreign Service jobs, or converting Foreign Service positions in Washington to Civil Service jobs, is not the answer. An informed and thoughtful review of which positions should be rotational and which can be non-rotational without too high a cost might be a very productive exercise," she said.

Kerry O'Connor is not too worried about the career trajectory she lost by converting to the Civil Service. "I was following my professional passion, and the kind of quality of work-life that I wanted," she said. "I figured the rest would work out as I follow my intellectual curiosity, perform compelling and valuable work, and treat my life holistically. The future isn't yet written. I make life choices with that in mind, and I don't let conventional wisdom stop me from doing things that need to be done."

The local staff – the 'backbone' of an embassy

Nihal Rizk was a 22-year-old newly minted mass communication faculty member at Cairo University in 1982 when she read a newspaper advertisement for a job in the press office of the U.S. Embassy. Against her father's wishes, she went for an interview and was hired on the spot.

Her first assignment as a TV specialist was to make contacts in the only two Egyptian TV channels at the time, both state-owned. Her second assignment was to help install a satellite broadcasting State Department-produced programs from Washington meant for foreign audiences. When all was said and done, she was tasked with recording an hour-long feed with a news and current affairs show every day and giving the tape to Egyptian television to air whatever parts it saw fit. "It was very difficult to put American programs on Egyptian TV, but we persisted, and they ended up using something almost every day," she said.

Three decades later, Rizk still works at the embassy as a *Foreign Service national* – or national of the host country – though she is now a senior media adviser and has two grown children. She has served under 10 ambassadors and hundreds of other Foreign Service officers. She is part of more than 1,000-strong local staff that is the embassy's institutional memory. Around the world, more than 44,000 host country and third-country citizens form what many diplomats call the "backbone" of each embassy or consulate.

"American diplomatic missions simply could not function without our remarkably talented and loyal locally employed colleagues," said Bill Burns. "Working with them at posts as diverse as Amman and Moscow has been one of the genuine highlights of my career." Frank Ricciardone, who was ambassador to Egypt from 2005 to 2008, said the local staff is "the secret to an officer's success," and some of his "oldest, dearest personal friends" are local embassy employees. "They unlock the mysteries and the hidden portals of their societies when treated with the respect and affection they richly deserve at all stages of a Foreign Service officer's career," he said.

I first met Rizk during a trip to Egypt with Albright in 2000, and every time I went back, whether with Powell, Rice, Clinton or on my own, she was a force of nature to watch and learn from. She seemed to know everyone in Cairo, including the right people in the government, the media, at airlines, hotels and other major companies. But more importantly, she knew what buttons to push and how to get things done with merely a phone call.

"Over the years, I've become more analytical and know very well not only the political and media landscape in Egypt, but also the changes in the society and public opinion that have occurred," she said. Working for the U.S. Embassy has been a double-edged sword, she added. "On one hand, Egyptians are suspicious, because there is a strong anti-American sentiment here. But on the other hand, it's very prestigious to work at the embassy, and I like helping to bring our two countries and peoples closer."

Burns and Ricciardone are just two of the many U.S. diplomats who fondly remember Rizk from their time in Cairo – actually, Burns has never served in Egypt, but he met her during his dozens of visits as assistant secretary for Near East affairs under Powell and still asks for her views and advice when he travels to Cairo as deputy secretary. "Nihal has always been an exceptional guide in understanding Egypt and the Egyptian media, and her skills and dedication are a reminder of the crucial role of Foreign Service nationals in our work overseas," Burns said. Ricciardone called Rizk "fearless, tough, shrewd, irreverent yet classy, politically savvy, a networker par excellence, news junkie, mistress of nuance and subtlety in two languages."

Contrary to the popular belief that local employees are only support staff, many of them perform duties typically assigned to Foreign Service officers – sometimes much better, in fact. While there are drivers, cleaners, cooks and mechanics, there are also legal advisers, economists, engineers, political analysts and financial specialists. Moreover, some like Claude How at the embassy in Mauritius literally keep their mission running. "The guy did the work of 10 people, repeatedly and adamantly turned down awards so more junior staff could have them, never lost his cool, and made miracles happen," said Virginia Blaser, a former deputy chief of mission in Mauritius who currently holds the same post in Uganda. How has been an embassy employee for 31 years, Blaser added.

Even though the State Department offers local employees "prevailing" wages and benefits in the respective country, many foreign nationals say they are deprived of basic workers' rights, and decisions about their employment are often taken without their input. AFSA's *Foreign Service Journal* wrote in its June 2012 issue about an unnamed post in Western Europe that unilaterally reduced the local staff's sick leave and vacation time, and changed the rules for termination of employment in 2008. Employees were given two weeks to agree to the new terms in writing or lose their jobs.[21] Their requests to the department in Washington to get involved were still unanswered as of the article's publication.

Several local employees in different countries noted their lack of career development – while they conceded that is unlikely to change, they suggested that simple incentives, such as their job titles and perhaps more training, would provide better motivation and a sense of being appreciated.

"Many of us are simply given an 'assistant' title, even though our duties actually include significant advisory functions," said Aneta Stefanova, a press specialist in Sofia, Bulgaria. "This may not seem very important, but given our role as liaisons between the embassy and the host society, it's important that we are perceived by our local contacts to be what we actually are, allowing us to maintain valuable contacts at high government and social levels. Other incentives should include familiarization with the country we work for – many of us have sent local contacts on programs in the U.S. and briefed them on places, events and institutions we don't know much about."

In addition, "the attitude of the Foreign Service officers plays a significant role as a motivating factor," said Stefanova, who has worked at the embassy since 1991. "Many of us have been on the receiving end of arrogant, disrespectful and often quite ignorant attitudes on the part of our American supervisors, which is due to a large extent to the unclear status of the local staff within the State Department system. The smartest and most successful officers I've met have been those who truly take care of their local staff and give credit where it's due. It all comes down to good manners and judgment, respect and loyalty to the people who teach you a big part of your job and introduce you to the right local contacts."

As in any large organization, not all employees deserve praise, and some foreign nationals have used questionable tactics to benefit themselves over the years. Tracey Jacobson, the ambassador to Kosovo and a former ambassador to Tajikistan, said her staff in the former Soviet republic "caught some of the patrol guards siphoning gas out of official vehicles to sell," and she fired 24 people. "Maybe petty theft occurs in Tajikistan, but not in the American Embassy – we are spending taxpayers' money," she said.

In spite of the problems, there are "remarkable stories" of local employees' dedication and commitment, said James Zumwalt, the former deputy chief of mission in Tokyo whom we met in Chapter 1. He told me about Akiko Otokita, a Japanese employee in the embassy's consular section who was among the many volunteers to work overtime after the 2011 earthquake and tsunami to help locate and evacuate American citizens. She kept working, even though she did not know for three days the whereabouts of her parents, "who lived on the coast and had been affected by the tidal wave." Zumwalt made it clear she could go home, but she wanted to stay and help someone else. "She later found out that her cousin had come in a car and taken her parents, and their house was destroyed after that," Zumwalt said.

Otokita was not the only Japanese staff member to go beyond the call of duty. "On the Sunday after the Friday earthquake, I saw one of our drivers running toward the embassy, and I stopped him to ask why," Zumwalt recalled. "He said he was about 15 minutes late for work. I asked him how he got in, because I knew the trains weren't running. He told me he had walked for three hours, and I was just blown away."

One of the best examples of Foreign Service nationals' heroism was the "unparalleled dedication and loyalty" of Afghan employees of the U.S. Embassy in Kabul from 1989 until 2001, as Colin Powell put it when presenting them with an award during a 2002 visit. For more than 12 years "with no American presence" while the embassy was closed, they "continued to protect and maintain United States Government property in Kabul" under "the most difficult circumstances," Powell said.[22]

Chapter 3

The Diplomat In Chief

Madeleine Albright was almost shouting. She could not hear me anymore, she said. The noise on her Air Force plane had, indeed, become more deafening, but she also seemed to be avoiding my question. And who could blame her? It was probably her happiest day as secretary of state – Yugoslav strongman and indicted war-criminal Slobodan Milošević had finally been driven out of power just hours earlier – and there I was, asking how she felt about having to leave office in three months.

It was October 5, 2000, and we were talking in the secretary's private cabin at the end of a trip to Europe and the Middle East. Albright's immense thrill of being America's chief diplomat was obvious to anyone who came in contact with her at the time. She knew her term would end soon, but until then she planned to "work every minute and extend the days." Representing the United States was "so much fun, and very energizing," she said, "and I think I've had a pretty good run. But we all occupy these jobs temporarily."

The first female secretary of state, Albright became a celebrity and attracted significant media attention everywhere she went. Some of the phrases she coined, such as "the indispensable nation," are still used quite often. At a time when few Americans and members of Congress were interested in foreign policy, Albright, with President Clinton's help, reinvigorated U.S. diplomacy and reasserted Washington's dominant role in world affairs. Upon leaving the State Department in January 2001, she left a handwritten note to Colin Powell on the secretary's desk that ended with these words: "I turn over to you the best job in the world."[1]

It may be the best, but it is also one of the most complex, and rather unusual compared with other cabinet posts – in fact, Eliot Cohen, the former State Department counselor under Condoleezza

Rice, said there is a "structural problem with that job." In most departments, the secretary is the chief executive. At State, he or she is also the country's chief diplomat – or operator, as Cohen put it – as well as the president's chief foreign policy adviser. To be truly successful, the secretary of state must give each of these roles the time and attention they deserve, which is even more challenging when one has various crises to resolve around the world and a 24-hour news cycle.

A chief executive needs sufficient resources to accomplish the organization's mission, and in this case, the White House and Congress control the purse. Unfortunately, as I pointed out in Chapter 1, the Clinton administration's huge international agenda and the growing demands of global engagement were in stark contrast to the very limited resources available to the State Department in the 1990s. When Albright took office in 1997, the foreign affairs budget was $18 billion, according to the Government Printing Office.[2]

Insufficient funds meant fewer, overworked and underpaid employees, old embassy buildings in desperate need of repair and security upgrades, as well as outdated technology. As a result, in spite of the important and exciting work, morale in the Foreign Service was low, hundreds of officers said. While some suggested that Albright could have fought harder for more resources, others said that would still have been a losing battle with Congress, and she would have had less time to focus on the rest of her job. It was not until the 1998 embassy bombings in Kenya and Tanzania, which killed more than 200 people, including 12 Americans,[3] that Congress agreed to provide more funding to beef up security overseas.

Although Albright reorganized parts of the State Department to reflect post-Cold War realities, the budget restraints did not allow her to undertake fundamental reforms of the Foreign Service. Aside from the funding issues, Eliot Cohen said it is common for a new secretary to think, "I have a limited time here, and fixing the Foreign Service looks like a huge task." That said, Albright had a soft spot for career diplomats, because her father, Josef Körbel, had been one back in her native Czechoslovakia, before World War II. "In another life, I would have been a Foreign Service officer. I come from a diplomatic family," she told me during that plane ride. "At dinner, most people talk about sports, and we talked about foreign policy. I grew up with it."

While the process of redefining American diplomacy we discussed in Chapter 1 began during Albright's tenure, the rebuilding of the service did not start until 2001.

Colin Powell

When Powell assumed office that year, he was shocked to discover how unprepared the Foreign Service was for the 21st century. Hundreds of positions around the world were vacant or had been eliminated, structured professional development of diplomats barely existed, and information technology was outdated – most U.S. missions abroad had only one Internet-capable computer for the entire building. Powell did not buy the "less is more" motto of the previous decade and decided to do something about it. An experienced and respected military commander, he knew that troops that are not cared for are less motivated and productive. "I came as a former soldier with a sense of responsibility to lead and manage the people," he told me.

Even before September 11, Powell was able to secure funding for hiring more Foreign Service officers – he called it the Diplomatic Readiness Initiative. "Hiring had stopped for a couple of years in the 1990s," he said. "You can't do that to an organization. You've got to have blood coming in – fresh blood, new blood." He also replaced the old computers and other equipment with modern technology. "I'm seen as a bit of a nut case on this, but there was more to this than just getting everybody the Internet-capable computer. It was to show them we are alive, we are well, we are in the 21st century," he said.

Next to increasing the size of the Foreign Service and modernizing its communications capabilities, introducing mandatory training during an officer's career has been a lasting legacy of Powell's tenure. "What I wanted to embed throughout the service was the concept of professional development from junior officer to ambassador, and particularly with respect to leadership and management," he said. "We found that many people who were in senior positions in the department didn't have the leadership – not just skills, but training in leadership – to do the kinds of jobs that we were giving them. In the military, you start out with leadership training as a second lieutenant. We didn't do that at State."

Powell's determination to give the Foreign Service the tools it needed to accomplish its mission earned him the service's admiration and loyalty. Hundreds of officers said that morale had not been that high since the days of George Shultz, President Reagan's secretary of state. "Powell was the mayor of the building," said Rena Bitter, whom I first met at the embassy in London in 2003 and visited again eight years later when she was director of the State Department's Operations Center, a 24-hour news and crisis-management hub. "People felt like they worked for him. They got the message that he cared about the institution. When people perceive loyalty from a leader, they are loyal, too." That has also been the case with Hillary Clinton, as we will see later in the chapter.

Another "factor the Foreign Service tends to look at in judging whether the secretary truly supports and believes in the service is the degree to which he or she relies on the career people," said Tom Countryman, the assistant secretary for international security and nonproliferation whom we met in Chapter 2. On that front, Powell also scored high. "He worked with the institution and made the institution work," said Richard Boucher, the former department spokesman under both Powell and Albright. While no secretary can do his or her job without the Foreign Service, some have turned to a small circle of trusted political appointees on the most important and strategic issues. The example of that style cited most often by career diplomats in recent decades is James Baker during the George H. W. Bush administration, and to a lesser extent Albright.

As thrilling as it was to travel abroad with Albright, visiting foreign countries with Powell was an experience like no other – both for us in the press corps and his staff. Thanks to his charisma, he won people over just by showing up. Yuri Kim, whom we met in Chapter 1, did advance work on some of Powell's trips. "He would walk into a room or hotel lobby, and people would spontaneously get up and start applauding," she said. "They didn't do it for the president, the vice president or anybody else I could see." On the plane, Powell was disarming, down-to-earth, talkative and often funny, but he rarely spoke about policy – his favorite topics were history and old cars.

While he relished the opportunities to meet with foreigners and represent the United States abroad, some media organizations liked to point out that he did not travel enough. During his four years in office, Powell flew just over 750,000 miles, according to his archived State Department website,[4] compared to the more than 1 million miles Albright says she traveled as secretary.[5] Rice beat Albright by about 20,000 miles,[6] and Clinton had flown about 860,000 miles by August 2012.[7]

Albright told me a "traveling secretary" is very important for achieving an effective foreign policy, because, in addition to "showing the flag," he or she is an "action-forcing mechanism" of sorts. "One, it creates the necessity for your own government bureaucracy to get its act together as to what the message will be, and then the place you are going to is trying to figure out how to respond," she said. Powell said he traveled as much as he needed to, and his executive assistant at the time, Craig Kelly, said the secretary tried to balance "going out and seeing as many people as he could" with "the huge agenda in Washington, where he was a major player." Kelly, who later became ambassador to Chile and has now retired from the Foreign Service, added that, like all of President Bush's principal advisers, Powell wanted to be in White House meetings, because there was "a lot at stake in there."

Some of those advisers, particularly Vice President Dick Cheney and Defense Secretary Donald Rumsfeld, often clashed with Powell on policy issues. "He had a very interesting cast of characters, and I think he had a hard time," Albright said. Another former secretary of state, who asked not to be named, said he "felt sorry" for Powell – "he had to fight battles with agencies that in the past weren't players in some of those issues. There is no more pure foreign policy issue than Arab-Israeli peace, and everybody was in the meetings on that over there. The secretary had to fight a very powerful coalition of opponents in the vice president and the secretary of defense, so it was tough."

Because Cheney and Rumsfeld claimed a lot of foreign policy turf, there was a perception that the State Department lost some of its importance under Powell. In reality, that depended on the issue. On North Korea, Bush initially sided with Cheney and Rumsfeld, but later accepted Powell's suggestions. "I got hammered early on for wanting to talk to the North Koreans," Powell recalled. "Nobody had told me we weren't going to talk to the North Koreans. What did we do a year later? Exactly what I suggested then." Bush also entrusted Powell with negotiating a new treaty with Russia to replace the Cold War-era Anti-Ballistic Missile Treaty, as well as many other important tasks.

"People are fond of pointing out that I may not be on the president's agenda," Powell told me at the time. "I am on the president's agenda. I know what he wants. I see him many times a week, in groups or alone. And the people who work for me respond to the direction that the president gives to me and I give to them." However, the Foreign Service often felt that its work was not valued by the White House, dozens of officers said, citing the "militarization of foreign policy" after September 11, which I mentioned in Chapter 1.

It was conventional wisdom at the time – and still is, to a large extent – that the State Department "marginalized itself" in the run-up to the Iraq war in 2002 and early 2003, because it was against the war. Powell "dealt himself out," said Eliot Cohen. Powell repeatedly brushed off suggestions to step down, some of which came from inside the administration. "I felt acutely that he did not agree with the president's Iraq policy," said a former Bush White House official. "He probably should have resigned, rather than end up in the position he was in, which forced him to sell a [policy] he didn't believe in." Several Foreign Service officers expressed similar sentiments, though that did not reflect the service's prevailing view.

After he left office, Powell said that what was interpreted by some as a policy disagreement was actually an effort to exercise caution before going to war. He recalled asking Bush, "Have you thought about everything you are going to get in here? It will be hugely expensive, and it will suck the oxygen out of anything else we are doing. You are now the proud owner of 25 million people. You are the government."

Bill Burns, at the time assistant secretary of state for Near East affairs, said there were "fairly fierce debates on how important it was to have a lot of company" going into Iraq. "The argument we tried to make was that the importance of having company going in had little to do with the immediate military challenge" of removing Saddam Hussein from power, he said. "The biggest challenge was going to be the day after, and it was very obvious that the more company we had, the better we could manage the situation. It wasn't a question of marginalizing ourselves, but about expressing concerns honestly. Sometimes, those concerns were being read as trying to slow down movement toward a [war] decision, or to avoid the decision altogether. The result was, you ended up with a pretty dysfunctional bureaucratic process."

Although the State Department had prepared a 17-volume project called "The Future of Iraq," the department's perceived distaste for a rush to war led to a decision to put the Pentagon in charge of postwar planning and management. "It's probably fair to say that the department was shunted to the side, but I don't buy the argument that it was somehow an abdication on the part of Powell or anyone else," Burns said. "I don't think that's true. He fought hard."

Even as some in the White House distrusted the State Department, Powell was chosen to persuade the world that Saddam possessed weapons of mass destruction during a presentation at the United Nations about six weeks before the war started. As widely documented and acknowledged by Bush administration officials, some of the information used by U.S. intelligence turned out to be false,[8] and illicit weapons in Iraq were not found after the invasion.[9] "It was your beloved State Department that went up there and made the case on weapons of mass destruction. And why did they pick the State Department? Why was I the agent?" Powell asked me. Perhaps credibility, I suggested. "You've answered the question," he said.

Condoleezza Rice

Hyatt Rickey's was a historic 16-acre hotel in Palo Alto, California, that welcomed presidents and celebrities during its nearly six-decade existence.[10] It was demolished in 2005 to make way for residential buildings, but five years before that, I stayed there on an assignment for the *Financial Times*. In the hotel's restaurant on a rainy January morning, I met for a breakfast interview with Condoleezza Rice, the main foreign policy adviser to Republican presidential candidate George W. Bush, who introduced herself as Condi. She was an accomplished 45-year-old professor and former provost at Stanford University, who had been director for Soviet and Eastern European affairs at the National Security Council during the administration of Bush's father, President George H. W. Bush.

As we made our way to our table, I suggested that to call a black woman's achievements "incredible" risked being condescending. With the friendly smile and relaxed manner of a West Coaster, Rice said she was used to such a reaction – she called it the "Condi in Wonderland" phenomenon. "I have a friend whose words for it are, 'My goodness, the monkey can read! It's amazing!'" she laughed. "I'm a package. I'm five-foot-eight, black and female. I can't go back and repackage myself. I can't do an experiment to figure out whether any of this would have happened to me had I been white and male, or white and female, or black and male. So I spend no time worrying about it."

I also suggested that, should Bush win the 2000 election, she could be his national security adviser or secretary of state. "I have no idea what my life will be like a year from now," she responded. During the three-hour conversation covering numerous foreign policy issues, Rice answered every question with the confidence and conviction of a true expert, even if a particular area was outside her expertise.

I was most fascinated by the fact that the person to whom Rice owes her decision to study international affairs was Albright's father, who was her professor at the University of Denver. "I like Madeleine very much," Rice said. "You can have the same intellectual father and different outcomes, but there are some powerful core values that we share. On issues of how you use power, we probably don't agree." The headline the *Financial Times* put on my story was, "Political Punch in a Package of Charm."[11]

Five years and two weeks after our first meeting, we were on a plane taking Rice on her first foreign trip as Bush's second secretary of state. There was no sign of my relaxed and easy-going breakfast companion. The woman on board was cautious, somewhat tense and buttoned-up – literally and figuratively – though still kind and polite. That was hardly surprising. An extremely private person, Rice was not used to the overwhelming public and media attention that came with her new job. At times during that first trip, she was startled by the dozens of TV cameras greeting her at press conferences in foreign countries. As national security adviser during Bush's first term, she had avoided the limelight and spoken at few public events. Her relatively brief government experience paled in comparison to the long careers of Cheney, Powell and Rumsfeld.

However, it took only a few months for Rice's confidence to return in full force, and she felt comfortable enough to predict future policy outcomes in private discussions with those of us in the press corps on her plane. The main reason for that was her close personal relationship with Bush, who trusted her more than he did his other foreign policy advisers. As has been revealed in books by Rice, Cheney and Rumsfeld since they left office, the two men often disagreed with the new chief diplomat but were overruled by the president.

In fact, in several stunning policy reversals, the administration did during its second term exactly the opposite of what had happened during the first. After the White House blocked active mediation in Israeli-Palestinian negotiations for four years, Rice spent more time and invested more of her credibility as secretary in that very issue than any other, with the possible exception of Iraq. Still, a peace agreement proved elusive.

In addition, not only did the United States continue its participation in six-party talks with North Korea that had begun under Powell, but Rice persuaded Bush to authorize lengthy one-on-one negotiations with the communist state, as well as incentives for Pyongyang to give up its nuclear weapons program, which Bush had earlier denounced as bribery. Despite significant progress, which helped Washington learn previously unknown details of North Korea's programs, their intended complete dismantlement was not accomplished.

Also on Rice's watch, Washington took part in negotiations with Iran for the first time in nearly three decades, alongside other major powers.

"There was a greater recognition of the importance of diplomacy in the second Bush term, and more attention to coalition-building," said Bill Burns. It will come as no surprise that the Foreign Service was thrilled that diplomacy was again the driving force of American foreign policy, after the focus on military might following September

11. The State Department as an institution was very pleased to be winning policy debates, and for its secretary to have the president's ear whenever she needed it. "People liked the fact that they had a very powerful boss," Eliot Cohen said.

On the management side, the Foreign Service did not give Rice as high marks as it did on the policy front. "She had a hard act to follow, because Powell was very beloved by the people, and the perception was that she didn't care about the troops as much as he did," said one senior officer who asked not to be named. "I don't think she was interested in institution-building," said another officer, who worked directly for both Powell and Rice. "I think she had other urgent business in mind, and it may have been that she was focused on those issues because she had a voice on them."

Several officers also said that Rice was less accessible than Powell. At the time, her aides explained that her style was to focus on a few of the most important issues – unlike Powell, who she thought had been involved in matters that did not deserve the secretary's attention. "Powell had a greater breadth of interests," one senior officer said in 2005. "Rice makes the big things happen. She is not into bringing every problem to the secretary."

Rice said she "found less resistance" in the service than she expected and actually "liked being CEO of the State Department and spent a lot of time on it." She cited institutionalizing transformational diplomacy, moving about 200 positions from Europe to emerging and less developed countries, which she labeled "global repositioning," as well as "changing the way we trained people and the requirements for promotions, so you had to serve in a hardship post" to get promoted. "We also tried to introduce in the selection of ambassadors from the career ranks some sense of a career path, so that you aren't just the next person in line for promotion, but you've actually gone through experiences that made you capable of handling" ambassadorial duties, she said after leaving office. She also noted that most of her closest advisers were Foreign Service officers, including five of the six assistant secretaries in charge of the department's regional bureaus. Several of those officers said they had access to Rice whenever they needed.

Perhaps the most controversial issue of Rice's tenure was service in Iraq. As noted in Chapter 1, the administration realized that the post-war reconstruction was not working with the Pentagon at the helm and decided to put the State Department in charge. That meant an urgent need for thousands of Foreign Service members to go to a war zone during Bush's second term, having received only two weeks of training and, of course, not carrying weapons.

When word came that the secretary might resort to "directing" people to serve in Iraq because not enough volunteers were coming forward, passions started running high. At a 2007 town hall meeting with the director-general of the Foreign Service at the time, Harry Thomas, several employees criticized the potential policy. "It's one thing if someone believes in what's going on over there and volunteers, but it's another thing to send someone over there on a forced assignment," said Jack Croddy, an officer for 36 years. "I'm sorry, but basically that's a potential death sentence, and you know it."[12]

Although most people in the Foreign Service, including those in the hall that day, did not agree with Croddy, his comment was published in hundreds of media stories and gave the public the impression that the service was disobedient and disloyal. Eventually, the vacant positions were filled voluntarily, and "I didn't have to direct people to serve in Iraq after all, even though I was prepared to do it," Rice said.

Hillary Clinton

About a month before the 2008 presidential election, I invited Madeleine Albright to an editorial board meeting at the *Washington Times*. On our way to the newspaper's offices, she said she had no idea who would be secretary of state if Barack Obama won the White House. "How about Hillary Clinton?" I suggested. "Not gonna happen," said Albright, who has been a close friend of Clinton's since the mid-1990s and advised her campaign for the Democratic nomination against Obama. Both women were surprised when he asked the junior senator from New York and former first lady to join his Cabinet, as were many others in Washington.

Clinton, who said she would serve only one four-year term, has maintained very high public approval ratings and impressed a diverse group of people, including Republicans. Among her biggest fans has been the Foreign Service, where she is widely viewed as the most effective secretary in decades – on all three fronts outlined earlier in the chapter.

As the country's chief diplomat, she has succeeded in reasserting U.S. leadership in many parts of the world. Kristie Kenney, the ambassador to Thailand, said, "Everybody in the world knows who Hillary Clinton is. They all want to meet and be photographed with her." Clinton has managed various crises rather well and maintained a brutal schedule. She has certainly had critics, who say either that she has focused too much on soft-power issues, such as women's

rights and Internet freedom, or that there has been no obvious diplomatic success on a specific issue for which she could claim personal credit. Clinton's aides disagree, pointing to her role in the NATO
air campaign that helped topple Libyan dictator Muammar Qaddafi
in 2011.

In terms of her style, she has displayed an ability to put herself in
the shoes of her foreign interlocutors, to understand where they
come from in defending certain positions, and then uses that insight
to bring them closer to the U.S. point of view, using arguments in
their own self-interest, several of her aides said. "She is very good at
dealing with powerful people, understanding their motivation, and
finding common interests with them," said Victoria Nuland, the
State Department spokesperson. While Clinton did not have significant diplomatic experience before becoming secretary, she quickly
mastered a huge number of complex issues, as well as the ability to
connect them in ways few people can.

As the president's chief foreign policy adviser, Clinton has had a
major voice in decision-making – though less so than Rice did, and
not on every single issue – largely because Obama and Clinton share
a vision for the U.S. role on the world stage, as I explained in Chapter 1. At the beginning of the administration, it did not take them
long to put their previous rivalry during the presidential primaries
behind them – in fact, they did so much faster than some of their
closest aides, according to administration officials who were not involved in the 2008 campaign.

Obama and Clinton also have similar instincts when dealing with
difficult issues, said people who have worked for both of them. Their
styles of chairing meetings – whether on policy or implementation –
are very much alike, too. "She couldn't care less whether she's talking to a Foreign Service officer with three years under their belt or
30 years," said Jack Lew, Obama's chief of staff whom we met in
Chapter 1. "Frankly, the president is the same way. When he is in a
room, he wants to talk to the person who knows most about the subject, whether it's the most junior or the most senior person." In addition, they both encourage dissent and invite opposing views during policy deliberations, said Bill Burns.

As chief executive of the State Department, Clinton has received
very high marks from employees, some of whom have posted in
their social media profiles what a great boss they have. She has se-
cured the largest budget the department has ever had, and expanded
the Foreign Service to a size never seen before, even though she
aimed for a 25-percent increase but managed about 17 percent. In
spite of that significant achievement, nearly 1,300 mid-level posi-

tions in the service remained vacant in 2011, according to the Government Accountability Office.[13]

"The stock criticism of people who come from Capitol Hill is that they haven't managed big organizations. I think she's shattered that stereotype," Burns said of Clinton. "It doesn't take much to motivate people in the Foreign Service. A little bit of attention from the political leadership can go a long way. She has provided that. She has really succeeded." Kristie Kenney said that Clinton had "organizational talent" and was "very open to us." Patrick Kennedy, undersecretary of state for management, said she is "a politician in the good sense of the word who knows how to get things done."

While Clinton commands the service's loyalty and admiration, for gay diplomats she is a true hero. Less than five months after taking office, she issued an order granting diplomatic passports, access to medical care and U.S. government jobs overseas, as well as other benefits, to same-sex partners of Foreign Service members. "Domestic partners of federal employees have for too long been treated unequally," she said in June 2009. "This change is the right thing to do, and it is the smart thing to do."[14] In a groundbreaking speech before hundreds of stunned old-school diplomats from around the world at the U.N. Human Rights Council in Geneva in 2011, Clinton declared that "gay rights are human rights," and that being gay "does not make you less human."[15]

Clinton told me the model she used in shaping her priorities as secretary was George Shultz. "He was obviously essential to President Reagan's foreign policy, but he also really paid attention to what we call *the building* – the Foreign Service and Civil Service – and I think you have to pay attention to the people that do the work," Clinton said. "I was very impressed that he got such high marks from everybody, because he could really manage and steward the resources of the Foreign Service and the Civil Service, but also be involved in all of the difficult issues of his time."

One of the most beneficial and consequential things Clinton has done for the State Department is articulating a vision for diplomacy and development as inseparable parts of national security, alongside defense. She calls them "the three Ds," and the equal components of the "smart power" the United States must exercise in the 21st century. She has also pushed for a "whole of government" approach to national security, with all relevant agencies working more closely together toward the same goals. Because "the size of our Foreign Service is dwarfed by the size of our military," there is "a dominance in the public imagination of one out of the three aspects of our foreign policy and national security," she said.

While that idea was not new, Clinton managed to institutionalize it by putting in the federal budget all "our international affairs, defense and veterans programs in the category of national security," said Jack Lew. "It's a concept we pioneered." That said, "we still have a way to go to connect up diplomacy and development" with defense in "the American consciousness about national security," Clinton noted.

As secretary of state, she has had a remarkably good relationship with the media, which has not always been the case in her career. Part of the reason for that is the professionalism of the State Department press corps – as self-serving as it may sound coming from a former 10-year member. But every secretary I have covered will agree with me. That group of journalists has a solid knowledge and understanding of international affairs and is very policy-focused. All you need to do is listen to the questions they ask at press conferences to realize that they are not interested in what the secretary wears, what she eats or other celebrity gossip so prevalent in today's media. If a reporter asks Clinton whether she would run for president again, chances are that person either does not cover the State Department or an editor made them do it.

But the bigger part of the reason for Clinton's popularity with the media has to do with her own skills as a politician, world-famous public figure and high-level policy-maker. The confidence and policy insight she exhibited during her very first trip as secretary in February 2009 surprised many of us in the traveling press corps, because unlike Rice, she was not the president's close personal friend. It was refreshing to work with a secretary who actually answered our questions, rather than recite talking points.

In fact, her candor got her into a bit of trouble on that trip. During a round-table discussion with us in Seoul just before we left for Beijing, she said that pressing China on human rights "can't interfere" with other important issues in U.S.-Sino relations.[16] Within hours, human rights groups started criticizing her.[17] But she said this: "It's worth being perhaps more straightforward and trying to engage other countries on the basis of the reality that exists in a number of these settings, to try to encourage more thoughtful deliberation about where we are going and how we are going to get there. And so that's how I see it, and that's how I intend to operate." However, that round-table discussion – a practice initiated by Rice, who liked longer and in-depth policy discussions – was the last one Clinton did. From then on, she gave five-minute interviews to individual reporters, mostly from TV networks, making little news. While she continued to be frank and speak her mind at times, she began using the "diplo-speak" that comes with the job.

In terms of contributions to modern diplomacy, Clinton has worked hard to humanize it by engaging the private sector and individual citizens – she called it "people-to-people diplomacy" – as well as by harnessing 21st century communication technology and social media, as we will see in Chapter 6. "She is great at seeing the leader of a foreign country, but she spends as much time when she's on the road trying to connect with people – doing town hall meetings, NGO events, and empowering that grassroots level to participate in civil society," said Victoria Nuland. "She says we need to know those people and be connected to them, and our programs need to address their interests. The kinds of events she does humanize diplomacy in a way that releases everybody else to be human as a diplomat. When she does that herself, embassies are having to do it, too."

On most trips I covered, the town hall meetings were the highlights, displaying Clinton's masterful public speaking skills and always yielding colorful questions of the type the media loves. During the first one in Seoul, she was asked about love. "I think if you can describe it, you may not fully be experiencing it," she responded, and then mused about her relationship with her husband and former president, Bill Clinton, whom she called her "best friend" for a very long time. "We have an endless conversation," she said. "We never get bored."[18]

So are America's diplomatic readiness and the Foreign Service better off as a result of the efforts of the three secretaries of state since 2001? While the full answer will have to wait until Part Four, there is no doubt that the service is in a better place now than it was a decade ago. Clinton has built on what Powell and Rice did before her, but her main contribution was articulating a vision and a sense of purpose for her institution and putting together the conceptual puzzle that is U.S. diplomacy today. The Quadrennial Diplomacy and Development Review (QDDR), which we discussed in Chapter 1, played a major role in forcing the department to think strategically about its long-term readiness, which has not been one of its strengths historically.

When I began working on this book in 2003, many Foreign Service officers could not explain how what they did every day fit in the big picture of American foreign policy – and how it related to the national interest. There are still such officers, but their number has decreased. The common approach to the Foreign Service of the three secretaries was to fix what they thought was not working, but essentially preserve the existing system, which was established by the Foreign Service Act of 1980.[19] A major shakeup of the system is politically difficult and bureaucratically unpopular, as most people at the State Department insist there is no need for it, though there are occasional voices arguing that a sweeping reform should be at least seriously considered.

PART TWO

DEALING WITH
THE WORLD AS IT IS

Chapter 4

Managing Foreign Relations

It was the strangest place to host a press conference by any of the four secretaries of state I have covered. But there we were by the baggage carousel at Andrews Air Force Base outside Washington just after 7 a.m. on December 5, 2005, with Condoleezza Rice reading a five-page statement about torture.

"The United States does not permit, tolerate or condone torture under any circumstances," she said. "The United States does not transport and has not transported detainees from one country to another for the purpose of interrogation using torture."[1] Rice was responding to media reports about secret CIA prisons in Europe, where Bush administration officials allegedly used "enhanced techniques" to extract information from suspected terrorists.[2] Some of the reports also claimed that the CIA was using European airports and airspace to move detainees to those facilities.

It was unusual for the secretary to make an on-camera statement at the terminal just before departing on a foreign trip, especially when there was no doubt that she would have plenty of opportunities to address the same issue during the trip. But this was not a usual circumstance. Dozens of European officials had expressed outrage and demanded answers from the Bush administration, and Rice tried to calm them down before seeing them in person. "I wanted to respond as soon as possible, and it seemed only reasonable to respond before I go to Europe, so that, if there are questions of the kind that you are asking, I can answer them," she said on the plane after takeoff.[3]

Following a dinner with Rice in Brussels two days later, European Union and NATO officials said she had "cleared the air" and they were satisfied with her answers.[4] Nine months later, Bush acknowledged the secret prisons' existence but insisted that detainees had not been tortured.[5]

As she flew from Germany to Romania to Ukraine to Belgium on that trip, Rice engaged in what amounted to high-level management of relations with other countries, resulting in thousands of media stories around the world. However, that was just the tip of the iceberg. Managing foreign relationships is a daily activity at the 275 U.S. diplomatic missions, which of course is the responsibility of the Foreign Service. It rarely produces media coverage – sometimes because the media does not find it interesting, and other times because the government prefers it to remain secret.

The public caught an unprecedented glimpse of that work through an unauthorized release of more than 250,000 State Department cables – some of them secret – by the website WikiLeaks in 2010.[6] The documents, written by American diplomats posted across the world, provided information and analysis on developments in other countries, foreign officials and U.S. embassy activities.

"Such reckless sharing of classified information jeopardizes our relationships and puts sources, such as human rights activists, in harm's way," said Michael Hammer, the assistant secretary of state for public affairs. "There is always an expectation that they talk to us in confidence. Diplomacy does need that space behind closed doors to take effect and produce results. People will be more willing to talk to you and do things for you if they are allowed that breathing space." At the same time, the cables made a surprising revelation to the public. "People suddenly realized three things," Hammer said. "First, that we are pretty good writers and provide sound and interesting analysis. Second, that we are passionate and determined to advance the U.S. national interest. Third, that we do what we say, and there isn't much variance between what we say in private and in public."

Kristie Kenney, the ambassador to Thailand whom we met in Chapter 2, said that some of her embassy's sources "felt betrayed" when they read the cables, but the "good news" is that many "still want to be engaged" with the United States. "Although there are certain people who will be more reticent with us, in general, they are interested in America and want to deal with us, so they are not going to shut us off," she said.

Although transformational diplomacy has received much attention in recent years, "traditional diplomacy is not a boogeyman and should not be undervalued," said Susan Johnson, the president of the American Foreign Service Association whom we also met in

Chapter 2. "It represents a huge body of international knowledge and practice that is still very relevant, and for many countries, the only kind of diplomacy they know and find acceptable. Loss of mastery of traditional diplomatic skills could weaken the overall effectiveness of diplomacy. Although concepts of sovereignty are being tweaked at the margins, the international system of nation-states is at the basis of global stability. Gradual evolution and better cooperation, collaboration and compromise through the auspices of diplomacy are likely to suit our interests better than the alternatives."

The embassy as a mini-government

On a snowy February morning in 2012, I arrived at the U.S. Embassy in Ankara for a Monday ritual – the *country-team* meeting, a Cabinet-like gathering of the mission's leadership, including the ambassador, his deputy, the various section chiefs and the heads of any consulates and other posts in the country. The sections are political, economic, commercial, consular, management, public affairs, security and others. Every embassy holds such meetings, though not on the same day of the week. They usually begin with a review of its activities during the previous week, followed by upcoming tasks, events, visits and deadlines. Along with specific and timely matters, the team discusses broad and strategic issues that may provide opportunities for advancing certain U.S. interests in the host country.

Yuri Kim, whom we met in Chapter 1, was the political counselor – and section chief – in Ankara. At the meeting I attended, she briefed the team on a recent visit of Turkish officials to Damascus, and explained how what they saw and heard fit in the picture of the Syrian government's crackdown on protesters that had been painted by the media and other diplomatic sources. She also suggested questions the ambassador, Frank Ricciardone, might ask a Turkish diplomat with extensive experience in Syria who was invited to dinner at the ambassador's residence that evening. The economic and commercial counselors, Laird Treiber and Michael Lally, updated their colleagues on an upcoming conference they saw as a good opportunity to promote U.S. trade and investment in Turkey. And the counselor for public affairs, Mark Wentworth, whom I had met in Romania during that 2005 "torture" trip with Rice, explained why I was visiting, following an introduction by Ricciardone.

The country team is much more than just a formal and hierarchical group – it is "one of the most effective expressions of the interagency process," said Bill Burns, the deputy secretary of state.

The practicality of having such a team is obvious given the growing number of federal agencies represented at embassies. In fact, State Department personnel are often outnumbered by employees of other parts of the government, such as the departments of Defense, Homeland Security, Justice, Commerce, Agriculture, the Treasury, as well as the FBI, the Federal Aviation Administration and the Centers for Disease Control. While all those representatives report directly to their home agencies in Washington, they also have to consult with the embassy leadership and keep it abreast of their activities, which must be part of its overall mission, Burns said. Other agencies get more things done if they work with the ambassador, he added.

The extraordinary depth and breadth of the U.S. engagement with foreign countries has been the most surprising discovery of my research. The level of intensity and the sheer number of issues being worked on at any given time make the U.S. Foreign Service the closest thing there is to a global diplomatic service. In fact, several foreign officials complained that the Americans have too broad an agenda and want too many things from their host government. Foreign Service officers did not deny that, saying it has become the reality of modern diplomacy.

"It's true that the U.S. government comes to them with all sorts of things, whether it's making a request or a complaint, and it never stops," said Hans Wechsel, the former restaurant manager whom we met in Chapter 2. "But many foreign governments have learned to filter through all that – they know that a certain issue is really important if it's raised by the ambassador or a higher-level visitor from Washington." The danger of that, Wechsel noted, is that some issues may not be taken seriously unless brought up by senior officials, which sometimes frustrates lower-level embassy personnel.

In addition, as mentioned in Chapter 2, many issues today can no longer be decided just by a country's Foreign Ministry or even its government. "We used to lobby the executive branch, but that's not enough anymore," said David Lindwall, one of the six diplomats we met at the beginning of Chapter 1. "In many countries, the center of power is not only in the central government, and we have to deal with a much broader field of players, such as legislatures, mayors, governors and even the private sector. We have to build constituencies." A campaign to do just that was the key to reforming Guatemala's child-adoption system, as we will see in Chapter 8. In such broad efforts, the contacts and contributions of the various U.S. agencies represented at a post are essential for a successful outcome.

An embassy's link to the interagency process in Washington is the country desk at the State Department. "We are in a position to advise the embassy, keep them apprised of what is happening here, which is where the major decisions are made, and shape their activities and outreach," said Timothy Lenderking, until recently director of the Pakistan Desk, officially known as the Office of Pakistan Affairs. "We also write directly to the secretary of state – rarely anything from the post goes straight to the secretary, so we need to be good at filtering." The Pakistan Desk is one of the largest, reflecting the huge challenges in that relationship – it has a staff of 21, including office managers, according to a department organizational chart dated May 7, 2012.[7] The Afghanistan Desk has 27 employees. Both offices are part of the Bureau of South and Central Asian Affairs. In that same bureau, there are eight India Desk officers, one for Bangladesh, and one for both Nepal and Bhutan.

The work of both the Pakistan desk and the embassy in Islamabad was hampered by several major events in 2011, said Lenderking and Cameron Munter, the ambassador at the time I visited Islamabad in early 2012. Just one of those events – the raid that killed Osama bin Laden not far from the capital – was planned, while the others were accidents.

As noted in Chapter 1, the fatal shooting of two Pakistanis in Lahore by a CIA contractor, Raymond Davis, preceded the bin Laden operation by about three months. Then in late November, a NATO air strike targeting terrorists killed 24 Pakistani soldiers. The prime minister at the time, Yousuf Raza Gilani, condemned the "unprovoked and indiscriminate" attack as "outrageous," and within hours, his government closed vital supply lines to NATO forces in Afghanistan, which remained shut for more than seven months.[8] The powerful army chief of staff, General Ashfaq Parvez Kayani, denounced the "blatant and unacceptable act" and demanded "strong and urgent action be taken against those responsible for this aggression."[9]

"It was a bad year," Lenderking said. "Many unforeseen things happened that exposed the thin veneer of the relationship. There was a pretty ambitious calendar set for 2011. President Obama was going to visit Pakistan, and President [Asif Ali] Zardari was going to come here, but all of that was run asunder by these events. We had other visits and exchange programs canceled. Our interaction with the Pakistani Embassy in Washington hasn't been affected too much. We still get visas done – we have a big embassy in Islamabad, and our people need visas to get there – but it takes time. Because of the Ray Davis incident, their embassy has a particular problem with our security staff, so they scrutinize those more carefully."

When short-term and long-term goals clash

General Kayani was seething. Ambassador Munter had just handed him a démarche from Washington with "a list of things" the Obama administration wanted the Pakistani army to do in the wake of bin Laden's death. It felt that now it had more leverage to secure better cooperation from the Pakistanis in the fight against extremists hiding in the country. The Pakistani government, having been kept in the dark, was still stunned by the raid, and Kayani knew that accepting the U.S. demands would be seen as capitulating to the Americans. So he "tossed the piece of paper" at the ambassador and asked him to leave. "I've rarely been insulted to my face as a diplomat, but he just threw me out of his office," Munter said. "Is this the way you treat people when they are down?" he recalled the general asking. "He is not a rude man, but it was about as rude as he gets."

For Munter, that one-on-one meeting was the culmination of a series of tense and emotional exchanges with Pakistani officials in May 2011. When the ambassador and his aides first went to see Kayani after the raid, what they heard was "congratulations." Then Kayani and Lieutenant-General Ahmad Suja Pasha, director-general of the Inter-Services Intelligence (ISI) at the time, "just sat there slack-jawed," Munter said. "They were absolutely amazed and didn't know how to respond. They didn't really get angry or resentful, or know what to do until they thought about it for a couple days."

Comments by Leon Panetta, at the time CIA director who later became defense secretary, that the Pakistanis were either "involved" in protecting bin Laden or "incompetent"[10] finally "drove them up the wall – partly because it was insulting, and partly because it was true," Munter noted. "Then they said it wasn't a question of incompetence or being complicit, but of violation of their sovereignty. So they completely switched the blame away from themselves."

Every American ambassador has two utmost priorities: protecting U.S. interests and building or maintaining a productive relationship with the host country. That does not mean that relations always have to be good at all cost – they should be at least business-like and respectful, so the two countries can work together when necessary. The key ingredient in any relationship, of course, is trust.

That was exactly what Munter had tried to build with Kayani for months before the bin Laden raid – not for the sake of having a good relationship, but because the Pakistani army's cooperation with the United States could help to save American lives. Thousands of al-Qaida militants are believed to be hiding in the border areas with Afghanistan, posing a threat to the U.S. troops on the other side of the border. Moreover, "al-Qaida can attack the homeland," so it is "vital" that the threat is eliminated, Munter said. "We could do it by invading Pakistan, but we have calculated that we probably wouldn't get every al-Qaida guy, we would radicalize this country in such a way that it would create new al-Qaidas, and we would radicalize the rest of the Muslim world." He had actually had success in gaining Kayani's trust. "He saw himself as someone committed to working with us – a nationalist who wasn't going to do our bidding but wouldn't betray us, either," Munter said. "He got hammered by some of his commanders for being too trusting of the Americans."

Pasha, the ISI chief, had a similar philosophy, which helped immensely in the Ray Davis case. After the shooting in Lahore, Davis was arrested and released six weeks later, but only after the victims' families received more than $2 million in "blood money," according to media reports.[11] "The ISI helped us get him out," Munter said. "They paid the blood money." However, U.S. officials in Washington were quoted at the time as saying that they would reimburse the Pakistani government.[12]

The bin Laden and Davis episodes, as well as the NATO strike that inadvertently killed Pakistani soldiers, are telling examples of how short-term U.S. goals in a foreign country can clash with the long-term American mission. Similar examples can be found around the world, including in Russia and China, where Washington has to play a careful balancing act between its advocacy of human rights and democracy, and the help it needs from Moscow and Beijing to address strategic issues, such as the North Korean and Iranian nuclear programs.

In Pakistan, "our main short-term goals are destroying al-Qaida and winning the war in Afghanistan," Munter said. To achieve these goals, the U.S. relies on Pakistan's help, but when it does not get it, acting alone or with NATO allies is the only alternative. One of the most controversial tactics Washington uses – to vocal protests from Islamabad – are drone strikes targeting militants. While the administration has refused to discuss the practice in public, U.S. officials were reported in June 2012 as saying privately that such an attack had killed al-Qaida's deputy leader, Abu Yahya al-Libi, in Pakistan.[13] The White House said the killing had brought al-Qaida "closer to its ultimate demise than ever before."[14]

The long-term U.S. goal in the region is a stable Pakistan, but also a stable Afghanistan, as well as India, Munter said. As it does in other countries, the U.S. tries to stabilize Pakistan through transformational diplomacy, which we will discuss in Chapter 8. It aims to improve governance, build effective democratic institutions and make people's lives better. It also helps to modernize and train the Pakistani military, in the hope that it would not allow Pakistan to be a safe haven for terrorists. A good working relationship with the local government is naturally very useful to make that happen.

However, "when the short-term and long-term goals are at odds with one another, you end up hurting your chances to achieve either one or both of them," said Munter. "I would do the bin Laden operation exactly the same way again – it was worth it, and the president had made the calculation that it was worth it. But let's not kid ourselves, it did damage the relationship very badly. There is a set of assumptions when you build a relationship, and when you talk with people, there has to be someone willing to listen. When that collapses, running an embassy and trying to get things done is very difficult, which is why this job is the hardest I've had in the Foreign Service by orders of magnitude."

Another complication, he noted, is that many people in Washington are "hugely frustrated" with the Pakistanis for not delivering, in spite of the large U.S. assistance they receive. Since 2001, Congress has approved about $20 billion in military and economic aid for Pakistan, according to the Congressional Research Service.[15] "We work hard on building trust," Munter said. "We give them assistance, whether it's money or wheat, and we airlift them out of their floods. But does it help us in the long run to build a dam here, so that these guys have hydro-electric power and don't have another flood?" Lenderking said that giving up is not an option, because "there is a lot at stake, and a failed state would be a disaster."

In a May 2012 report, the State Department's Office of the Inspector General gave Munter and his team "great credit" for managing the "fallout" from the events of 2011. The "embassy leadership has forged effective working relationships with and among the unusual assemblage of agencies at post," the report said. "The success of these team-building efforts is also reflected in a shared view within the country team on how the United States should approach and advance its sometimes competing interests in Pakistan."[16]

An ambassador's autonomy

Since September 11, 2001, the U.S. ambassadors to Pakistan in both the Bush and Obama administrations have had a close working relationship with the secretary of state and even the president, because of that country's importance in the fight against al-Qaida. The bin

Laden raid and the other episodes discussed above further magnified the interest in Pakistan at the very top of the U.S. government.

"Many of the decisions regarding Pakistan are presidential decisions," said a senior White House official who asked not to be named. "In making those decisions, the president consults with his national security team, and the ambassador is part of that. When we are in the Situation Room having a meeting on Pakistan, it's not always a great time of day in Islamabad, but the ambassador is always there [via video-conference], because it's important to have him in the conversation. The president has spent more time with the ambassador to Pakistan than with most of our ambassadors. You just can't take your eyes off the ball when it comes to Pakistan. This is not your typical relationship with a foreign country."

Munter's predecessor in Islamabad, Anne Patterson, continued to have a relationship with Obama "at the closest level," because he sent her to Egypt next, where she has dealt with "some of the toughest issues of our generation," the senior official said. Following the popular uprising that ousted former President Hosni Mubarak as part of the so-called Arab Spring in 2011, the Egyptian authorities accused U.S. pro-democracy activists in Cairo of working for groups receiving illegal foreign funding, and barred them from leaving the country. They were released after weeks of intensive diplomacy.[17] "When we were dealing with the challenge of the potential charging of the Americans in Egypt, the work that our Foreign Service officers did was critical, and there were briefings a few times a day, often directly from the ambassador," the official added.

Constant high-level interest in another country is a double-edged sword for the Foreign Service. The inspector-general's report on Embassy Islamabad criticized "Washington's intense and at times intrusive involvement, and its voracious appetite for information on the situation in Pakistan," as "one of the embassy's greatest challenges." "While it ensures that mission concerns receive both timely and top-level attention, it also consumes extraordinary amounts of the mission's time and energy and adds significantly to the stresses at this already stressed post," the report said.

In most countries, the U.S. ambassador rarely enjoys presidential attention, which may seem a negative, but it usually means that the relationship with that country is doing just fine. It also means that the ambassador has greater autonomy – not to make policy, but to take decisions concerning policy implementation. "In general, there is an inverse relationship between the amount of autonomy an ambassador has, and the degree of controversy around what's happening" in a particular country at a certain time, said Jack Lew, the chief of staff in the Obama White House whom we met in Chapter 1. "If you were in Eastern Europe in the 1990s," you did get presidential attention, he noted.

There are large and influential countries, such as China and Russia, that occupy the minds of the secretary and the president every week, because of bilateral problems and global issues they are involved in as permanent members of the U.N. Security Council. Then there are nations like Greece, which has not been traditionally controversial, but its serious financial problems since 2010 have received worldwide attention due to their impact on economies and markets far and wide.

Daniel Smith, the U.S. ambassador to Greece, said that the policy on how the United States could help the troubled EU member and NATO ally was designed through the interagency process in Washington. "That's where we all get our instructions and guidance, but within that broad parameter and strategic framework, a lot of flexibility flows to the ambassadors in terms of how you work the issue, who you partner with, and how you move forward," said Smith, who joined the Foreign Service in 1983 and was previously executive secretary of the State Department.

Sometimes, the direction set by Washington is so broad that an ambassador's hand is much freer in shaping U.S. engagement. For example, when James Jeffrey was ambassador to Albania from 2002 until 2004, the policy objectives were a stable, secure and democratic country that developed its economy toward future EU membership. Albania has never been deemed vital to the U.S. national interest, so when explosive disputes broke out between the government and the opposition, Jeffrey saw no reason to bother senior officials in Washington. "Every day during that period, I had to get on the phone with the head of the opposition, the prime minister or the president and say, 'You are about to throw the country into total chaos and violence, and you might drag down the entire Balkans. Could you please take the following six-point action program that we just developed this morning and apply it?' This is what I got to do for almost two years," said Jeffrey, a former ambassador to Iraq and Turkey who retired from the Foreign Service in 2012 after 35 years.

Richard Boucher, whose many posts in the service included ambassador to Cyprus, said the diplomats he learned from as a young officer used to say that "an ambassador should never receive an instruction he hasn't written."

Cameron Munter may not have had great autonomy in Pakistan, but he certainly did in Serbia, even after the 2008 attack that burned down a part of his embassy, as mentioned in Chapter 1. The events around Kosovo's independence from Serbia were "difficult, but that was something we managed on our own," he said. The attack was in response to Washington's recognition of Kosovo as a sovereign country, and it led to a costly embassy evacuation and the destruction of millions of dollars' worth of communications equipment by the U.S. staff, which is a standard procedure in such cases, Munter said.

Once evidence surfaced that Serbian Prime Minister Vojislav Koštunica had personally approved the assault by a "gang of hoodlums," Munter decided that he was "going to ensure the prime minister was gone," and that "the best revenge was making sure this guy lost the next election," which was less than five months away. Koštunica was the last president of Yugoslavia before it ceased to exist in 2003, having replaced Slobodan Milošević in October 2000 – about three months before I interviewed Koštunica in Belgrade for the *Financial Times*.[18]

Munter determined that the key to weakening Koštunica's 2008 re-election chances was taking away the support of the Socialist Party of Serbia, once led by Milošević. Its new leader was Ivica Dačić, who had once challenged Milošević for the top post. "We got him to flip over and join the pro-Europeans," Munter said. "We didn't pay him off; we just persuaded him. What he really wanted was international legitimacy. So we got [José Luis Rodríguez] Zapatero, the Spanish prime minister at the time, and George Papandreou, the future Greek prime minister, who ran Socialist International at the time, to invite Dačić to visit them abroad, where they wined and dined him. They told him they would let him in if he joined the pro-European forces, and he did. He put a knife in Koštunica's back." Koštunica's party lost the July 2008 election. Dačić's party did not join Socialist International, the global organization of left-of-center political parties,[19] but he became deputy prime minister and rose to prime minister four years later.[20]

To ambassadors' delight, Hillary Clinton has tried to ensure that they have the authority and flexibility to operate as chief executives. "Chiefs of mission must be empowered and accountable as CEOs of multi-agency missions," says the Quadrennial Diplomacy and Development Review (QDDR), which we discussed in Chapter 1.[21] Some of those authorities are quite meaningful – for example, a new position cannot be created and a new employee cannot be sent to post without the ambassador's approval. Tracey Jacobson, the former ambassador to Tajikistan whom we met in Chapter 2, said she refused an initial request from Washington to add positions at her embassy because there were not enough management officers to take care of the post's personnel. "I made a decision that we would not allow the American staff to increase until our management platform was appropriate for the mission," she said. "I went on a lobbying campaign, which was ultimately effective. Then I was able to accept additional positions."

At the same time, chiefs of mission have significant limitations that make it difficult to be true CEOs, many of them said. "The full meaning of that word I don't believe is possible in the U.S. government," said Frank Ricciardone. "We don't have that degree of license within our law. We have a lot of people looking over our shoulders, who can and do exert statutory authority over what we do. The budget is directed from Washington, and we can't allocate resources in the way that a CEO can on behalf of the shareholders."

The art of suasion

In July 2003, armed Filipino military officers took over an apartment tower in Manila, in a peculiar attempt to overthrow the government of President Gloria Macapagal Arroyo.[22] Ricciardone, who was the ambassador to the Philippines at the time, was alarmed by reports that Arroyo was considering a military response, which most likely would have resulted in civilian casualties. Having received permission from Deputy Secretary of State Richard Armitage, he called Arroyo to plead with her not to use force.

"I had to tell her she shouldn't send tanks in and blow up the building," which was not too far from the American Embassy, Ricciardone recalled. "I said, 'You have time on your side, just wait them out. Tell me, Madam President, you are not going to do this. I will wake up President Bush if you think you are going to do this. We can't just stand by.' She didn't do it. She waited it out. She later told Bush that she made the decision based on what I had told her. It was the right decision."

Persuasive arguments are the bread and butter of classic diplomacy, and at the end of the day, they are the Foreign Service's main tool – it cannot afford to dangle military power as a stick or foreign aid as a carrot all the time, and it certainly does not carry weapons around. "All we have are our wits and bare hands," said Carolyn Johnson, whom I met in Brussels in 2003. Yuri Kim questioned the widely accepted meaning of the word "diplomatic" as nice and tactful. "It's not about being nice to people or not saying hurtful things. In fact, in the jobs that I've had to do, we've had difficult and sometimes combative conversations," she said. "In the most acute cases, like North Korea or Iraq, it's about talking to someone so that guns don't get pulled out. It's a way to avoid or end conflict, and to get people to compromise."

The QDDR uses the word "suasion," which correctly describes a daily activity in pursuit of an ambitious global agenda. Of course, not the whole world is friendly to the United States, so there is groundwork to be laid sometimes.

"Generally, we try to move countries from being enemies to neutrals to supporters to allies," said James Jeffrey. Textbook examples of that continuum are the former communist countries of Central and Eastern Europe that are now NATO and EU members. Some relationships develop in the opposite direction, as is the case with Venezuela, which used to be a good friend of the United States but has become a passive enemy under President Hugo Chávez. When I visited the U.S. Embassy in Caracas in 2003, significantly reduced access had made the work of American diplomats very difficult, and some of the post's Venezuelan employees told me they often had to hide where they worked for fear of retribution.

Several Foreign Service officers spoke of a prevalent view in many countries after September 11 that the "militarization" of U.S. foreign policy had hurt the "moral authority" of the U.S. Along with that, they added, there was a perception that it had become very difficult for American diplomats to get other countries to do things, as discussed in Chapter 1. However, while that was the case around the start of the Iraq war, relative normality has been restored, they said. More importantly, it has never been that easy for U.S. diplomats to secure international cooperation in the first place, they noted.

For example, Turkey's refusal in 2003 to allow use of its military bases in support of the Iraq war – and to open its airspace to U.S. and allied aircraft on their way to Iraq until the last minute – became a major irritant in the relationship and produced numerous media stories.[23] "But I don't remember a time when Turkey was compliant, in the sense that we could simply say something, and they would do it," said Ricciardone, who had served there twice before becoming ambassador in 2010. "We asked them to help pressure the Soviet Union not to invade Afghanistan in 1979, and they weren't very receptive, at least at the beginning." Kim agreed that "it was always tough with Turkey," as did Douglas Silliman, a former deputy chief of mission in Ankara under both Ricciardone and Jeffrey.

In spite of the difficulties, however, "the size of the Turkish economy has nearly tripled in the last decade, and the U.S. has had a huge impact. Turkey values that, even if they don't say it in public,"

Silliman said. In addition, "Afghanistan is NATO's biggest mission, and Turkey is a big player in that mission. I think Turkey has influenced both us and Europe, and we've also influenced Turkey," he said.

"In absolute terms, we have more power than ever before, but in relative terms, there are other countries on the ascendance," Silliman said. "I don't think we've declined, but there is a lot of competition." Ricciardone agreed. "It's a multipolar world, and the way that we have to make arguments is different from the old days," he said. "Countries' interests are much more varied, and in general, diplomacy is much more work now than it used to be."

The intricacies of diplomatic reporting

Christopher Harris is a very lucky mid-level Foreign Service officer – a cable he wrote from Islamabad in January 2012 was discussed at a Principals Committee meeting at the White House, and the action proposed in it was given a green light personally by President Obama. The Principals Committee is chaired by the national security adviser and includes the secretaries of state and defense, as well as the director of national intelligence and the chairman of the Joint Chiefs of Staff, among others.

The Pakistani parliament was preparing a debate on the future of relations with the United States, following the events discussed earlier in the chapter, and Washington was eager to put the problems behind and move forward. Harris was tasked by Munter with trying to predict the main points likely to be raised during the debate, and to suggest if and how the U.S. government should address them, drawing on input and expertise from across the embassy. "This is something the National Security Council does at the White House, but one of the things we can add is an on-the-ground perspective, and we thought it would be useful," Harris said. "It was a long cable – five or six pages – that included 16 points." He declined to be more specific because the document was classified.

The inspector-general's report on Embassy Islamabad mentioned earlier praised the post's reporting. At all levels, it "has provided a clear-eyed assessment of realities in Pakistan, as well as sober advice to Washington on how to deal with those realities, even when the message was not what Washington might have wanted to hear," the report said.

Hundreds of reporting cables are sent to Washington every day, and their authors often wonder if anyone – let alone the president –

reads them. Doug Silliman, who after Ankara went to Baghdad, where I met him, said he edits more cables than he writes as the embassy's political counselor, and also teaches the intricacies of cable-writing to young officers. "I've found that there is some great political and economic reporting that is sent back to the department, but it's either too long or doesn't touch on an issue that's interesting, or people don't understand it, so it doesn't get read," he said.

Richard Hoagland, Munter's deputy in Islamabad and a former ambassador to Kazakhstan and Tajikistan, has written up more than two pages of tips he shares with his younger colleagues. They sound remarkably similar to the rules I was taught as a young journalist. Among them are: "concise and intriguing headlines," "colorful writing, despite what some in Washington will tell you," as well as avoiding passive verbs "like the plague" and "long, complex sentences with multiple embedded clauses." In fact, Hoagland says that "good cables should copy journalistic style, rather than academic models."

Sumreen Mirza, whom we met in Chapter 2, was one of Silliman's young officers in Baghdad. "I write almost every day – cables, meeting notes, spot reports or other messages," she said. "Having served in Washington, I know that a good number of people read the cables." The political tradecraft course she took at the Foreign Service Institute "gives you the basic tools, and then you come here and pick up the style and template that suits the management, the interlocutors and the conversations we have," Mirza added. "The WikiLeaks episode has changed a bit of our writing. We are more careful about protecting sources and other people."

In Baghdad, she covered the Kurdish political parties. Although there is a U.S. consulate in the Kurdistan region in northern Iraq that does its own reporting, "my job is to understand the Kurds' role in national politics," she explained. "The Kurdish Alliance has almost 60 seats in the parliament, and they have been a mediator in political crises, as well as a kingmaker in the political formation. I meet with them almost every day – in the parliament, the ministries, in non-governmental organizations."

How does one report on a country without having a physical presence there? The United States has no diplomatic relations with Iran, but it has several "Iran watchers" based in different countries with ties to the Islamic Republic. Hans Wechsel was one of them – in Istanbul – until the summer of 2012 and was nominated for an award for "impact and originality in reporting." He said he made contacts with Iranian asylum-seekers in Turkey, as well as "people who still live in Iran but travel to Turkey, and Turks who visit Iran or maintain connections there." During his time in Istanbul, Wechsel met with Iranian opposition leaders, journalists, academics, student activists and human rights lawyers, he said.

Many more agencies than just the State Department make use of the reporting from overseas missions, and the "quality of the reporting, the details, the analysis that goes into the average cable is really value added," Hillary Clinton said. "I read a lot of cables," she said. "Obviously, what gets to me is a small percentage of what is written and sent in every day, but I think that these cables are widely read."

When WikiLeaks published the cables mentioned earlier, "we had to change our distribution pattern to other agencies," because the leak had come from outside the State Department, said Patrick Kennedy, the undersecretary of state for management whom we met in Chapter 3. "On more than one occasion, I was approached by officials from other agencies to make sure we didn't cut off our feed to them."

Who sets the agenda?

There is a refugee camp in Iraq that looks nothing like the camps you have probably seen on the news – it may actually no longer exist by the time you are reading this. Rather, it resembles a small town, with modern buildings, the latest communications technology and even its own university, said David Lindwall, who was the political-military counselor in Baghdad when I met him in early 2012. When Lindwall first visited Camp Ashraf six months earlier, he was impressed by a "huge mosque with a monumental blue dome, a museum, water park, several monuments, a large conference center, and a tree-lined main boulevard."

Camp Ashraf has been the headquarters of the People's Mujahedin of Iran, which is also known as Mojahedin-e Khalq or MEK, an Iranian resistance group designated by the State Department as a foreign terrorist organization "for the assassination of several U.S. military personnel and civilians in the 1970s."[24] Following the 2003 U.S. occupation of Iraq, the American military disarmed the camp, which had about 3,400 residents, according to the department. The post-Saddam Iraqi government was under pressure from Tehran to close Ashraf for years, but the MEK refused to leave. The Iraqi army attacked the camp more than once, killing several Iranians and provoking an outrage in Congress.[25]

So it fell on the United States to help find a new home for the refugees and close Ashraf. That was the reason for Lindwall's visit – the first of many over nearly a year. "I was surprised to be received by a group of polite, well-educated interlocutors who could have passed for Western diplomats," he said. "The conference room where we met had communication equipment that would be the envy of any U.S. embassy."

A direct link between Ashraf's future and the U.S. national interest is difficult to find, but it was the issue that occupied more of Lindwall's time in Iraq than any other, and the "U.S. government spent an incredible amount of time and resources on it," he said. He explained that paradox with "an effective lobbying campaign that a few vocal MEK supporters" mounted in Washington. "Somehow, they persuaded 98 members of Congress to sign a letter" to Hillary Clinton calling for the group's removal from the terrorist blacklist. "These were very serious people," Lindwall said of the legislators, "so there was a great deal of pressure on us to resolve this problem, even though 99 percent of Americans couldn't care less about it."

In 2012, hundreds of Ashraf residents moved to a former U.S. military base near the Baghdad airport, Camp Hurriya. The rest were supposed to follow suit shortly, but complaints about the living condition delayed the process.[26]

While the executive branch of the U.S. government usually sets the country's diplomatic agenda – and overseas missions often have flexibility in the daily management of foreign relations – the field has become more competitive, as the Ashraf case shows. Congress plays a major role in foreign policy through legislation, foreign travel, and of course by appropriating funds. In addition, the Senate must confirm every ambassador, as well as assistant secretaries and higher-ranking officials at the State Department.

Many U.S. priorities in a foreign country have an obvious connection to the national interest, such as working to stop the flow of terrorist financing, defending and promoting human rights and expanding business opportunities for American companies. Other priorities like Camp Ashraf may be less evident, but they "have certain constituencies in the U.S.," Lindwall said. "The largest program we have in Guatemala is to improve child nutrition. Part of the reason is that some members of Congress are very interested in child survival, so there are always funds put in the appropriations bill."

In many cases, the Foreign Service does not need to be told by Washington that something should be a priority. As a junior officer in Brussels in 2003, Hans Wechsel was responsible for the counterterrorism portfolio at the embassy, which led to frequent interactions with various parts of the Belgian judicial system. In the process, he came upon an unusual law that, until then, the United States had little reason to worry about. "Belgium came up with the idea that, for certain crimes against humanity, regardless of where they took place and who committed them, Belgium had the obligation and competence to pursue a case," Wechsel said. "It's commonly referred to as 'universal jurisdiction.' That concept was mixed with the idea that any citizen could bring a criminal complaint, and force at least a cursory investigation."

Shortly before the Iraq war started, victims of a Baghdad bombing during the first Gulf War in 1991 filed a complaint against top U.S. officials at that time, including President George H. W. Bush, Defense Secretary Dick Cheney and Colin Powell, who was then chairman of the Joint Chiefs of Staff.[27] Although arrests could not be made just on the basis of a complaint, Wechsel explained, "at a certain point during an investigation, a judge could decide that there was enough evidence to make an arrest, but they would not make an announcement, so how do you know? While arrests were hugely remote possibilities, there was no absolute guarantee that they wouldn't happen" if the named officials went to Belgium, which of course hosts both the EU and NATO headquarters, Wechsel said.

Before the story appeared in the media, he got the attention of his superiors at the embassy and in Washington, who decided on a dual course of action. First, get the complaint, and any others that might be filed, dismissed. Second, repeal the law.

The diplomatic work paid off. By the time the press focused on the issue, a parliamentary commission had changed the law to allow the government to block such cases. The long-term solution, however, took several months, during which Washington threatened to seek moving the NATO headquarters to another country to avoid visits to Belgium by affected U.S. officials. Powell called the law a "serious problem."[28] It was repealed in August 2003,[29] following some not very pleasant public exchanges between the U.S. and Belgian authorities.[30]

Even as a junior officer, Wechsel played an important role. "Both my government and the Belgian government recognized me as an expert on the issue, and I was in meetings with the Belgian prime minister," he said. "I had contacts with different perspectives and agendas. I knew the lawyer for the NGO that was helping file those complaints, as well as the member of parliament who had authored the law. I had contacts in the Justice and Foreign Ministries, and also had a working relationship with the federal prosecutor. So I had the whole circle – everybody who had a major stake. There were never strong personal friendship, but we were friendly."

Fighting common battles

Perhaps the most complex part of the Foreign Service's work is so-called multilateral diplomacy. As mentioned in Chapter 1, the U.S. has permanent missions at several international organizations, such as the United Nations, the EU and NATO. In the EU, many decisions are made not in national capitals, but at the headquarters in Brussels. For every U.N. Security Council resolution Washington wants passed, American diplomats must lobby other council members for their votes. Of the 15 council members, the five permanent ones – the U.S., Britain, France, Russia and China – have veto power.

At NATO, all 28 members in effect have veto power, because decisions are taken only by consensus. When Victoria Nuland was ambassador there during the Bush administration, the most pressing issue was beefing up the international forces in Afghanistan so other countries could share the burden with the U.S. At the same time, the most important long-term matter was expanding the alliance's "global partnership beyond its traditional European theater, to countries like Morocco, Jordan and the United Arab Emirates," Nuland said. "We wanted to encourage them to see NATO not as a four-letter word or an aggressive military organization, but as the core of a global security community in service to global peace and other U.N. objectives. We also wanted them to understand that NATO was changing at light speed compared to how it started in 1949."

Multilateral diplomacy is not practiced only at international organizations. On transnational issues like human trafficking and climate change, American diplomats work with individual countries around the world every day. In addition, the U.S. has often been a mediator in resolving international conflicts. David Lindwall recalled that the U.S., Argentina, Brazil and Chile were guarantors of the Ecuador-Peru peace process that emerged from a month-long war the two neighbors fought over a disputed border area in 1995.

A much longer peace process – between the Israelis and Palestinians – also has four active outside observers in the United States, the U.N., the EU and Russia, known as the Quartet. The Middle East is, of course, a historically volatile and oil-rich region where the major powers have long had strategic and economic interests. Because Washington wants to be kept in the loop on other countries' policies, and sometimes cooperates with them, Foreign Service officers at U.S. embassies in Europe have been tasked with being Middle East watchers. James Miller was one of them when I met him in Paris in early 2012. "France plays a role in the Middle East, and we have some competing and many overlapping interests," he said. "The person in this job is usually a Middle East expert who has served in the region, who knows the people in Washington to reach back to, and who can work with the French on moving the ball forward the way we want it to go. There are very talented people in Paris who have deep understanding and extensive training in the region and speak Arabic well. They come to meetings with us and make very good arguments."

At many U.S. embassies, even though they are bilateral missions, dealing with multilateral issues is a daily activity. As a member of the EU and the 17-nation euro zone, which uses the euro as its common currency, Greece became everyone's problem when its massive debt crisis started in 2010, dragging down the European economy as a whole. The bailout packages that followed sparked controversy across Europe and provoked different views among the EU members, which were faced with potentially the first departure from the euro zone.

The United States was keenly interested in the outcome not only because its economy is tightly linked to that across the Atlantic, but also because it is a member of the International Monetary Fund, which played a major role is trying to resolve the crisis. "In order to deal with this, you have to understand the dynamics in each of the countries and the factors in play," said Daniel Smith, the ambassador to Greece. "In bilateral diplomacy, it's easier to understand what motivates everyone. In multilateral, you have more players, it's much more complicated, and there are more things to take into consideration."

Another less controversial but very important long-term security issue Smith has worked on in Athens is piracy – the real kind, with pirates and guns, not the theft of intellectual property, which we will discuss in the next chapter. Piracy is a global problem, but in addition to trying to mobilize the world through multilateral diplomacy, Washington engages individual maritime powers.

"While not a big country, Greece is a heavyweight in terms of shipping and has the world's largest merchant marine," he said. "So we have an ongoing dialogue with the Greek government, shipowners and others on how to address these issues. I recently gave a speech at one of the biggest shipping conferences in the world, and we had American firms on hand that can provide security assistance to Greek companies to protect them from piracy. Since this has become an organized criminal activity, we have to trace the money, and we need their cooperation to do that."

One of the largest multilateral diplomatic efforts Washington has mounted in recent years is its push to widen international sanctions against Iran as punishment for its nuclear program, which the West fears is aimed at building a weapon. In 2012, the United States and the EU effectively imposed an oil embargo on the Islamic republic. Faced with the risk of being denied access to the American banking system, many countries observed the sanctions. That July, for example, Kenya canceled a deal to import 4 million tons of Iranian crude oil a year. "There is an embargo on Iranian oil," Patrick Nyoike, permanent secretary in the Kenyan energy ministry, was quoted as saying by wire reports. "We don't want to get involved in the intricacies of international inter-governmental issues."[31]

Chapter 5

Economic and Business Diplomacy

Kristie Kenney, the ambassador to Thailand, always seems upbeat and chipper, but on the day I visited her in Bangkok in February 2012, she was especially excited, in anticipation of a rare event the next day. The Boeing Company was flying in its newest commercial plane, the Dreamliner, which she saw as an excellent opportunity to promote the U.S. aircraft industry, and American business in general. An added bonus was the fact that the president of Boeing for Southeast Asia was Ralph Boyce, one of Kenney's recent predecessors at the embassy in Bangkok, whom many Thais still remembered because of his superb command of their language. As it happened, I had met Boyce in Jakarta in 2004 while he was ambassador to Indonesia, and visited him in Singapore just three months before the Dreamliner event.

An event with the U.S. ambassador in almost any country would attract significant media attention, and Kenney used the chance to showcase issues important to American interests. Promoting U.S. business and expanding trade was one of the top issues on her agenda. "Every single day of the year we promote American companies and help to find new opportunities for Americans to do business here," she said. "It starts with me wearing a Coca Cola T-shirt at a basketball game or carrying a Starbucks cup." Not long after the Boeing event, Kenney gave a speech at Cotton Day, organized by Cotton USA to promote American cotton exports. She wore a dress made entirely of U.S. cotton.

As we saw in the previous chapters, diplomatic success is often difficult to measure – many results are long-term, and the absence of conflict is rarely seen as a reason to reward someone. If there is one area where the results are obvious and almost immediate, it is economic and business diplomacy. Helping U.S. companies to generate more revenue abroad, so they can contribute more to prosperity at home, is always a priority. At a time of economic woes and high unemployment, it becomes an urgent necessity. President Obama has made that link very clear and direct, and has been pushing for more bilateral and regional free trade agreements. In 2010, he created the National Export Initiative aimed at "doubling exports over the next five years by working to remove trade barriers abroad, by helping firms – especially small businesses – overcome the hurdles to entering new export markets, by assisting with financing, and in general by pursuing a government-wide approach to export advocacy abroad."[1] Two years later, the Department of Commerce reported that, for the first time in U.S. history, annual exports of goods and services exceeded $2 trillion. It estimated that, in 2011, jobs supported by exports increased to 9.7 million, up 1.2 million since 2009. Also in 2011, every $1 billion of U.S. exports supported 5,080 jobs, it said.[2]

In 2012, Hillary Clinton designated June 14 Global Economic Statecraft Day, on which American embassies and consulates hosted over 250 events in 130 countries, the State Department said.[3] The series of events – mostly conferences, seminars, webinars and round-table discussions – continued around the world. One of the more interesting ideas was a cooking contest among leading hotel chefs in Japan to promote the use and export of U.S. agricultural products. In addition to the activities abroad, U.S. diplomats visited "their hometowns to explain how local companies can connect with markets overseas and attract foreign investment to their communities," the department said.

"I've worked to elevate economic issues to the forefront of our diplomacy," Clinton told me. "We are very focused on ensuring that the Foreign Service is an active partner with the rest of the American government, and with the American private sector, to promote jobs and opportunities that will benefit certainly first and foremost the United States, but by extension the rest of the world."

Seeking a level playing field

In his message to the Foreign Service on the first Global Economic Statecraft Day, Obama urged U.S. diplomats to "ensure that everybody plays by the same rules, so that our companies can compete on a level playing field."[4] That is the main job of the economic sections at embassies.

In the past, those sections mostly analyzed the host country's economy and reported back to Washington, but that "has been de-emphasized, partly because there are many consulting firms and others who publish such analyses," said Tom Countryman, whom we met in Chapter 2. "There are also many nuts and bolts in terms of trade, regulations and environmental issues that an economic section has to deal with today, and they get priority. No matter how good a bilateral relationship is, those issues are often challenging to work through, because they affect the pocketbook on both sides."

Jimmy Mauldin, the former Alabama sales and labor manager we also met in Chapter 2, reported on Pakistan's transportation sector while working as an economic officer in Islamabad, but the biggest part of his portfolio had to do with trade and investment, as well as entrepreneurship, he said.

The most recent global financial crisis gave new prominence to financial diplomacy, which has existed since the 1947 Bretton Woods Agreements that established the International Monetary Fund and the World Bank. "Some economic decisions made in one country have an outsized impact on jobs and growth here in the U.S. and around the world," Lael Brainard, Treasury undersecretary for international affairs, said in a June 2012 speech in Washington. "By determining whether currencies and stock markets plunge or stabilize, it can make the difference in whether families can afford to send their children to college, buy a home, or retire comfortably. Convincing leaders of other countries to change their domestic economic policies can be challenging and intensely political, yet it is essential when it has an economic impact on our shores."[5]

Lobbying foreign governments to improve business conditions for U.S. companies is necessary in both developing and developed countries, said John Nylin, the economic officer in Tokyo whom we met in Chapter 1. "Many American companies have issues with tariff and non-tariff barriers here in Japan, and the economic section deals with that – they work with different agencies both in Tokyo and in Washington," he said.

In Greece, strict regulations and high fees have caused "enormous difficulties" to U.S. cruise lines to "operate in Greek waters," said Daniel Smith, the ambassador there. "We facilitated a dialogue between the Greek government and the cruise-line companies. This is a win-win situation – the companies are willing to make investments if they can operate in Greek waters, and they will make money, but they will also bring tourists and other economic benefits to Greece. Everyone will be better off. But the Greek government will have to resolve the legal issues and address the infrastructure and security in the ports."

In many countries, the problems American businesses face are much more fundamental. They have to do with culture and values, often making bribery and corruption a big concern, said Julie Chung, the economic counselor at the embassy in Bangkok. "We may have high standards, but companies from other countries don't have the same value systems," she said.

Violating intellectual property rights, for example, is a huge problem in Thailand, as well as in China and across Asia, "and we'll be working on it for years," Chung said. "The U.S. Patent and Trademark Office has been coming here to conduct training. The Thais don't pay for that, but if it makes it easier for American companies to sell billions of dollars more of their products without extra fees or bribes, it's worth it. We seek transparency and reforms, but we can't change an entire culture or country overnight – we have to chip away at it little by little. Now, there are Thai innovators and inventors, so we asked them, 'Do you want your intellectual property to be pirated by the Vietnamese and the Chinese?' That suddenly hit them a little bit closer to home. It's not just about copying American movies and music, but it's about Thai products as well. So we are changing up the conversation to be about Thailand, as it faces its own intellectual property issues."

Among the most lucrative – and controversial – trades the U.S. does around the world are the sales of weapons and other military equipment, and they are overseen and authorized by the State Department. Officers like David Lindwall, who was the political-military counselor in Baghdad when I visited the embassy there in early 2012, "do the screening and paperwork," he said, though the Pentagon "originates the deals." Since Saddam Hussein's demise in 2003, Iraq has made U.S. arms purchases worth more than $15 billion, Lindwall said, citing a single recent order of over $2 billion for 18 F-16 aircraft. "They are about to order 18 more. They ultimately want to have an air force to match their neighbors' who have hundreds of planes apiece. That creates a lot of jobs in the U.S.," he said.

Globally, American arms sales are booming – 2011 was a record-setting year, exceeding $30 billion, and an increase of at least 70 percent was expected in 2012, the State Department said, noting that "these sales support tens of thousands of American jobs."[6] When authorizing deals, the department said that it takes into account the overall situation in the purchasing country, including its human rights record, potential weapons proliferation and regional security.

Whether working with a foreign government or U.S. businesses in any industry, American diplomats aim to make those activities "more than episodic," said Laird Treiber, the economic counselor in Ankara. "We try to create a strategic economic and commercial relationship with Turkey," he said. "The point is to make it enduring, get companies here for the long haul, and get the Turkish government to focus on long-term ties."

The Foreign Commercial Service

Since 1993, Michael Lally has spent each workday helping U.S. companies to start or expand their business in foreign countries. He began in the former Soviet republics of Ukraine, Kazakhstan and Azerbaijan, where free markets were a novelty after decades of communist-style planned economies, and trade relations with the U.S. were almost non-existent. Things were very different in Mexico, whose trade with the U.S. exceeded $1 billion a day. During his three years there, Lally conducted hundreds of briefings and arranged numerous meetings between American businesses and Mexican companies or government officials, complete with "matchmaking services" that resulted in deals worth billions of dollars.

Unlike most Foreign Service officers, whose jobs often vary from post to post, Lally has done trade and business promotion all his career – he is a member of the Foreign Commercial Service and works for the Department of Commerce, rather than the State Department. He is one of about 260 officers in more than 75 countries, though the service also has about 1,200 employees in over 100 U.S. offices. In addition to matchmaking, it provides trade counseling, market intelligence and advocacy.[7]

"The Foreign Commercial Service is part of American diplomacy," Lally said in Ankara, where he moved after Mexico City. "We help mainly small and medium-sized companies, which really need the help and are the primary engines of growth in the U.S. economy. For example, the president has made renewable energy a priority, and we recently had 16 American companies here. We took them to three Turkish cities and arranged 350 meetings for them at 200 Turkish companies. We brought banks along as well to try to pull the deals together."

Those services are not free. "A large company we charge about $2,300 a day, a small company, about $700 a day, and if you are a first-time person to the commercial service, it's $350," Lally said. "When a benefit accumulates to the greater good of American business, there is no charge. For example, we don't charge for a market briefing – they can come in and talk to us. But if there is a benefit that accrues to a specific company for their business development, they should be charged, and that's why Congress has mandated it."

Among the recent deals Lally and his colleagues in Ankara helped facilitate was a joint venture to manufacture and commercialize carbon fiber and derivatives between the Dow Chemical Company, based in Midland, Michigan, and Turkey's Aksa Akrilik Kimya Sanayii. "Total investment in the project is expected to reach $1 billion in five years and create up to 1,000 jobs," the Associated Press reported in December 2011.[8] Another joint venture that Embassy Ankara supported was a coal project in southeastern Turkey between the AES Corporation, an Arlington, Virginia-based global power company, and Koç Holding, along with Oyak, Turkey's largest pension fund.[9]

The Foreign Commercial Service has a list of "success stories" on its website, including a $3 billion Australian contract awarded to the U.S. Navy to supply Seahawk helicopters. Sikorsky Aircraft, "the airframe manufacturer, and Lockheed Martin, the avionics and mission systems integrator, are the primary industry partners," the website said. "General Electric, Raytheon, CAE and 30-40 smaller American suppliers also have a role in the sale." In another case, the service "helped Air Products, a specialty gas supplier located in Allentown, Pennsylvania, to overcome a foreign trade barrier that threatened to exclude it from Taiwan's market."[10]

In countries that are smaller trading partners with the United States and where the Foreign Commercial Service has no representation, the embassy's economic section performs those functions. John Nylin did just that in Slovenia from 2004 to 2006 as an economic officer. "I spent a lot of time reaching out to American businesses, because that was the ambassador's priority," he said.

When Tracey Jacobson, whom we met in Chapter 2, became ambassador to Tajikistan in 2006, there was no American Chamber of Commerce in the former Soviet republic, so she tasked her economic officers with mobilizing the business community to establish a chamber. "You want business people coming together and lobbying the government to create the best business environment," she said. "We started by using the embassy's convening authority to set up business forums. Some of the business leaders told us that they had never talked to each other until we brought them together." In the absence of a dedicated commercial section, officers and contractors from the U.S. Agency for International Development stepped in to help "improve the business environment, reduce the bureaucracy, and make it easier to start and grow a business," Jacobson said. "We had advisors working with various ministries, and we also did entrepreneur training."

Helping American companies may seem a win-win proposition, but not everyone in a foreign country agrees. In 2009, the embassy in Haiti got involved in a dispute between Haitian senators and U.S. textile manufacturers over workers' wages. Just weeks before Senate elections, several lawmakers proposed tripling the minimum wage, which was then 22 cents an hour. Contractors for American companies making T-shirts, bras and underwear for clothing giants, such as Dockers and Nautica, were worried that their costs would increase too much and some factories might have to be closed, so they asked the embassy for help. It mounted an effort to limit the pay raise, and wages ultimately doubled.[11]

Media organizations, having learned about the embassy's role from the WikiLeaks cables, depicted U.S. diplomats as unsympathetic to the plight of workers in the Western Hemisphere's poorest country, choosing instead to help American companies get richer.[12] Some even attributed one of the cables, which argued that the proposed increase "did not take the economic reality into account," to David Lindwall.

In reality, Lindwall was in Guatemala at the time and did not become deputy chief of mission in Port-au-Prince until two months after the issue had been resolved. He said that both the embassy and Haitian President René Préval "feared that such a big increase would kill that key sector of the economy, as it would make Haitian exports much less competitive – the manufacturing sector was just beginning to pick up speed and create jobs." Préval and the embassy "apparently weighed in with the senators to tell them that, while tripling the minimum wage might get them some votes, it would hurt exports," Lindwall said. After the parliament doubled the minimum wage, "the manufacturing sector stagnated until 2012," when things started looking up "thanks to U.S. assistance, as part of the 2010 post-earthquake recovery program," he added.

The Foreign Agricultural Service

Clay Hamilton grew up on a farm in Texas, and as soon as he graduated from college, he decided to dedicate his career to helping American farmers. He began as a "county extension agent" for the Department of Agriculture, "reaching out to farmers to share scientific research, provide economic training, answer questions and offer any assistance they might need," he said. An exchange program he did in Europe got him interested in working overseas, and upon his return home, he started looking for a job combining both his passions. He found it in the Foreign Agricultural Service, where he could help U.S. farmers by expanding market opportunities for them abroad. Consistent with U.S. global development goals, it also helps other countries improve their agricultural sectors, which in turn makes them better trading partners.

Hamilton received his first assignment, at the U.S. Embassy in Bulgaria, in 1992 – less than three years after the collapse of the country's totalitarian regime and the end of the Cold War. One of his first tasks was to help Bulgarian wheat growers make a profit, which they were not doing at the time, he said. In fact, free-market economic reforms had just recently started. "Bulgaria had many well-educated people, even infrastructure, but they weren't familiar with the Western way of doing things. Once they did start catching on, they were making a profit. It was exciting. Now they are part of the EU," he added.

The Foreign Agricultural Service has 122 officers in 58 countries, and they are responsible for entire regions.[13] Hamilton, whom I met in Turkey, having completed assignments in Italy and Japan after Bulgaria, also covered Central Asia from Ankara. "I recently came back from Azerbaijan, where we did training on food safety, plant and dairy health, working through one of the agrarian universities, which is a long-term program," he said. "If you look back at South Korea, we did a lot of the same things decades ago, and now they are one of our biggest trading partners. We want the rest of the world to develop into better customers."

The chief mission of the Foreign Agricultural Service is to "expand exports of U.S. agricultural products through trade and development," Hamilton explained. "American farmers are our main constituency, and we frame everything through how it helps farmers."

For example, the Turkish dairy industry "pretty much collapsed in 2003, and they ended up slaughtering a lot of cattle," he said. "Here, they rely on excess dairy cattle for meat, so meat prices went through the roof – they were among the highest in Europe. We had been working with the government to get them to buy U.S. breeding cattle, and they finally got so worried about meat prices that they opened up the market. We've seen huge increases in trade every year. Last year, we saw $200 million worth of live cattle. They realized that cattle bred for meat tastes better than dairy cattle and started to diversify," Hamilton said.

"The next step is opening the market for beef," he added. "They have a huge need for cheaper beef, but politically they don't want to buy much from the United States because of issues like hormones, though we'd like to open the market for hotels and restaurants. It's a small market, but it's important for the U.S. beef industry. They barely break even from what they sell in the U.S., but exports bring them a profit, because it's usually a higher-quality product, and they get paid more for it. They also export things we don't particularly want. If you sell tongues for dog food, it's $2 a pound in the U.S., but it's $27 a pound in Japan, because it's a delicacy. There are a lot of other things, such as chicken hearts and feet, that we don't eat in the U.S., but they do in Asia, so that's a huge business for the poultry industry."

I did not expect to get a crash course in cattle exports during my research on the Foreign Service, but as odd as it may seem, everything Hamilton described is an important part of American diplomacy. It also clearly shows the direct impact of the service's work across the world on the quest for prosperity at home.

The Foreign Agricultural Service has its own success stories. In 2009, it helped several California companies to drastically expand their exports of stone fruit, including peaches, plums and nectarines, to China, reaching $3.3 million, a 73-percent increase from the previous year. It also made it possible for apple-marketing companies in Pennsylvania and New York to break into the Indian and Southeast Asian markets, respectively.[14] In 2012, the Pakistani media reported on U.S. programs in the country aimed at increasing "agricultural productivity and economic development through training, the introduction of disease resistant seeds, and vaccination for foot-and-mouth disease."[15]

Not only does the Foreign Agricultural Service not charge for its services, but it often gives funds to trade associations to promote U.S. products overseas, Hamilton said. Food security has become a top agenda issue for both the U.S. and the U.N., and Washington is serious about helping American farmers first, but also their foreign colleagues. Based on population-growth projections, "we have determined that agricultural production has to increase by 75 percent by 2050, and we can't do that in the U.S. alone," Hamilton noted. "We've done pretty well so far, but we need all countries to step up and produce better and more efficiently."

Chapter 6

Public Diplomacy

Côte d'Ivoire, also known as Ivory Coast, is a former French colony in West Africa with nearly 22 million people.[1] Its most frequent appearances in the Western media in the last two decades had to do with a 1999 coup d'état and a two-year civil war that began in 2002. Although the term of the incumbent president, Laurent Gbagbo, expired in 2005, he repeatedly delayed elections until November 2010, when his challenger, Alassane Ouattara, was declared the winner by the country's Electoral Commission. Ouattara was recognized as the new leader by the United Nations and other international organizations, but Gbagbo refused to hand over power, igniting months of violence.[2]

From Washington, Bruce Wharton watched public support for Ouattara decline in the weeks after the election – the main reason, he determined, was the lack of a communication strategy. Wharton, a Foreign Service officer since 1985, at the time was deputy assistant secretary for public diplomacy in the State Department's Africa bureau and decided to help. He flew to Abidjan, Côte d'Ivoire's largest city and former capital, to design and begin implementing the missing strategy. "I started by identifying the primary channels of communication, the audiences and the messages that would be most effective," he said. "Then I suggested specific communication strategies to Ouattara and his team – dressing the set of the television station they were using a little differently so he looked presidential and painting a vision of the future that most Ivorians were willing to support."

Ouattara belongs to the 39 percent of the population who are Muslim, while Gbagbo is Christian, like 33 percent of Ivorians. "In speaking to Christian members of civil society, I became aware that they were worried that Ouattara was an Islamist and was going to force people to convert to Islam," Wharton said. "So I suggested to him that he needed to emphasize religious tolerance and make clear that there was room in Côte d'Ivoire for people of many faiths. As Easter drew nigh, I suggested that he put out a message to Christians wishing them a peaceful holiday. That had a very positive effect on public confidence." Even though the standoff was resolved militarily by the U.N. and France in April 2011,[3] the new communication strategy did make a difference, Wharton said, because by then most people had accepted Ouattara's vision. "He was able to move fairly quickly into the full powers of being the president and lead the country, both in terms of economic and political development," Wharton added.

What were the U.S. interests that motivated Johnnie Carson, the assistant secretary of state for African affairs, to send Wharton to Abidjan? Washington saw Côte d'Ivoire's election "as part of a wave of democratic reforms in West Africa," a troubled region whose stability is important both politically and economically, Wharton said. As the world's largest producer and exporter of cocoa beans and a major producer and exporter of coffee, Côte d'Ivoire attracts significant American investment, he explained. As we saw in Chapter 5, a stable and transparent government is essential to U.S. business interests. The Obama administration supported Ouattara because he was "the rightful winner of the election," Wharton said. Still, the U.S. diplomat met with Gbagbo's team as well – "I didn't want us to be identified as supporting a specific party or candidate, but the principle of having the democratic process followed as faithfully as possible," he said.

Wharton, whom Obama nominated to be ambassador to Zimbabwe in 2012, was the first deputy assistant secretary for public diplomacy in the Africa bureau. Such a position in each of the State Department's six regional bureaus was created in 2010, with the goal of using public diplomacy to better carry out various policies. Wharton said that having that title helped him get access to all major players in Côte d'Ivoire that he would not have had otherwise. The access to Carson and the decision-making process in Washington was just as important, he said.

A seat at the policy table

Judith McHale grew up in the Foreign Service, and though she did not follow in her diplomat-father's footsteps, her international upbringing has played a major role in her career. A lawyer by training,

McHale eventually became president and CEO of Discovery Communications, where she spearheaded an ambitious global expansion. The small company that began with a single U.S. cable channel grew to a media giant, with 147 networks in 45 languages, and 1.7 billion subscribers in 209 countries and territories.[4] It had succeeded at communicating with its audiences by understanding their needs and interests, and by providing programs in foreign languages that were also influenced by cultural nuances – not simply feeding them subtitled American content.

In 2009, three years after McHale left Discovery, Hillary Clinton appointed her undersecretary of state for public diplomacy and public affairs. It was McHale who created the public diplomacy positions in the regional bureaus. Why did she see a need for those posts in the already large State Department bureaucracy? Because U.S. public diplomacy efforts lacked a strategic focus and had to be better aligned with the country's foreign policy objectives, she told me.

So she went back to the core national interests of security and prosperity, as well as the dual mission of American diplomacy of dealing with the world as it is and making it more secure and prosperous, which we discussed in Chapter 1. McHale asked herself and her new team: How can public diplomacy better support that mission, and how can U.S. diplomacy in general benefit from the tools public diplomacy has to offer?

Like the Foreign Service's mission, McHale's vision had a short-term aspect and a long-term one. In the short run, she set out to "integrate public diplomacy in policy formulation," in order to maximize the chances for a particular policy's success. She also wanted to strengthen the State Department's global media operation to respond quickly to breaking stories and to correct inaccuracies. In the long run, she sought to "create strong and lasting relationships" with foreign publics and "influence their behavior," in the hope that they would provide the "support and help we need to move our agenda forward."

One of McHale's predecessors in the Bush administration, Karen Hughes, made an effort to "incorporate public diplomacy into everyone's consciousness" at the State Department and other parts of the government, Hughes said. Building on that foundation, McHale's more ambitious plan was to secure a seat for public diplomacy at the policy table. "Public diplomacy needs to be at the front of policy formulation, so decisions can be informed from the beginning as far as foreign attitudes towards a particular subject," she told me. "This is not to say that our foreign policy is driven by foreign popular opinion at all, but with an understanding of it, we can better formulate policies and have a greater chance of success. If you are doing something, you want to understand how it's going to impact the people who will be directly affected by it. If you are going to have a negative reaction, wouldn't you want to know that up front?"

That was the function McHale envisioned for the six new positions. In reality, the officials in them have focused more on implementing existing policies, rather than helping craft new ones, said Bruce Wharton. But he added that McHale's efforts marked "the first time in a decade that anyone took a serious look at the structure and mechanics of public diplomacy, as well as the management and the administrative support that's necessary to make it work." The last major structural change was in 1999, when the United States Information Agency (USIA) was folded into the State Department.

The agency's "Cold War mantra was telling America's story, and the idea was to put something out that we would then contrast to the Soviet way of doing things," said Walter Douglas, a Foreign Service officer since 1986 who was McHale's executive assistant. "After the Soviet Union collapsed, there was nothing to replace that, so USIA was still telling America's story, even though there was nothing to contrast it with, but we did that for a lack of anything better to do."

Indeed, for years after the Berlin Wall fell in 1989, the U.S. government was not quite sure how USIA fit in Washington's foreign policy puzzle. There was nothing wrong with the agency's mission – "to understand, inform and influence foreign publics"[5] – but what purpose did it serve? In the 1948 Smith-Mundt Act, information meant for foreign audiences was considered propaganda that should be kept away from Americans, as I mentioned in Chapter 1, and in effect separated USIA from the policy process. "Americans consider propaganda a dirty word, although every successful politician, president, business and NGO engages in it daily," said Mark Helmke, a former senior staff member on the Senate Foreign Relations Committee.

In recent years, the concept of public diplomacy has often been misunderstood. After September 11, 2001, its mission was viewed as improving the U.S. image abroad, and the State Department produced an expensive ad campaign about how Muslims live in America, among other marketing initiatives. Some TV stations in the target Muslim countries refused to air those ads and documentaries despite the lucrative revenue they would have received. Many Foreign Service officers dismissed the campaign as a solution to the wrong problem. "Muslims don't like America not because Muslims in the United States are treated poorly," a senior officer in Europe said at the time.

"I'm not on a campaign to make people like us," McHale told me in 2010. "This is not a branding or marketing exercise. It's about building relationships with people and becoming woven into the fabric of their daily lives. We have to make sure we understand and make clear to people that we are listening to their needs and aspirations. If, at the same time, we can succeed in improving the reputation of our country in certain parts of the world, then that would be good, too. But that's not the primary driver."

According to the Pew Global Attitudes Project, "positive views" of the United States jumped by as much as 20 percent in many parts of the world when Obama was elected in 2008, though those highs retreated by 2012, particularly in Muslim countries. That year, only 19 percent of surveyed Egyptians held positive views of the U.S., while that number was even lower – 12 percent – in Jordan and Pakistan.[6] "Public diplomacy in this particular situation can make changes at the margins, but to move the needle you have to have policies or conditions change," said Andrew Kohut, president of the Pew Research Center, which conducts the annual survey. "Big changes in public opinion are not consequences of misunderstanding, but of big events."

Running a global media operation

Using public diplomacy to achieve policy goals can be tricky, many Foreign Service officers said. During President George W. Bush's first term, for example, some administration officials viewed public diplomacy as a vehicle for selling unpopular policies, particularly the Iraq war. "We always think we have to put a spin to convince people," a senior Foreign Service officer in the Middle East told me in 2003. "There is a certain manipulative quality to the way we buy and sell and deal with each other. We think we can deal with the world that way, but we can't, because people see us as hypocrites. What they are dying for us to do is trust them enough to be honest with them."

Long before top officials in Washington admitted it publicly, career diplomats warned that the Bush administration's policies – not the Foreign Service's inability to sell them – were the main problem. Many people in the Middle East regard U.S. policies "as sour milk gone bad," one mid-level officer in the region said, referring to widespread opposition to U.S. support for Israel and use of military force in Muslim countries. "It doesn't matter how you package it and how much money you spend on an advertising campaign. When you open the package, it will still smell bad," he said. "Sometimes, however, you have to make a decision that the policy is upsetting, but it's in our interest to maintain it, so we have to live with the upset it causes."

Within days of becoming undersecretary for public diplomacy in 2005, Karen Hughes, a trusted Bush adviser and close friend, set out on a "listening tour" of Egypt, Saudi Arabia and Turkey and invited several of us in the press corps along for the ride. But the trip was marred by a string of critical articles in the U.S. and Arab media. Some fellow reporters ridiculed her then-limited knowledge of foreign affairs and mocked references in her public remarks to her religious faith and personal experiences as a mother. Having realized that she would not change minds about the Iraq war or other administration policies in the region however articulate she might be, Hughes tried to connect to her mostly female audiences on a personal level. But they would have none of it – they wanted to talk about Iraq and the Palestinians.

After that experience, Hughes continued to travel around the world, but on commercial jets and without American reporters in tow. She made a point of letting Bush know what she saw and heard abroad, which may have influenced the president to lend a more sympathetic ear to other countries' grievances and viewpoints – and possibly nudged him closer to some of the more moderate policies advocated by Rice during his second term and mentioned in Chapter 3. "Generally, after a big trip, I go and share with the president my impressions," Hughes told me in 2007. "I'm very aware that our words are viewed skeptically, and witnessing the intensity of some of the negative views is difficult. But that doesn't mean that we can't forge common interests and values, or that we shouldn't invite people to come and see what America is like. Our deeds, particularly the things we are doing in the areas of health, education and economic opportunity to improve people's lives around the world, resonate."

While "selling" policies has been officially rejected as a function of public diplomacy, today Washington engages in "messaging" to foreign publics more than ever – whether to "explain" policies or promote various U.S. projects around the world. "It's not a question of selling your policies, but rather explaining your policies to people," McHale said. "It's very difficult to sell something to somebody they don't want to buy." Tara Sonenshine, McHale's successor under Clinton, shared both women's philosophy. "The challenge of public diplomacy is to explain America: What are its policies, practices, values, ideals and ideas," she said in a speech in Washington in June 2012.[7]

The State Department today runs a 24-hour global media operation.[8] It publishes every word the secretary of state utters in public, holds in-person and teleconference briefings with U.S. officials and facilitates interviews with them, comments in real-time on breaking news and foreign countries' statements and actions, manages a wide Internet platform and maintains several active social media feeds.

"I have to be aware that the media is so much a part of foreign policy," said Mike Hammer, whom we met in Chapter 1. As assistant secretary for public affairs, he essentially runs the media operation. "There are numerous reports that are erroneous, and it's important to correct as many of them as possible, so people have accurate information about our policies and actions." Moreover, McHale said the U.S. should be "more proactive and less reactive" in framing its "narrative." In addition to its main operation in Washington and the public affairs sections at overseas missions, the department has regional media hubs in London, Brussels, Dubai, Tokyo, Johannesburg, as well as a domestic-based hub in Miami for Latin America.

The Bureau of Public Affairs' activities are separate from the U.S. government's international broadcasts, such as the Voice of America, Radio Free Europe, Radio Free Asia, and the Arab-language TV network Al Hurra, among others. Those outlets are overseen by the Broadcasting Board of Governors, on which the State Department holds one of nine seats.[9]

As I pointed out in Chapter 3, Clinton has put a strong emphasis on using social media for diplomacy purposes, though the department is still learning how to harness that new phenomenon most effectively, as are many others around the world. The news media no longer has a monopoly on reporting on U.S. foreign policy, though there is no replacement for good journalism – the State Department can easily make an announcement or explain an action in a format millions of people can read on their computer screens without the traditional media's filter. Senior U.S. officials have taken to Facebook and Twitter to respond to citizens' questions in real-time.

The department, which also maintains a blog called "DipNote," tries to respond to the global appetite for information about what the U.S. does across the world, though there is room for improvement. Press releases and blog posts still follow the public relations model, rather than a journalistic style, which would be much more effective regardless of who the target audience may be. The most basic example is the inverted pyramid concept familiar to every journalism student – you begin a story with the biggest news to come out of an event, not by stating that the event took place.

Despite social media's many advantages, such as mobilizing assistance for victims of the 2010 Haiti earthquake, in many countries it is not as ubiquitous as it has become in the developed world, said Walter Douglas, who is now the public affairs counselor in New Delhi. In developing nations, "television is everything, and nothing else has the numbers of people who can be reached via broadcast TV," even in 2012, he said. "My colleagues out there are saying, 'I go on TV and get 40 million viewers, then I go on social media and get 1,000.'"

Even in the West, the power of television – and traditional media in general – should not be underestimated, said Victoria Nuland, the State Department spokesperson, who has embraced social media. "As ambassador to NATO, I started going on morning talk shows and women's programs, and gave interviews to women's and youth publications – in English, French, whatever it took," she said. "It used to be just the ambassador and the deputy who spoke publicly, but everybody in my mission from a second-tour officer on went out and did speaking events – whether it was at public schools in Belgium or back here at home. You can't just work in a cubicle anymore. If your ideas don't survive in the outside world, they need some reflection."

'Ignorance is our number one enemy'

In September 2003, five Americans took up assignments as English teachers thousands of miles from home, determined that, by the end of the school year, their students would not only speak some English, but know much more about the United States. "They welcomed us with open arms," Craig Dicker, a Foreign Service officer who helped to place the newcomers, said of the schools that hired the teachers. "They were thrilled to have Americans teach there." There would have been nothing exceptional about the teaching assignments had it not been for the particular schools: Islamic institutes in Indonesia that prepare teachers for the country's large network of religious high schools, known as madrassas.

Dicker said the idea came from Nur Fadil Lubis, vice rector of an institute in Indonesia's third-largest city, Medan. He had hosted a Fulbright scholar before and thought that his students would benefit from having an American in the classroom. Indonesia, the country with the world's largest Muslim population, is a major U.S. concern, because rising anti-Americanism has made it a breeding ground for terrorists. "It's an opportunity for us to share more of our culture

with a very important constituency," said Dicker, at the time a regional language officer at the U.S. Embassy in Jakarta. "Is that a
wise expenditure of money? I believe so. After working with an
American for two or three years, those future teachers will have no-
tions and ideas about America they would not have had if that person hadn't been there. We are dealing with people who will have an
impact on an audience that we keep on hearing is so important to
us."

Teaching English has been among the most successful U.S. public
diplomacy efforts for decades, along with other cultural and exchange programs, said dozens of Foreign Service officers and political appointees. When I first met Dicker in 2003, he said there were
only 16 language officers in the Foreign Service. In 2012, there were
25, though the growth of the programs had far outpaced the increase
in officers, he noted. Not only was the program in Indonesia "still
going strong," with about 20 new teachers arriving that summer, but
"we get about 100 proposals from Indonesian universities every
year, so the demand is far greater than what we are able to supply,"
said Eran Williams, the language officer in Jakarta at the time.

"Language teaching gives us access to audiences that otherwise
we can't reach," said Dicker, who joined the service in 1992 and has
also been posted to South Africa, Hungary, Turkey and Azerbaijan.
"We provide them with access to information they might not otherwise have. If people are dependent on the local media and a relatively limited and controlled set of information resources, they are more
likely to be swayed in one direction. We care, because ignorance is
our number one enemy."

Dicker credited Judith McHale with actively engaging the private
sector in teaching English overseas, including Microsoft, Cisco Systems and several publishing houses. They use modern technology,
such as "interactive games, learning opportunities on mobile phones
and one-stop portals for teachers," he said. In late 2011, the State
Department "deployed 6,000 Amazon Kindle e-readers, centrally
loaded with tailored content, to over 700 global American spaces"
through a partnership with Amazon.com, the department said.[10]

Building lasting relationships

Both Judith McHale and Karen Hughes said that program expansion – not only in English teaching, but in all areas – was a top priority for them. "Our education and exchange programs, I'm convinced, are the single most valuable public diplomacy tool," Hughes

told me. "It's been the most effective over the last 50 years, because we can prove that they make a lasting difference, not only in people's lives, but also in their attitudes." The State Department's exchange programs have more than 1 million alumni, including dozens of Nobel laureates and hundreds of current and former heads of state and government.[11]

In addition to the Fulbright program, which brings foreigners to study in the U.S. and sends Americans to other countries, the department runs short-term programs that allow foreign journalists, politicians, scholars, human rights activists and others to visit some of their U.S. counterparts and exchange knowledge and experience.

"Every time there is a Cabinet reshuffle in a country, the embassy tallies up how many of the new ministers have been on an American program," Walter Douglas said. "It's great, but most of those people did that 15-20 years earlier, so you don't have an immediate impact. You are playing a long-term game, and you are trying to pick leaders showing promise while they are young. Somebody picked Tony Blair, Margaret Thatcher, Nicolas Sarkozy and others back when they were junior politicians," Douglas said in reference to the former British prime ministers and former French president. There is no guarantee, of course, that all participants in those programs will become friends of America and will have pro-U.S. policies if they ascend to top government positions in their countries.

Some educational and other exchange programs have recently come under increased scrutiny because of reported abuse of young participants. In 2011, several hundred foreign students on a summer work and travel program in the United States protested the working conditions at a plant in Pennsylvania that packs Hershey's chocolates. They said they were forced to work on grueling production lines lifting heavy boxes, often on night shifts, and had little time and money left for travel. Several months later, the State Department revised the types of jobs students can do, banning them from most warehouse, construction, manufacturing and food-processing work.[12] In 2012, media reports said that dozens of high school foreign exchange students had been sexually abused by their American host parents.[13] In both cases, the department identified as the main problem the outsourcing of the programs to numerous companies and organizations, which seriously hurts oversight, transparency and accountability.

The State Department also runs speaker programs, though several officers said that the department has paid less attention to them in recent years and not allocated enough resources for them. More funding has gone to building online platforms, social media content and video production, so Washington can reach foreign audiences directly, "over the heads of embassies," as one officer put it.

Many public affairs officers abroad do not wait for U.S. speakers in order to organize events. When I visited the consulate in Erbil, the capital of Iraqi Kurdistan, in March 2012, Matt Ference, the public affairs officer we met in Chapter 2, hosted a program about democracy and federalism in Iraq for political science students from the University of Kurdistan. The speaker was an Iraqi Ph.D. candidate and son of a prominent Islamist political leader. "We invite people to the American Cultural Center, so we can stimulate discussion on politics, society and culture," Ference said. "We've had talks about language, the environment, music and other subjects. It's a place where Americans and Iraqis can get together and share their views on different topics, where we can learn from each other. Even if I'm the only American in the room, it's often the first time our audience has ever had the chance to talk to a U.S. government official."

Apart from the official public diplomacy programs abroad, which also include concerts, poetry readings and exhibitions, some officers have taken it upon themselves to make a difference in the lives of young people in other countries. Michael Guinan, a former lawyer whom I met in the public affairs section of the embassy in Islamabad in early 2012, said he volunteered to teach essay-writing and public speaking to college and high school students interested in studying in the United States. "I like to work seven days a week, so I do it in my spare time," he said. "I try to get them to a point where they are more likely to be successful in their admissions. Public speaking is a lost art in Pakistan. No one teaches it to the kids, and some colleges and universities have reached out to us and have asked us to help, so I stepped in and filled the gap."

American celebrities have been used to promote the United States overseas from time to time, but those initiatives have not been very consistent, and Karen Hughes tried to institutionalize them. In 2006, she enlisted the State Department's first "public diplomacy envoy" – Olympic skater Michelle Kwan – and traveled with her to Russia and China. The envoys named since then include former baseball star Cal Ripken Jr. and actress Fran Drescher.

"If you use icons of American culture judiciously and selectively, you can have a big impact," said Charles Rivkin, Obama's ambassador to France whom we also met in Chapter 2. Rivkin has used his personal connections from years in the entertainment industry to introduce world-famous American actors and singers to French youth in a very different light from what those audiences see in the media.

"When Samuel L. Jackson was here, I asked him to come with me to the *banlieues*," the French term for suburbs that has become synonymous with low-income housing areas, Rivkin said. "He got out of the car, and these kids in one of the most disadvantaged suburbs of Paris yelled, 'Le Big Mac, Le Big Mac!,'" a reference to one of the actor's famous lines in the 1994 film "Pulp Fiction." "He said, 'I grew up in Tennessee, where I drank out of a different water fountain from the white kids. I had to work three times as hard as my white neighbors. But you know what, I did it.'" Another black American Rivkin took to a *banlieue* was singer William James Adams, Jr., better known as Will.i.am. He talked to the youngsters about his upbringing in the housing projects of East Los Angeles by a single mother. Oscar-winning actress Jodie Foster, who "speaks perfect French, gave a speech to aspiring filmmakers," Rivkin said.

Other distinguished guests of his in Paris have included filmmaker Woody Allen, musician Herbie Hancock, and Richard Parsons, a former chairman of Time Warner and Citigroup. "Celebrities are two-dimensional figures when they are on screen or in your headphones," Rivkin said. "But when they appear in person and say 'I'm proud to be an American,' and 'America's a good place,' that has a huge impact."

Combating violent extremism

Malala Yousafzai was born in the scenic Swat valley of northwestern Pakistan in 1998. She used to think that going to school was a "useless exercise." She "realized the importance of education" in 2007, when the area near the border with Afghanistan was partially overrun by Islamic militants who banned education for girls.[14] Swat became a battleground between extremists and Pakistani government forces, "creating such devastation that no tourist could come here," Yousafzai recalled in a recent video clip.[15] "I used to wonder why, with such atrocities being committed against us, none of us was speaking out and standing up for our rights," she said.

"At that time, to speak up against terrorism was a very bad thing," her father, Ziauddin Yousafzai, said in the same clip. "Malala was the only girl to speak her mind to the media. She used to send her diary entries to the BBC." She said she saw it as an "opportunity to reveal to the world the injustice we were facing at the hands of terrorism." In 2011, Pakistani Prime Minister Yousuf Raza Gillani awarded the girl the first annual National Youth Peace Prize, which was named for Yousafzai. "The only reward I wished for was peace in Swat. I wanted to be able to attend school again," she said. "My purpose is to serve humanity, and the path I've chosen to fulfill this purpose is that of politics, because politics will enable me to reach out and help the whole of Pakistan. This country needs good leaders. I hope to become one such leader."

The video that told Yousafzai's story is one of several short documentaries produced by Black Box Sounds, a Pakistani media company, with funding from the U.S. Embassy in Islamabad. Others feature Pakistan's first female diving instructor, Rosheen Khan, and 84-year-old Abdul Sattar Edhi, who created the country's largest network of shelters and medical services for the poor. The stories have aired on 14 TV stations, said Irfan Saeed from the embassy's public affairs section. The company's YouTube channel, "Think Twice Pakistan," has been viewed nearly half a million times, as of the summer of 2012, Saeed added. With the embassy's help, Black Box Sounds has ventured into scripted television, starting with "Dhamak," a drama series "conceived to illustrate the devastating effects of terrorism on the families who have lost their loved ones," according to the company's website.[16]

Saeed's job in Islamabad was unique for any U.S. mission abroad – he was tasked with creating a pilot program to counter violent extremism. Although the embassy already had numerous contacts in many parts of Pakistani society, and worked with them on various programs and projects, there was a section it was not reaching: religious, tribal and other leaders with influence on a segment of the population at risk of turning to terrorism.

"What we do is try to find such leaders and increase our contacts with them, and then amplify their voices to create a narrative" that offers a more positive and peaceful vision for Pakistan, Saeed said. "We also try to find good-news stories that promote national pride, tolerance and equality. For example, there are some amazing stories of courageous women here that few people know about. That may not be a direct 'Terrorism is bad' message, but it changes people's mindsets. So we ask media companies to come to us with good stories to tell, and we provide funding through a competitive process." Saeed said he did not consider that propaganda, because the goal was not to promote a pro-U.S. agenda but an "anti-violence narrative." The May 2012 State Department inspector-general's report on Embassy Islamabad, which I mentioned in Chapter 4, praised the pilot program as a "creative" new approach that "may serve as a model elsewhere."[17]

A Pakistani-American fluent in Urdu, Pakistan's national language, Saeed was hand-picked for the job by Judith McHale, even though he is not in the Foreign Service and works for the Department of Homeland Security. Concerned that previous U.S. efforts to counter violent extremism had included activities that targeted audiences who were never at risk of becoming terrorists, such as teaching English, McHale wanted to refocus those programs more narrowly. "If we identify in a particular area a group of individuals who might be at risk of becoming a threat, then we would develop programs specifically aimed at them," she said.

Karen Hughes kept a paper clipping under glass on her desk at the State Department. It read: "A man has made at least a start on discovering the meaning of human life when he plants shade trees under which he knows full well he will never sit" – a reminder that the mission of public diplomacy often takes a lifetime to accomplish.

Chapter 7

Consular Affairs

A teenage girl lay on the tile floor, in a pool of her own blood. Curled up on the coffee table beside her, and also bleeding, was the girl's little brother. Muslim fanatics had broken into their house on the outskirts of Baghdad and shot the children in the head as their parents and siblings watched in horror. The reason: They were Christians.

The killers had carried out a threat made a day earlier in March 2004, when the family received a note from Ansar al-Islam, a radical Kurdish Islamic group that had backed Saddam Hussein's regime in Iraq, and has documented links to the al-Qaida terrorist network.[1] The computer-typed, printed and then photocopied message warned that the family would be killed and "doomed to hell" unless it stopped selling alcohol, a reference to a small liquor-delivery business the father was running to make ends meet. In Iraq, only Christians were allowed to sell alcohol. The lives of the parents and their other offspring were spared.

By the time Willis Witter, the *Washington Times*' deputy foreign editor at the time, arrived at the house about a week after the murders, the two children had been buried, but "there were still specks of brain and blood on the walls," he recalled later. For years, he kept on his desk in Washington photos of the children lying in their blood, which a neighbor had snapped once the gunmen were gone. Two uncles had moved in to protect the family after the tragedy. One of them, "disheveled after another sleepless night spent clutching his AK-47," pleaded with Witter for help as his eyes filled with tears. "How can you guarantee we won't be killed? We can't sleep. We can't go out to work. We are so scared that we are carrying our guns all the time. It all happened in less than 10 seconds," he said. The mother, "rail-thin beneath her black mourning dress, sat quietly with her surviving children." Witter himself was "terrified," he said, that his visit "would expose them to even more danger." The parents asked him not to publish their names or other personal details.

Journalists are supposed to report on events rather than help to shape them, but covering stories like the Iraq war often leads to breaking that rule. The grief and terror Witter saw in that mother's eyes could not leave him indifferent. In an e-mail message to me several days after his visit to the house, he suggested that I ask my contacts in the State Department's Bureau of Consular Affairs to connect us with the only consular officer in Iraq, who was assigned to the Coalition Provisional Authority (CPA) that governed the country in the year after the 2003 U.S.-led invasion.

Witter, convinced that the family would not survive unless it left Iraq, wanted to know if the consular officer, Beth Payne, could help them move to the United States. In an e-mail message, she told him that they would have to be outside Iraq to apply for asylum. In Washington, I was told that, if the parents wanted to apply for U.S. entry visas, they would have to go to Amman, the Jordanian capital, because the Baghdad office was not a visa-issuing post at the time. That was not an option for the family, which barely had money for food, let alone for travel. Witter could not afford to pay, either. For him, Payne was a heartless bureaucrat who did nothing to help a family escape almost certain death. "I still have this nagging sense of failure that I wasn't able to do more to follow up for this poor family," said Witter, who has no idea what happened to them. "It would be unfair for me to blame Ms. Payne. Still, she did deal with my request as if I were a cockroach, to be crushed and swept into the garbage."

When saving lives means breaking the law

When I spoke with Payne in 2006 – at the time, she headed the consular section at the embassy in Dakar, Senegal – she said she did not remember Witter's case, noting that she received several similar requests every day during her year in Baghdad. "Unfortunately, this became a very common occurrence, and it's a very hard choice," she told me. "My consular assistant's brother was assassinated – a woman I worked with and loved dearly who had her life threatened, but there was nothing I could do." Most of those tragic cases, she added, involved Iraqis who were not eligible for non-immigrant visas, and did not qualify for immigrant visas, which are granted on the basis of family ties or employment in the United States.

"To be eligible for a non-immigrant visa under U.S. law, you have to overcome a presumption that you intend to immigrate, by demonstrating significant ties with your country," Payne said. "Someone fleeing Iraq would have a terrible time overcoming that presumption, because their ties are tragically severed. Then you have a much larger issue. It's a philosophical question: Do I start saving individual people, because I think their lives are in danger, by violating the law I swore to uphold? When I was asked to do it in Rwanda after the genocide in the 1990s for the victims who lived next door to the people who raped them – they were using U.S. visas to go to Canada and seek refugee status – it was the same issue."

But the issue was different, she said, from the famous case of Hiram Bingham IV, a U.S. diplomat who issued visas to about 2,500 European Jews against official U.S. government policy during World War II.[2] Bingham, Payne said, "is a hero of mine." There are many questions you have to answer, she said: "How do you choose which ones? Where does it stop? Doesn't this go way above me?" In the end, she said, she felt "lucky" she "didn't have the power" to grant visas in Baghdad, which meant she "never really had to make that decision."

Payne, a former criminal lawyer who had served in Kuwait, Israel and Rwanda since joining the Foreign Service in 1993, was asked to become the first U.S. consul in Iraq under the U.S.-led occupation in 2003 by Maura Harty, assistant secretary of state for consular affairs at the time. "The idea was very exciting," Payne said. "I couldn't say no to that." She won an award for valor for helping casualties of the October 2003 bombing of Baghdad's Al Rashid hotel, where she lived. Her parents attended the award ceremony at the State Department, and Harty said she met them "with some trepidation," because it was she who had sent their child in harm's way. But Payne's mother took Harty's face in her hands and said: "Thank you for letting our daughter serve her country."

As grand as it may sound, the job of consular officers in the Foreign Service is to help Americans abroad and to protect America's borders. Helping Americans does not necessarily mean getting them off the hook for something wrong they might have done – it means making sure they are treated humanely and fairly under the host country's laws and any relevant internationally accepted rules. Visiting Americans in foreign jails is a frequent duty for consular officers, but the bulk of their work has to do with more mundane tasks, such as issuing temporary U.S. passports and registering newborn U.S. citizens. Actually, there is nothing mundane about an American who has been mugged and robbed in a country he or she is visiting for the first time, and needs a new passport to get home. As for protecting America's borders, that function of consular work is done through issuing U.S. entry visas, which has become rather complex and critical, as we will see later in this chapter.

Payne's main duty in Iraq was to assist American citizens. That part of her job got her involved in a very high-profile case that put her in the media spotlight at about the same time Witter contacted her. She was trying to locate a missing 26-year-old American, Nicholas Berg, who had gone to the war-torn country to seek work and was abducted by al-Qaida in Iraq. Berg was later beheaded by a man the CIA claimed was terrorist leader Abu Musab al-Zarqawi.[3] In a gruesome video of the execution posted on the Internet, masked men were heard linking their action to the widely publicized abuses of prisoners by U.S. service members at Abu Ghraib prison.[4] Zarqawi was killed by U.S. forces in 2006.

Several days after Berg's death, his parents provided the Associated Press with copies of e-mail messages they had received from Payne, informing them that their son had been held by the U.S. military before his capture by al-Qaida.[5] "I have confirmed that your son, Nick, is being detained by the U.S. military in Mosul," she wrote on April 1, 2004. "He is safe. He was picked up approximately one week ago. We will try to obtain additional information regarding his detention and a contact person you can communicate with directly." When the story broke about a month later, the State Department said that Payne's information had been wrong. Berg had been held by Iraqi police – not the U.S. military – but Payne was not informed of that detail until a week after she had sent the message to the parents.

Now Payne teaches entry-level officers the lesson she learned from that case. "I stress to them that any e-mail you send to any client, read it twice and make sure you wouldn't mind seeing it on news wires and it's something you are comfortable standing by later, if anybody questions it," she told me. "I'm very proud of those e-mails that they were professional and exhibited the compassion I was feeling for the parents. At the time they were written, they were written accurately."

It took her "a long time personally to recover" from the Berg case, Payne said, pointing out that a consular officer's top priority is to protect Americans abroad. "We have Americans in our consular district, and our job is to protect and assist them," she said. "But we have no ability to force anybody to do anything. We can only give people information in such a way as to allow them to make an informed decision. If a person makes a decision that costs them their life, that's hard on a consular officer. I questioned myself: Was there different information I could have provided? Was there any way I could have had that person – without crossing a line – change their decision that obviously resulted in a tragic death? We deal with people's lives, but we don't control them."

'Any American, any problem, any time'

Gavin Sundwall stood beside the grave, a Bible in hand, and read John 11:25-26: "I am the resurrection and the life..." A local embassy employee said a prayer. Two taxi drivers, who had become the deceased woman's chauffeurs during the last years of her life, shared memories of her and shed tears. They sprinkled the woman's ashes over the graves of her two husbands, which were just a few feet apart. The impromptu ceremony at the Corozal American Cemetery outside Panama City was over.

Sundwall, the Foreign Service officer with the Satanist killer experience from the beginning of Chapter 1, had never met the elderly American woman when she was alive, even though she had lived in Panama for decades. He saw her for the first time when he went to the morgue to identify her body after she had died from natural causes in the summer of 1998. That was no unusual duty for him as a consular officer in Panama City, but the funeral he organized was certainly not in his job description. "I informed her family back in the U.S. of her death, but they didn't want to come down and have anything to do with her burial, although they sent money," Sundwall recalled. "They told us that her last wishes had been to be cremated and have her ashes sprinkled over the graves of her two husbands. All her friends were elderly and didn't want to come. So who else would have done it if I hadn't?"

Also during his tour in Panama in the late 1990s – his first in the Foreign Service – Sundwall received a call one day from an Indiana couple who had just adopted a girl from the Central American country and wanted to take the baby to her new home in the United States. But the airline they flew on refused to allow the infant on the plane. She did not have a U.S. entry visa, and though she was now the daughter of American citizens, she was still a national of Panama.

As it turned out, the couple "had done all the adoption paperwork through the Panamanian system, but had done nothing on the American side," Sundwall said. "She was an abandoned and burned girl who had been put in a trash can and set on fire. The [adoptive] parents had scheduled hospital treatment for her the next week and had appointments for reconstructive surgery. So it was very hard, but I had to sit them down and tell them that there was nothing I could do to help them out of this situation that day, since the Immigration and Naturalization Service declined to allow them to enter the U.S. without a visa under humanitarian parole. It was one of the hardest things I've had to do in my career."

Sundwall explained to the new parents that they had to go back home and apply for adoption, which includes visits by social workers to determine whether they would be capable parents. Then, they had to file an application for an immigrant visa for the girl, which would make her a permanent U.S. resident, and later an American citizen. "At the end of the day, they had to put the child back into the orphanage, go back to the United States and start the process. I told them they could call me anytime to talk about anything they wanted," Sundwall said. But the process dragged on, and the couple got frustrated with the immigration authorities who seemed to come up with hurdle after hurdle. At Sundwall's suggestion, the couple took the matter to the office of their U.S. senator, Richard Lugar. "They were back in my office within a month after that first time, and we issued the visa," Sundwall said.

According to the State Department, the U.S. "welcomes more children through adoption than any other nation" – more than 230,000 from 1999 to 2011.[6] In 1994, the Bureau of Consular Affairs created the Office of Children's Issues, which assists "parents as they seek to provide a home to orphans abroad through inter-country adoption by offering country-specific information about the adoption process, and by advocating for greater protections for adoptive parents and children abroad."[7]

Sundwall's stories from Panama may seem extreme and not quite representative of daily consular work, but they are actually very common. Almost every consular officer has similar life-changing stories, and they certainly do not always end happily.

There was no happy ending – at least not yet – to the story of a 24-year-old U.S. graduate student who went missing while hiking alone in southern China in August 2004, about a week before I first met Sundwall in Beijing. He was chief of the American Citizens Services section at the embassy, having served in Kuwait after leaving Panama. The student, David L. Sneddon, was a Mormon missionary from Utah traveling through China at the end of his study there when he vanished in the Tiger Leaping Gorge. His family flew to China and, with the help of the embassy, recreated his last steps and met with senior local officials. The U.S. ambassador at the time,

Clark Randt, raised the issue at the highest levels of the central government in Beijing. Robert Bennett, a Republican U.S. senator from Utah at the time, also got involved. Although the family did not find Sneddon or his remains, it was "very grateful for the full cooperation and support" of both the embassy and the State Department. "The ambassador was most gracious, considerate and interested in our situation," the student's parents wrote on a website created to help find David. "The embassy and staff of American Citizens Services have gone beyond the 'second mile' in their continuing efforts to help."[8]

Sundwall has many other stories about Americans abroad to tell. There was the elderly Chinese-American woman who got lost in Beijing with $3,000 in her pocket. Then there was the American man and his Chinese wife who were being blackmailed by their landlord. And of course, there are suicides, traffic accidents and other fatalities, as well as passports and visas for new American spouses and children. Sundwall, together with one entry-level Foreign Service officer and three local employees, covered a consular district in China larger than Western Europe – and, as he pointed out, "it's much harder to do business in China than in Western Europe." While there are "limitations on what we can do and how much we can get involved," Sundwall said, "our job is really any American, any problem, any time."

Getting 'beaten up' for 'doing things right'

Dozens of Foreign Service officers around the world said that helping fellow Americans out of danger was one of the highlights of their careers. "It may not be a big deal for you when you see hundreds of people a year, but it is a big deal for a little lady from Des Moines who has never traveled overseas and has had her bags grabbed and has been pushed around," said Virginia Blaser, the deputy chief of mission in Uganda whom we met briefly in Chapter 2. "I love to be the one who can solve her problems."

Blaser was chief of the American Citizens Services section at the embassy in London when I first met her in 2003. She later became acting consul-general in El Salvador, where I also visited her, and then deputy chief of mission in Mauritius. She began her first foreign assignment in Madrid in 1993 with an experience that went far beyond what she was required to do. She was the embassy duty officer when a call came in from two Midwest teachers who had brought a group of teenage students to Spain on their first trip abroad.

A boy from the group was nowhere to be found, and the teachers wanted the embassy's help to locate him before word about his disappearance reached his parents back home. Blaser alerted the police but could not just sit and wait for something to happen. "I remember thinking that the child might be out there hurt or scared," she recalled. "So my husband and I literally walked the streets for two days, hoping that we'd find him just by sheer luck, but of course we didn't. Eventually, we got a call from the police saying that they had been driving along a highway outside the city and found him – traumatized, dehydrated and sunburned." In the meantime, the boy's parents and their congressman's and senator's offices had been calling several times a day.

When the boy arrived at the embassy, Blaser, herself a mother, took him home against official rules, phoned his parents, fed him, gave him clothes and a bed for the night. "Finally the next day, the group leader came to pick him up. We gave him another set of clothes, they left and we never heard from anyone again – not from the parents, not from the senator or congressman, not from the school. I suppose in a way that was a compliment, if everybody was satisfied and had no complaints. I don't usually feel that we need thanks for doing our job. But it was one of the few times I actually wanted someone to call and say that the kid was all right." No one returned the clothes, either.

Blaser did hear back from two Colorado women she had helped in London in the spring of 2003 – but only through the media. The women, whose rental car had been broken into and their purses stolen with their passports and money, called on a Friday morning to ask for help. A local British employee at the embassy explained to them the procedure for applying for a temporary passport so they could return home, telling them they needed to submit photos and pay a fee. They arrived at the embassy, with their luggage, a few minutes before it was to close. Visitors are usually not allowed in the building with more than a small bag or purse for security reasons, but the guards saw the women were frustrated and let them bring the suitcases into the lobby of the American Citizens Services section.

Even though the embassy was closing for the week and most of Blaser's staff were preparing to go home, she asked for volunteers to work overtime so they could start processing the women's passport applications.

"This wasn't a true emergency, because they weren't leaving the country until Monday, and there was time to do everything that morning, but because they were so upset and angry, I wanted to do as much as we could that night," Blaser said. One local employee was recovering from cancer and needed rest, yet she offered to stay. Another one did, too, although his father had just had a heart attack that afternoon and the son was expected at the hospital, as Blaser learned three days later. Most of the paperwork was done, and the only thing left before the passports could be issued was mandatory name checks, which could take hours. Since her staff had already put in an extra hour, Blaser requested the name checks and asked the women to return first thing Monday morning to receive their passports. They did and made their flight back home later that day.

A couple of weeks passed, and one day an article appeared in the *Denver Post*. The two women, high school teachers Jennifer Tompkins and Irma Sturgell, had told columnist Diane Carman their story – it was about the "hell" they had endured with the "nightmare embassy staff." Blaser's heart sank as soon as she glanced at the headline: "Travelers see Brits' best, Yanks' worst."[9]

"The embassy staff was unconscionably rude. The women didn't have the money and the photos required to get new passports, the bureaucrats said. They refused to allow them to make any calls," Carman wrote. "We were still pleading, but they physically took our suitcases and put them on the street," she quoted one of the women as saying. "They said if we had been beaten or raped, they could help us. That would have been considered an emergency. It was unbelievably inhumane."

Both Blaser and the embassy spokesman at the time, Lee McClenny, told me that Carman had not contacted them to ask for their version of the story. Carman confirmed that in an e-mail message to me but offered no explanation why not. "That was such a small case, and there have been thousands since then," Blaser said, "but it still bothers me, because it was my staff that made sacrifices and did everything right, only to get beaten up in that article."

The case of the Colorado women is hardly an isolated occurrence. Almost every member of Congress has heard complaints from constituents about callous bureaucrats at embassies who care more about obeying rules and going home on time than helping people in need. Then there are the accusations that the State Department often chooses to cozy up to a foreign country rather than help an American citizen resolve a personal matter. Sometimes, those accusations are founded.

Child abduction battles

"My family's lives depend upon my silence," Patricia Roush wrote me in a 2006 e-mail message that left me speechless. The woman who had spent most of the last two decades waging a very public battle to bring her two kidnapped daughters back home from Saudi Arabia had no interest in speaking out anymore. In the years before that, she had accused the U.S. government of betraying her children "for Saudi oil" – during high-profile congressional hearings, in numerous media interviews and a book titled "At Any Price."

"People still e-mail me often for advice," Roush wrote me, "but I have moved on with my family and trying to bring them here on different grounds now." She was not more specific, but from my conversations at the State Department it was clear that officials from both countries had finally persuaded her that, if she wanted to see the girls again, she should work things out quietly with their Saudi father. Khalid al-Gheshayan, Roush's former husband, had taken them secretly to his homeland in January 1986, when Alia was 7 years old and Aisha was 3, and not allowed them to return to the United States ever since. "I have tirelessly pioneered the issue of American children kidnapped and taken abroad," Roush told the House Committee on Government Reform in 2002. "My relentless efforts over the years led to the creation of the Office of Children's Issues at the State Department, intended to advocate on behalf of the littlest American citizens snatched to foreign countries, and to enactment of the International Parental Kidnapping Act in 1993."[10]

Roush's name has become known to hundreds of members of Congress, American and Saudi diplomats and other government officials. She has harshly criticized both Republican and Democratic administrations for "sacrificing" her children in order to maintain good relations with an oppressive regime whose support is vital to the United States in a hostile Middle East. "All I could do was continue to expose this evil, and lead the campaign to free them and all the other American women and children dying a little each day inside the tortuous walls of the totalitarian kingdom while the U.S. State Department continued to make excuses for the Saudis, and pandered to their slightest requests – at any price," she wrote in 2003 on her website, which no longer exists.

Roush repeatedly depicted State Department officials in Washington and Saudi Arabia as cold-hearted and uninterested in freeing two helpless American citizens from a society that affords them no rights. "My daughters have become victims of the endless gamesmanship between U.S. diplomats and the Saudi family princes," she wrote. "Ties between the U.S. and Saudi Arabia are long and deep-rooted, cemented by long-standing military and economic interests. The U.S. is the leading supplier of defense equipment and services to the kingdom. Billions of dollars of U.S. merchandise are exported to Saudi Arabia each year."

Child abductions have become a huge problem not only in countries like Saudi Arabia but around the world, including in western U.S. allies such as Germany and Austria. As of January 2012, the Office of Children's Issues had 1,326 open cases involving 1,908 children, the State Department said. Since the late 1990s, more than 5,000 abducted children have been returned to the United States, it added.

Beth Payne, who worked in the Office of Children's Issues before going to Iraq in 2003, became its director in 2011, following a tour as consul-general in Kolkata, India. She said she fully understood why American mothers are frustrated with U.S. diplomats. "If I had a child and it was taken from me, I would do anything in my power to get that child back, and any government bureaucrat who appeared to stand in my way would become someone I would detest," she said. "We have to learn that there will be people who are angry with us, they don't like us and say terrible things about us in public. So it comes down to this: In your heart, are you doing the best you can and working as hard as you can, knowing that it's not appropriate to break the law in the United States or another country?"

Congress has been deeply involved in child abduction cases for years. One of the most vocal critics of the State Department's handling of those cases has been Indiana Republican Congressman Dan Burton, who has accused the department of doing "very little" to help parents get their kids back. "If we are not willing to stand up and fight for American citizens whose children have been kidnapped, what kind of priorities do we have?" he asked in 2002.[11]

Payne said that the State Department's approach to resolving child abduction issues has more to do with a quiet negotiation than a public campaign. "Because we are not police and we don't have access to Black Hawk helicopters to go and pick up children, it becomes all about information, persuasion and working to find a common ground," she said. Following that path, she "got more than six kids back from Saudi Arabia" in the two years before she left for Iraq in 2003, she said, and "never lied to the Saudis or violated the law." She advised those children's mothers not to go to the media with their stories. "We don't need to win some public campaign," she said. "We just need to go home at night and be comfortable with ourselves."

"Gentle pressure relentlessly applied at and with the cooperation of the highest levels of the Saudi government has provided us the ability to do what we could not do before," said Maura Harty, the assistant secretary of state for consular affairs from 2002 until 2008 whom we met earlier in the chapter. "The critical element that had previously not been present was the very vigorous engagement of Congress. Their ability to shine a searingly bright spotlight on this issue is always welcome."

Harty's successor as assistant secretary, Janice Jacobs, said that Congress's involvement has made the child abduction issue "a lot more public" and difficult to keep quiet about. "In a perfect world, it would all be done very quietly, but these stories are often heart-wrenching stories that the media loves," she said. Official U.S. policy is not to take sides in child-custody disputes, but at the same time consular officers have a duty to protect U.S. citizens. That apparent contradiction makes these cases even more difficult, several officers said. They protect the interests of the American parent and child, they explained, by negotiating – they actually try to avoid using that word – on their behalf with local authorities and sometimes with the other parent.

Gavin Sundwall exhausted all his persuasive skills over three days in the fall of 2002 in a hotel room in central China, where Camille Colvin and her 4-year-old son Griffin were held by police at the request of the boy's Chinese father, Guo Rui. He had kidnapped his son from New York, after a U.S. divorce court had awarded custody to his ex-wife. She had hired a detective and found Griffin in Guo's hometown of Zhengzhou but was not allowed to leave the country – or even the hotel – unless she left the child behind or reached an agreement with Guo. "She was besieged," recalled Sundwall, who flew down from Beijing to handle the case. "The Chinese said it would have to go through the Chinese court system, which was going to take awhile, and she agreed, but there was a lot of pressure on her to make one of those informal deals to settle things with the father. At one point, I was trying to persuade the Chinese to let me take the child to my house in Beijing not to be trapped in that hotel." In the end, Colvin had to pay $60,000 in "blood money," Sundwall said, even though she won custody in a Chinese court.[12]

September 11 and the shakeup of the U.S. visa system

At first glance, David Donahue's experience on September 11, 2001, was not much different from that of most other Americans. "I heard the first plane had already hit the World Trade Center, and then watched the second live on television, like everybody else," he recalled.

But while most Americans were at home or at work when the terrorists struck the twin towers and the Pentagon, Donahue was in Afghanistan. He had been sent in from Islamabad, the capital of neighboring Pakistan, where he was the U.S. consul-general – the United States had no diplomatic relations with the Taliban regime, which had provided safe haven to Osama bin Laden since 1996.

Donahue was on a mission to rescue two American citizens, Dayna Curry and Heather Mercer. The Christian relief workers, along with six Germans and Australians, had been detained five weeks earlier on charges of proselytizing and faced possible death sentences. At the time, I actually followed the case for the *Washington Times*.

"We had a beautiful morning," Donahue told me in 2003 in Manila, where he had moved from Islamabad a year earlier. "We were out with a Taliban official, visiting the old German school where his son went. In the middle of the tour, we received a call that we had been granted permission to visit the girls, talk to them in depth and discuss legal representation for the first time." Donahue was unable to secure the release of the women, who were freed only when the Taliban were overthrown in a U.S. operation in November 2001,[13] but he continued to monitor their case from Islamabad. "The war was going on, and I would call the Foreign Ministry as bombs rained down on the city. They would check on them and give us reports back," he said.

As a Foreign Service officer since 1983, Donahue, who later became consul-general in Mexico City, knew immediately after the attacks that the work of American diplomats overseas was bound to change. Nowhere have those changes been as visible as in consular affairs and, more specifically, the issuance of U.S. entry visas to foreigners. That function, which is now performed at 222 missions around the world, came under intense scrutiny in Washington after it was discovered that the 19 hijackers who carried out the attacks had entered the United States on legally obtained visas.

But even the harshest critics, who immediately after the attacks demanded that the State Department be stripped of visa-issuing responsibilities, later conceded that the fault lay less with individual officers than with a system that lacked basic coordination with intelligence and law-enforcement agencies. "There was nothing in our consolidated database that would have said, 'Don't let these individuals in the country because they are terrorists,'" Colin Powell told the 9/11 Commission investigating the attacks in 2004.[14]

In the years after the events of September 11, the Bureau of Consular Affairs underwent unprecedented changes. It tried to strike a balance between "secure borders and open doors," as Powell defined the policy, but in the early days the "open doors" part lost out to the demands of heightened security. As many consular officers around the world told me, before September 11, you could do no wrong by issuing a visa; after September 11, you could do no wrong by denying a visa.

The new regulations included fingerprinting and photographing visa applicants, followed by personal interviews with everyone except children and the elderly, as well as security clearances from Washington that sometimes took months. That resulted in long waiting times first to schedule an interview, then for an applicant's turn in huge lines snaking around embassies and consulates – often in sweltering heat or biting cold – and finally for visa approval.

Esteemed international scholars missed conferences where thousands of participants hoped to hear their presentations. First-rate foreign students missed the start of classes or never made it to the United States. The lengthy and costly application process, which for many ended with a rejection, changed America's reputation from a welcoming country that attracted the world's best and brightest to a fortress that, in effect, told foreigners to stay away. The numbers reveal a telling picture. In the 2001 fiscal year, a record of more than 7.5 million non-immigrant visas were issued worldwide, but by 2003, the number dropped to 4.8 million.[15]

For the State Department, there was no room for mistakes – letting another terrorist in the country because of an oversight became its recurring nightmare. "We weren't going to err on the side of letting in one or two people who shouldn't be here," said Richard Boucher, the State Department spokesman during Powell's tenure. "We were going to err on the side of keeping out 1,000 who should have been here." In spite of all government efforts and new security procedures, however, other terrorists did manage to get on planes destined for the United States with the intention of blowing them up – fortunately, no one succeeded.

In 2002, Richard Reid, the so-called shoe-bomber, tried to detonate explosives hidden in his shoes on a flight from Paris to Miami, according to his indictment issued by a U.S. district court in Massachusetts.[16] As a British citizen, he did not need a visa, so no one blamed the State Department.

That was not the case, however, in 2009, when Nigerian Umar Farouk Abdulmutallab attempted to explode a homemade bomb hidden in his underwear on a Christmas day flight from Amsterdam to Detroit.[17] He actually had a valid U.S. visa in his passport, so many fingers were pointed at the State Department. The visa had been issued in 2008 by the embassy in London, where Abdulmutallab was a student, and the consular section there had performed all necessary checks. But at the time, there was no information in the system linking Abdulmutallab to terrorist groups, Patrick Kennedy, the undersecretary of state for management, told me in early 2010 for a story I wrote in the *Washington Times*.[18] A previous visa had been issued by the embassy in Nigeria in 2006.

It was at that same embassy where Abdulmutallab's father reported his son missing in November 2009 and expressed concern that he "might have fallen under the influence of extremists in Yemen," as a State Department official put it to me. In its first message about the case to the National Counterterrorism Center (NCTC), the State Department did not include visa information, but that was corrected several days later. The NCTC determined that "the information was insufficient to make a judgment" about revoking the visa, which is why the State Department did nothing, Kennedy said. The undersecretary for management oversees the Bureau of Consular Affairs.

Even though the NCTC did not recommend visa revocation, some people in Washington were reluctant to exonerate the State Department completely, because it has full authority to cancel visas without permission from other parts of the government.

President Obama blamed the failure to prevent Abdulmutallab from boarding the plane on a lack of inter-agency coordination. "The U.S. government had the information – scattered throughout the system – to potentially uncover this plot and disrupt the attack," he said days after the incident. "Rather than a failure to collect or share intelligence, this was a failure to connect and understand the intelligence that we already had."[19]

Often derided in the past for "stamping passports" and doing little of significance, consular officers now have no trouble convincing anyone that they are truly America's first line of defense and their work matters greatly. "We may not deal with the highest foreign policy, but every one of these cases has a chance to become that, if we don't handle it as ably and professionally as we can," Maura Harty said. "We have pushed our borders as far from the United States as possible. As visa adjudicators abroad, our goal is to stop questionable or dangerous travelers from ever reaching our shores."

Fortress America?

Goverdhan Mehta, a highly respected professor of organic chemistry at the Indian Institute of Science in Bangalore and the institute's former director, prepared for his two-week lecture tour in the United States in February 2006 at the invitation of the American Chemical Society. So he went to the U.S. Consulate in Chennai for a visa interview. At 75 and with a good track record of multiple visits to the United States, Mehta had no reason to be nervous. So he was stunned when his visa was not approved on the spot. He went to the press and said that he had been refused a visa, because the consular officer conducting the interview had determined that he posed a risk of chemical warfare and bioterrorism.

As often happens with prominent figures being denied U.S. visas, Mehta's case went all the way up to the ambassador at the time, David Mulford. It turned out that a visa had not been issued because, "as part of a standard visa-processing requirement for those working with sensitive technologies, the consulate required additional information," embassy spokesman David Kennedy told me at the time.

A couple of days later, Mulford personally called the scientist to apologize and offer him a visa. But Mehta had already canceled his trip and declined the offer. "In spite of my track record, I was surprised to be denied a visa this time, though all the relevant papers were in order. I was embarrassed at the way they conducted the interview. I felt humiliated. I decided there was no point in arguing," he said at a press conference. "The issue is a generic one and relates to the free interaction of scientists and their participation in various international activities without being subject to any restriction or humiliation. It is not only an issue concerning scientists in India but all over the world."[20]

Mehta is one of thousands of visa applicants who require special security clearances every year, because their field of study or work is deemed highly sensitive by the U.S. government. The journal *Physics Today* wrote in June 2003 about Irving Lerch, director of international affairs at the American Physical Society, who had become "a clearinghouse for those fighting the visa wars and has personally intervened in about 200 visa cases."[21]

Lerch told the publication about a Chinese student in the United States who went back to China when his parents were killed in an accident and was refused a visa to return to school. He also cited the case of a Russian woman who had worked as an associate scientist at the U.S. Department of Energy's (DOE) Ames Laboratory in Iowa for 11 years. "She went to Germany with her 2-year-old child and wasn't allowed to return. Her husband at Ames hired an attorney who used loopholes in the law to reunite the family," the journal wrote. It noted that even a former Russian minister of science "couldn't obtain a visa in time to attend a scientific conference" in New Mexico.

The list of sensitive fields and technologies was expanded after September 11 to include "everything from nuclear engineering and chemistry to biotechnology and urban planning," *Physics Today* wrote, and most such cases are referred to Washington for review by the FBI, CIA, DOE and other agencies. It was not unusual for that process to last several months in the years following the terrorist attacks, though it was gradually shortened to weeks or even days, as the backlog decreased and more resources became available to the government. Both the academic and business communities have publicly criticized the system for hurting millions of legitimate travelers – and costing universities and companies millions of dollars. The media has published many stories about foreigners going to study in Britain, Australia and other English-speaking countries, disillusioned with the stringent U.S. rules. Educators and business leaders have written numerous articles urging the government to do something about the process.

According to data from the National Center of Education Statistics, the number of foreign students enrolled at U.S. colleges and universities dropped in the 2003-2004 academic year for the first time in more than three decades, compared to the year before. It continued to fall in the following two years. Once things settled down, however, and the new visa system began working better, the number started climbing again in 2006 and reached a record of more than 723,000 foreign students in 2010-2011.[22]

Another recurring theme in media coverage worldwide since September 11 has been the treatment of visa applicants once they arrive at a consulate for their interview. *Financial Times* reader Piyush Jain wrote in a letter to the editor in September 2006 about his experience at the consulate in Mumbai, India, after waiting 10 weeks for an appointment.

"Finally, when I was called at a specific time with at least 100 people, we all waited outside the consulate building on the street," Jain wrote. "After I got into the building, I had to wait for three hours for an interview. During the interview, I had to disclose all my personal and financial details to the interviewer. Officials even looked at my wedding photo album to ensure that the marriage certificate I produced was not a fake. Out of two weeks of my vacation, I spent about three days on my visa-related activities. Having served very prestigious U.S. organizations during my career, I expected to be treated with some dignity in the U.S. consulate. Even if this level of scrutiny is required, visa-seekers could still be treated with some respect."[23]

For many visa applicants around the world, their interviewing consular officer may be the first American they have ever met – and for some, maybe the last. Their impression is lasting, and it should be positive, Maura Harty said. "People who come to our consulates because they want to travel to the U.S. should have a dignified experience," she said. "That doesn't mean that they have a right to a visa. But I have called officers off visa lines when I've found them to be rude to people."

In fact, "our entire system needs to get friendlier," said Craig Bryant, whom I met in 2011 in Singapore, where he headed the consular section. "If this is the only face of America these people are seeing, it's not just the consular officer who needs to be friendly to them, but also the guard who takes their cell phones. The system that mandates their appointment weeks in the future is not a friendly system."

Holding 'lives in the balance'

A young Chinese man leaned forward and assumed all the seriousness of someone determined to achieve his goal. "You see, sir," he told the consular officer on the other side of the window. "My mother has a prosthetic leg. I want to study chemistry so I can build a better polymer and make a better artificial leg." The officer, who had asked why the visa applicant wanted to continue his education in the United States, said, "This is the most compelling reason I've heard all day," and granted the student a visa.

The next day, another student showed up at the embassy in Beijing and gave the "prosthetic leg" speech – and then another one, and another one, until there were hundreds of them. All interviewing officers were bewildered, but it did not take them long to figure things out. After the applicant who had first used the story the day before received a visa, he decided to share his experience in an Internet chat room, where thousands of Chinese students posted various tips on how to obtain a U.S. visa. In fact, "there is this whole game in China, because the students think they have to give us a story in order to get a visa," said Gavin Sundwall, who was one of the interviewing officers. "They also try to steer each other to certain officers, and even gave us nicknames," he added. Some of the nicknames were "baldy," "too tall baldy," "beautiful girl," "handsome guy" and "cousin of handsome guy."

In Bogota, Colombia, in 2001, Eric Watnik interviewed a man "wearing a very ill-fitting suit" that was obviously not his. "Several minutes later, somebody wearing the same suit came in," Watnik told me in 2011 at the embassy in Singapore, where he was the public affairs counselor. "Apparently, there was somebody outside saying, 'The only people who get approved are people wearing suits, and you are not wearing a suit, so you need to rent this suit from me.' We also had people come in wearing glasses that weren't theirs – someone thought people in glasses had a better chance of getting a visa because they looked smarter."

Students all over the world worry that, after working hard for years to secure admission in prestigious American colleges and universities, they might never see the campus because they cannot get a U.S. visa. After all, Sundwall said, an acceptance letter from Harvard is not enough for a consular officer to issue a visa.

Every applicant must prove that he or she is not an intending immigrant, as required by U.S. law – that means that they have enough established links to their country and community, such as a family, home, vehicle, job, so that they have a compelling reason to return. But a young, single student who does not own property or a car can have a hard time overcoming the law's presumption. This is why students come up with stories that they hope would convince the interviewing officer that they will go back to their country after graduation.

Qing Liu did not try to pitch a story. She simply went to the embassy in Beijing and said that she had been awarded a presidential fellowship by the University of Buffalo in upstate New York to pursue graduate studies at the Department of Romance Languages and Literatures in 2003. Her specialty was Spanish, which she had studied for most of her life at specialized language schools in China. But her interviewing officer told her that it made more sense for her to go to school in a Spanish-speaking country and refused her a visa. She tried again, with the same outcome, wrote the university's newspaper, *The Reporter*. Liu was perplexed – why was it the officer's business to decide where she would study, she wondered.

"It is extremely difficult for me to make this decision; however, I feel that I would like to quit," she wrote in an e-mail message to Assistant Professor William Egginton. "Each time I tried, I wished I could win. You can't imagine how stressful it is to prepare for such an interview, and how disappointed I am after getting rejected. Now,

I just want to stop torturing myself (also you, to some extent). It is not an easy decision for either of us. Dating back to college, I have been preparing for study in the U.S. for several years and already reached the last step. It is so hard for me to give up something that I have been longing for."[24]

Sundwall was not involved in Liu's case, but he said that officers in China have to be very careful to whom they give visas because, according to the embassy's estimate, 95 percent of the Chinese students in the United States end up staying, most of them legally. But he added that "it's OK to say, 'I don't know what I'm going to do,'" when an officer asks about an applicant's intentions. "It's our job to judge the intent," he said. "We have to make the best decision we can at the time of the interview." A good indication that a student plans to return is his or her field of study, Sundwall explained. "There are growth fields in China," he said, "and we know the local context and what makes sense." He acknowledged, however, that just because there is high demand for certain specialists in China, it does not mean that such professionals are not wanted in the United States.

Maura Harty likes to say that the best commercial for America is America. "We have an abiding interest in welcoming all sorts of travelers to the United States, but we have a special emphasis on students, because that is a long-term investment in the security of this country," she said. Good consular officers, she added, not only understand the law and know how to apply it, but are also familiar with the language, economic and political situation of the country in which they work. They also know the travel patterns and overstay rates of candidates from that country, as well as the parts of the United States with large communities of that nationality, which could provide a social safety net for new immigrants.

Even with all the rules and regulations, the decisions officers make on visa applications are often subjective, many of them said. They understand that in denying a visa they might be frustrating an applicant's lifelong dream. "It's hard, because you have lives in the balance," Sundwall said. "These are decisions that affect people through the end of their lives. That's something we are all conscious of."

The visa mill

I was somewhat confused. The building resembled a huge hangar, but inside it felt more like the Department of Motor Vehicles (DMV).

Hundreds of people were waiting for different services, and when someone's turn came, their number appeared on an electronic board – accompanied by a ding, just like at the DMV – and they were directed either to one of 18 stations around the hall or to one of 15 windows at the end.

"This is our waiting room," said Laura Clerici, the consul in Mexico City, as she ushered me through the visa section in the fall of 2003. I have visited many such operations around the world, but very few come close to the size of this one. After waiting in line outside the embassy and going through security, applicants handed all their forms and documents to a local Mexican employee at one of the 18 stations, where they were also fingerprinted and photographed. After more waiting, they went to one of the windows to be interviewed by a consular officer. Those who were approved for a visa had to stop at another table outside the hall where a courier service had set up shop to collect payment for sending the stamped passports back to their owners.

Things have changed a bit since my visit, and digital photographs and fingerprints are now collected at an Applicant Service Center outside the embassy in Mexico City, the State Department said. There are 10 more such centers outside the capital, it added. Mexico is by far the country with the most visa applications every year, with over 1 million non-immigrant visas issued.

U.S. Non-Immigrant Visas Issued by Country (2011)

Country	Number of Visas	Rejection Rate
Mexico	1,315,116	12.8%
China	945,040	12%
Brazil	801,371	3.8%
India	554,267	30.1%
Colombia	234,700	21.7%
Russia	204,315	10.3%
Venezuela	198,422	16.1%
Argentina	194,533	2.5%
Philippines	155,150	33.8%
Taiwan	149,731	1.9%

Source: U.S. Department of State

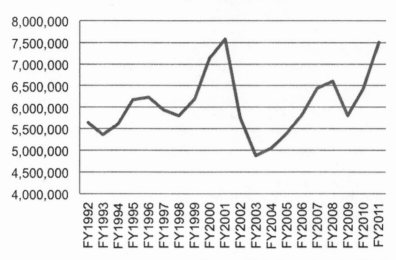

U.S. Non-Immigrant Visas Issued

Source: U.S. Department of State

Worldwide, 9.6 million non-immigrant visa applications were submitted in the 2011 fiscal year, 7.5 million of which were approved, according to preliminary State Department data.[25] That puts the rejection rate at about 22 percent. In addition, about half a million immigrant visas are granted annually.[26]

A typical U.S. consulate has three sections – American Citizens Services, Immigrant Visas and Non-Immigrant Visas – but officers usually spend most of their time on non-immigrant visas. Every entry-level Foreign Service officer is required to do a consular tour, regardless of his or her career track, which is not surprisingly a controversial decision. Over the years, there have been suggestions that there be a separate Consular Service with its own work force, or even that consular work be contracted out to private companies, perhaps under the State Department's supervision.

"I've always thought that having people stamp visas for two years really does turn off a lot of very smart people" from the Foreign Service, Condoleezza Rice told me. The late Warren Christopher agreed. "We should find a way to minimize the amount of time spent doing the bureaucracy of immigration," he suggested in 2004. "There is no reason why highly educated and trained Foreign Service officers ought to be doing as many routine tasks as they are now. It should be possible to have contract employees doing some of the less challenging work at posts."

Although dozens of officers who are not in the consular career track said they would have preferred not to do consular work, they noted that it has become much more challenging and intellectually stimulating since 2001. Still, many of them said they had not joined the Foreign Service to do visas, and their consular tours did not provide the correct impression of the rest of a diplomatic career. "My first tour was as bad as it gets," said an officer whose consular assignment was in Latin America. "I seriously considered leaving the service. I admire people who do consular work as a career."

Janice Jacobs, the assistant secretary and former ambassador to Senegal and Guinea-Bissau who joined the Foreign Service in 1980, acknowledged that many new officers are "impatient" and "just want to get into their area of specialty and show what they can do." But while "it's always been a challenge to convince people about the importance of consular work," she said, "the skills they learn as consular officers are going to serve them well throughout their Foreign Service career. You have to gather a lot of information, you have to know about the country you are serving in, you have to know the law, you have to look at that individual in front of you and figure out in about two minutes, 'Is this person going to come back after a short visit to the U.S.?' And you have to be able to make quick decisions. I've found all of those skills served me well as a deputy chief of mission, and even as an ambassador."

Jacobs also said that what makes consular work particularly rewarding is that "it's very tangible" and produces immediate results, which is often not the case in diplomacy. "You are working with people and helping people, and at the end of the day, you know exactly what you've accomplished. You also get immediate feedback on your performance" from American citizens or visa applicants, she said.

'Worked to death'

Consular officers not always prefer to receive "feedback" from their customers. "Even if you say 'no' nicely, some people still yell at you and try to spit on you," Virginia Blaser said of visa applicants. "It took me weeks not to take that personally, because I'd never had anyone speak to me that way before. Sometimes, they even threaten your life."

Another source of frustration for consular officers, especially before September 11, was the interference of their colleagues from other parts of the mission in visa issues. Gavin Sundwall had an applicant in Kuwait in the early 1990s whose name was on a watch list, so he submitted the application for clearance through the proper security channels. But the person "was very well connected, and within 20 minutes, the economic counselor came down screaming at me that I didn't know what I was doing, and how dare I refuse a visa to this outstanding friend of his," Sundwall recalled. "I tried to explain to him what the system was, but he wouldn't listen to me, so I had to take it to the deputy chief of mission. I thought it was completely inappropriate that this had happened, and I got fairly good coverage, but not an apology."

It is almost impossible for such an incident to occur in the post-September 11 environment, but since then, consular officers have had plenty of other challenges. The most serious of them has been a huge workload under severe budget constraints and personnel shortages. "We had more than 2,100 people requesting visas every day, so we were upping the number of interviews [our section] did from 700 to 1,000 to 1,200 to 1,400, and we were worked to death," a junior officer in Latin America told me in 2003. An officer in East Asia said: "I wish we could just shut everything down sometimes to make a statement." An officer interviewing more than 100 applicants a day became standard at many posts around the world.

Although things have improved significantly because of recent hiring increases, officers in China, Brazil and other countries still "interview 100-120 people a day," said Janice Jacobs. "I worry about those officers. In these big countries, it's almost the norm."

The public, of course, sees the other side of the visa application process and often complains about extended wait times for interviews and high application fees. The current fee for a tourist or business visa is $160, which is a lot of money in many countries, and of course it is non-refundable if the application is denied. "Every time we raise the fees, there is always the fear that we are going to be discouraging travel," Jacobs said. "But [the Bureau of] Consular Affairs is fee-funded, so we have to charge whatever it costs us to provide the service."

The wait for visa interviews in most countries has been reduced significantly to just a few days. As of March 2012, Nigeria was an outlier with up to 90 calendar days for tourist visas, though student visa applicants had to wait just over a week.[27] Jacobs said that 75 percent of applicants worldwide were "seen in three weeks or less," and President Obama tasked her bureau with increasing that number to 80 percent, in an executive order in January 2012.

In certain places, there is not much that can be done to shorten the wait, Jacobs said, because of restrictions imposed by the host government. "For example, in Cuba, we have personnel ceilings – we have a lot of difficulties getting people in, and getting equipment in, so those wait times really stretch out," she said in reference to the 900-day wait for interviews at the U.S. Interest Section in Havana. Because the United States and Cuba have no diplomatic relations, the U.S. mission there is not an embassy but an interest section. "There is a similar [visa-processing] situation in Venezuela," where the wait exceeds 200 days, Jacobs said. In other consulates, while there are no official restrictions, the limited space makes any personnel increases very difficult, she said. In Recife, Brazil, where in early 2012 the wait was often over three weeks, "there is no way for us to add [interview] windows" in the building the consulate currently rents, "so that's going to stay high until we can get into a new building," she added.

Overall, there are measures the State Department can take – and has taken – to provide better and more timely services to visa applicants, and to lessen the burden on overworked consular officers. For example, any applicant whose previous tourist or business visa has expired in the last four years is exempt from a new interview – it was just one year until 2012. In addition, applicants younger than 16 and older than 79 do not have to be interviewed, even if they have never had a visa before.

The Foreign Service hiring surge under Hillary Clinton benefited the Bureau of Consular Affairs immediately, making it possible for every consular position worldwide to be filled, according to Jacobs, and even for new positions to be created. In addition, to address the growing needs in countries like China and Brazil, the department started hiring hundreds of "visa adjudicators" – people who speak Mandarin Chinese or Portuguese but are not Foreign Service officers – on five-year renewable contracts. They undergo the same visa training given to consular officers and have the same responsibilities and authorities in the visa process, Jacobs said.

Domestic pressures

Consular officers are in a very peculiar position. They are tasked with keeping dangerous people from reaching the United States, and with helping to increase the number of foreign visitors at the same time. They are supposed to deny visas to potential immigrants – a description that many young students fit – but not to stand in the way of boosting the numbers of foreign students in U.S. colleges and universities. These very different objectives are not necessarily mutually exclusive, but accomplishing them is extremely challenging.

On the security front, there is "always a possibility that we are going to issue a visa to someone who is not on anyone's lookout system, someone with a clean identity who comes here and does something awful," Jacobs said. "It doesn't keep me up at night necessarily, because I honestly believe that we've put in a lot of very, very good security measures. But the people that we don't know about are still an issue. I worry about that."

Her bureau's biggest immediate challenge, Jacobs said, is "keeping up with the demand [for visas] and responding to the pressures – satisfying U.S. stakeholders by bringing more visitors to the United States." The travel and tourism industry is naturally the most vocal about boosting the number of foreign visitors – in a National Travel and Tourism Strategy released in May 2012, the White House set a goal of increasing those numbers to 100 million annually by the end of 2021.[28] Jacobs said she understood why. "International travelers contributed about $153 billion to the U.S. economy in 2011," she said in reference to data released by the Department of Commerce. "We know that, for every 65 visitors, one job can be created in the travel and tourism industry. So lots of interest in this on the part of those interested in growing the economy and creating jobs." The Department of Commerce said that 62 million foreigners visited the United States in 2011, of whom 21 million were Canadians who participate in the visa-waiver program.[29]

As of May 2012, that program applied to 36 countries, whose citizens could visit the United States for up to 90 days without a visa stamped in their passport. However, their passports must contain biometric data, and they need what amounts to an electronic visa that can be processed within minutes online, through the so-called Electronic System for Travel Authorization (ESTA). The countries included in the program are: Andorra, Australia, Austria, Belgium, Brunei, Czech Republic, Denmark, Estonia, Finland, France, Germany, Greece, Hungary, Iceland, Ireland, Italy, Japan, Latvia, Liechtenstein, Lithuania, Luxembourg, Malta, Monaco, the Netherlands, New Zealand, Norway, Portugal, San Marino, Singapore, Slovakia, Slovenia, South Korea, Spain, Sweden, Switzerland and the United Kingdom.[30]

The State Department can nominate new countries, but the Department of Homeland Security (DHS) has to approve them. There has long been political pressure to add more countries to the program, but Jacobs said those countries must meet strict security requirements. "They are supposed to share information on known or suspected terrorists, on criminals, and to share data on lost or stolen passports with Interpol," the largest international police organization, she said. "They have to be producing a certain kind of passport, and have certain kinds of border controls in place. So there is a lot more to it than just reaching a level on the visa refusal rate below 3 percent."

Another measure the travel and tourism industry has been pressing the State Department to take is conducting visa interviews remotely via videoconferencing. The industry's argument is that many applicants now have to travel long distances just to show up for an interview. In vast countries like China, India, Brazil and Russia, people have to fly thousands of miles sometimes to get to the nearest U.S. embassy or consulate. "We don't think it's a good idea, and we don't want to do it," Jacobs said. "The problem is that when you talk to people, you can't size them up on a TV screen. You just can't. Looking at the person, looking at the documents, touching, feeling, listening to their responses, watching their reaction, their breathing – all of that enters into a situation about whether or not to issue a visa. You lose so much of that when you are doing it from afar."

At no other time is the Bureau of Consular Affairs under more intense pressure than during a huge crisis in a foreign country with a high number of visiting or resident U.S. citizens. A task force is formed immediately to receive phone calls and e-mail messages from relatives and friends of anyone who may be in harm's way. "In the case of Haiti, we had 300,000 phone calls in the first three weeks" after the January 2010 earthquake, Jacobs said. More than 316,000 people died, according to Haitian government figures,[31] though that figure has been questioned as exaggerated. The State Department said the number of American fatalities exceeded 100.[32] In 2011, Jacobs' bureau had several task forces – after the March earthquake in Japan, and during the revolutions in Tunisia, Egypt and Libya. The bureau also coordinates the evacuation of U.S. citizens from those locations.

The bureau often receives accolades for its handling of such crises, which was not what was directed at it during what became known as the 2007 passport fiasco – possibly the darkest hour of Maura Harty's five-year tenure as assistant secretary. A backlog of more than 2 million passport applications was created when Harty's bureau underestimated by 1.5 million the expected increase in applications as a result of a new law requiring Americans to have a passport when traveling to neighboring countries in North and Central America and the Caribbean, which had not been the case before. The law actually passed three years earlier, with delayed implementation.

Harty got an earful of Congress's anger at a hearing of the House Foreign Affairs Committee in July 2007. Tom Lantos, the late Democratic congressman from California and committee chairman at the time, called the passport crisis a "travesty" and "national embarrassment." He said that "congressional offices across the land are being flooded with phone calls from outraged citizens." Until then, many of those citizens had no idea that the State Department was in charge of the passport system. "Millions of Americans, our constituents, have been reduced to begging and pleading, waiting for months on end simply for the right to travel abroad," Lantos said. "Endless delays in exercising every citizen's right to a passport are outrageous and unacceptable."[33]

The problem was "fixed in less than half the time even we projected might be needed to address it," Harty recalled later. However, as often happens in Washington, for many people the passport episode overshadowed the consular bureau's many achievements under Harty's leadership. Among them were implementing new standards for visa and passport security, and evacuating thousands of Americans after disasters, such as the 2004 Asian tsunami and the 2006 conflict between Israel and Lebanon.

As of May 2012, passport applications were being processed in about four to six weeks, according to the State Department.[34] Expedited service took about two to three weeks, though some of the 25 passport agencies around the country could issue passports within five business days if applicants appeared in person.[35]

The visa-selling business

Gons Gutierrez Nachman, a 37-year-old Costa Rican-born naturalized American citizen, joined the Foreign Service in 2003. His first assignment was as a political officer at the embassy in Kinshasa, the capital of the Democratic Republic of the Congo. Although his portfolio at work focused on human rights, in his government-provided residence he liked to have sex with underage girls – one as young as 14 – according to U.S. court documents cited by the Associated Press in 2008. He wrote about his escapades in a journal and filmed them. One seized tape was labeled "2004 Congo Sexual Adventures."[36]

Nachman's first tour ended in 2005, but he did not want to part with a certain Congolese woman – it is not clear if he ever had sex with her. So he helped her file a false refugee application with the Brazilian government, which made it possible for him to hire her as a domestic employee at his next post, Rio de Janeiro, where he arrived in 2006. Apparently, he found his new position as a consular officer a convenient vehicle for continuing his extracurricular activities. According to the federal charges filed against him, he consistently pressured female visa applicants into having sexual relations with him. He also made his Congolese employee film his sexual encounters with the Brazilian girls, some of whom were as young as 15. In 2008, Nachman, then 42, pleaded guilty to possessing child pornography and misusing his diplomatic passport, and was sentenced to 20 years in prison. Before the sentencing, he asked the judge to marry him to his fiancé, 21-year Brazilian Ana Carolina Pereira Porcher, but the judge refused.[37]

Selling U.S. visas – for money, sex or other favors – is probably the most common crime committed by Foreign Service officers. That does not mean it happens often, but when it does, it generates significant media coverage, which influences the public's perception of diplomats. The Bureau of Diplomatic Security, the State Department's law-enforcement arm, investigates such cases and has the power to make arrests. Diplomatic Security is also responsible for protecting the secretary of state, ambassadors and foreign officials visiting the United States, as well as for the overall security of all American missions abroad, as we will see in Chapter 12.

The visa fraud scheme that yielded the biggest financial benefits in the last decade was the doing of a married couple: Long Lee, a Foreign Service officer, and her husband, Acey Johnson. According to the Department of Justice, Lee first started accepting bribes in exchange for visas in 1995, while serving as a consular officer at the embassy in Hanoi, soon after President Clinton restored full diplomatic relations with Vietnam.

Lee wanted to continue the scheme at her next post, the embassy in Fiji, but there she was a management officer, with no authority to issue visas. Conveniently for her, at the time the State Department had a program that allowed U.S. missions to hire family members of American embassy personnel as "consular associates," to compensate for the shortage of officers caused by slashed budgets in the 1990s. Those temporary employees had almost the same authority as officers, including the power to adjudicate visas, which was taken away after September 11. So Johnson became a consular associate in 1997, and the fraudulent operation proceeded as planned. It also went on in Sri Lanka, where the couple moved in 2000 – until Lee was arrested there in 2003.[38]

A total of about 200 visas were sold. As part of the scheme, "visa brokers" located in Northern Virginia, Los Angeles and Sacramento, California, "collected bribes from foreign nationals, ordinarily from India or Vietnam, and steered the nationals through the visa application process, including travel to the U.S. embassies where Lee and Johnson were posted," the Justice Department said. "On instructions from Lee and Johnson, the brokers broke bribe payments into transactions under $10,000 to avoid scrutiny by financial institutions and law enforcement, and then forwarded payments to Lee, Johnson and their family members. Using the bribe payments, Lee and Johnson, among other things, amassed $350,000 in cash (deposited in various bank accounts or secreted in their Oregon home), sent a series of payments to their children, and acquired and/or maintained two separate properties – a seaside home in Port Orford, Oregon, and a vacation home in Bailey, Colorado."[39]

In 2004, Lee was sentenced to five years in prison, while Johnson's jail term was three months longer. In addition, they "were ordered to forfeit $750,000 in seized cash and properties purchased with ill-gotten gains," and to each pay a fine of $12,500. Each was "also ordered to serve a three-year term of supervised release following release from imprisonment," the Justice Department said. Ten "visa brokers" were convicted, too.

Most other such cases pale in comparison. In 2003, Alexander Meerovich "admitted to issuing at least 85 visas illegally" while serving as a consular officer at the embassy in Prague from 1999 to 2002, and was sentenced to two years in prison and fined $5,000.[40] In 2007, Matthew Christ was sentenced to two years in prison for selling visas while a consular officer at the embassy in Lithuania in exchange for "restored motorcycles."[41]

Then there is the bizarre case of Michael John O'Keefe, who was 62 and a 22-year veteran of the Foreign Service when he was sentenced to one year in prison in 2009. The bribes he accepted from the CEO of a jewelry company, STS Jewels Inc., while working at the consulate in Toronto, included trips to New York and Las Vegas, complete with "exotic dancers," accommodation, "expensive meals" and other "entertainment," the Justice Department said. In exchange, he issued 21 visas to people sponsored by the company.[42]

"Protecting the integrity of the U.S. visa is a top priority," the State Department said. "We will continue to investigate all allegations of visa fraud vigorously and seek to prosecute and punish those people involved to the fullest extent of the law."

PART THREE

MAKING THE WORLD
A BETTER PLACE

Chapter 8

In Pursuit of Good Governance

When David Bustamante arrived in Chile in the fall of 2000 for his assignment as the U.S. Embassy's cultural affairs officer, he was given a task that had nothing to do with culture and the arts. His charge was to lead the embassy's support for a sweeping judicial reform underway in the Latin American country. Those efforts would take up about one-fifth of Bustamante's time in Santiago – more than he spent on any other single issue. They were a big part of the work of the post's leadership, the political section, the legal attaché and representatives of other law-enforcement agencies. In fact, most of the embassy community helped in some capacity, because the reform's success was a top U.S. priority.

Why did Washington dedicate such significant resources to another country's domestic agenda? The first reason was practical: "American citizens and corporations in Chile were subject to an unpredictable and arbitrary system of justice, in which they could be found guilty without even knowing that they were being investigated for committing a crime," Bustamante said. That is the case in many countries, but the United States does not offer the support it gave Chile to all of them.

There was a more strategic and complex reason. Washington was looking for "a leader in Latin America at making government better serve the public," Bustamante said. A decade after the end of General Augusto Pinochet's military regime in 1990, Chile was "quickly emerging" as such a state. "The U.S. saw Chile as one of the few countries in the region that was improving the quality of its government services and fighting corruption, and saw support for the new justice system as a way of assuring the success of both initiatives," Bustamante added.

However, "when the Ministry of Justice looked around its own shop, it quickly identified as the weakest link in carrying out its mission the failure of the criminal justice system," he said. "Its sad state so discredited the efforts to improve government efficiency in the eyes of its own people, that it endangered all the other reforms being put into place."

The new judicial system Chile began implementing in 2000 had been approved by parliament five years earlier, so U.S. officials had time to prepare an in-depth plan and secure the resources they needed to assist the Chileans. Under the country's old "secret and inquisitional system" in place since 1907, "the tasks of investigating, indicting and adjudicating a criminal case were in the hands of a single investigating judge," the Georgetown Journal of International Law pointed out in a 2010 article.[1] The new system, Bustamante explained, is based on the German model, "in which investigation of crimes is left to the police and coordinated with a national public prosecutor's office." Defendants can see their accusers and respond to the charges during trials "in a single-judge Guarantee Court or before a three-judge panel in an Oral Trial Criminal Court" – there is no jury – the Georgetown Journal wrote.

So what did the U.S. Embassy do to help the new system's implementation? Over several years, it sent Chilean parliamentarians and Ministry of Justice officials to the United States, and "the laws creating public prosecutors' and defenders' offices were drafted based on knowledge of how these offices functioned in the U.S.," Bustamante said.

One of the biggest challenges for Chile was building courthouses, because the lack of first-round trials under the old system – the trials on appeal were very few – meant that there were no large and secure courthouses with modern transcription systems. "We brought U.S. court architects, administrators, reporters, translators, bailiffs and others in contact with their new Chilean counterparts," Bustamante said. "Sometimes we sent Chileans to the United States, sometimes we brought their U.S. equivalents to Chile, but more often we organized digital video conferences. The courthouses got built – most of them real pictures of efficiency – and a transcription system was eschewed in favor of a computerized audio recording system." The embassy also helped design programs to train new prosecutors and defenders led by U.S. academic institutions, including the California Western School of Law, the University of California's Hastings College of the Law, and Georgetown Law School, Bustamante added.

In the end, how did the U.S. benefit from that exercise? "The Chileans pulled off the huge judicial reform on budget, on time, and with tremendous success," said Bustamante, who has since retired from the Foreign Service. "The public – even those charged under it – were impressed at their ability to participate and influence the outcome of the system. Whenever journalists wrote about it, lawyers discussed it, administrators got things done, or architects critiqued courthouses, they all gave credit to the U.S." The experience resulted in closer cooperation with Chile in other areas of government reform, and U.S.-Chilean relations "greatly improved" overall, Bustamante said. "Our access to the government of Chile became such that some of us were received as true friends when we visited ministries, and almost treated as if we were employees there," he said. "To this day, no matter which party is in power in either country, Chilean and American officials trust each other and openly discuss difficult issues, in part because of this seminal cooperation."

The mission of transformational diplomacy

The success of Chile's judicial reform is a good example of how U.S. diplomats helped transform societies even before Condoleezza Rice articulated her vision of transformational diplomacy and charged the Foreign Service with making it more than an episodic effort. In her first major speech on the subject in 2006, Rice called for "bold diplomacy" that "seeks to change the world itself" through "doing things" *with* other countries, not *for* them. "We seek to use America's diplomatic power to help foreign citizens better their own lives and to build their own nations and to transform their own futures," she said.[2]

Rice defined the mission of transformational diplomacy this way: "To build and sustain democratic, well-governed states that will respond to the needs of their people and conduct themselves responsibly in the international system."

As I explained in Chapter 1, such states tend to be more stable and economically viable, which contributes to making the world more secure and prosperous, and advances the U.S. national interest of maintaining security and prosperity at home. Good governance is a key condition, because government accountability, providing essential services and economic opportunity, guaranteeing safety and respecting human rights offer citizens a much better alternative to the cycle of poverty and violence that is all-too-familiar to many developing countries. That cycle disenfranchises people, who may turn

to terrorism and other criminal activities, and produces internal instability that could easily spill into a regional conflict and harm U.S.
interests. "The idea of transformational diplomacy is to give people a
stake in their own future," said Richard Boucher, the former State
Department spokesman.

While Chile was not a poverty-stricken and lawless country in the
1990s, it was hardly the prospering and vibrant democracy it is today. It needed help and was happy to receive it from the United
States. Transformational diplomacy aims to benefit not only Africa
and other places most often viewed as needing foreign aid, but any
nation willing to improve its governance. That willingness may not
be immediate, and sometimes American diplomats have to persuade
foreign governments to undertake reforms.

For years, the U.S. Embassy in Baghdad has been helping the
Iraqi government to improve and expand the country's oil-
producing infrastructure and to enhance the protection of pipelines.
But it has not been easy. Even though the Iraqis "want the oil revenue and are willing to pump, they are not very forward-looking" and
have been reluctant to invest in better infrastructure, said David
Lindwall, the former political-military counselor at the embassy.

Why does Washington care? Because Iraq, whose oil output was
reported at about 2.5 million barrels a day in June 2012,[3] "could
produce as much and possibly more than Saudi Arabia's" 10 million
barrels a day, "which could have a huge impact on what Americans
pay for gasoline," Lindwall said. As was the case with Chile, there is
a strategic reason here, too. The U.S. would like Iraq's economy to
grow and lift more people out of poverty, and increased oil revenues
would create such conditions. "Since 2003, we've been trying to
build within the Ministry of Oil a cadre of people who would understand this," Lindwall said. Some improvements have been made, but
there is a lot more to be desired, he added.

Beginning in the 1990s, the U.S. Embassy in Guatemala tried for
more than a decade to persuade the Central American country to
reform its child-adoption system. Rampant corruption was hamper-
ing many Americans' attempts to adopt Guatemalan children – from
1999 to 2011, U.S. citizens adopted more children from Guatemala
than from any other country except China and Russia, according to
State Department data.[4] The corruption "created a situation where
babies were being stolen" without the future American parents'
knowledge, said Lindwall, who was deputy chief of mission there in
the mid-2000s. Congress put "an incredible amount of pressure" on
the embassy to push for changing the system, he said – "Guatemala
was a historic violator of human rights, but on that we didn't get

nearly the pressure that we did on adoption." Lindwall and his colleagues mounted an intensive lobbying campaign among Guatemalan legislators, government officials and others involved in the issue and finally succeeded.

It is not surprising that some governments, mostly those not democratically elected, resent the notion of the U.S. trying to transform their countries, though many of them still happily receive financial assistance from Washington. Others take the aid begrudgingly.

Byron Tsao was a political officer in Nicaragua in 2007 when the embassy there "tried to help the police force get basic equipment, because many of the cops didn't even have proper boots," he said. "We wanted to improve their law-enforcement organs so they could do their jobs better. We also tried to buy them a computer system" with a broad database of records, he added. However, some members of the administration of socialist President Daniel Ortega denounced the proposal as an "insult" that failed to "make up" for the harm the U.S. had done Nicaragua in the past, an apparent reference to the Reagan administration's funding of a right-wing militia, the Contras, to overthrow Ortega's first government in the 1980s.

"I had some interactions where people were shouting at me, getting so close that their spit was landing on my face," Tsao recalled. "I'd say, 'I'm sorry you are not interested. I'll tell Washington to assign the funds somewhere else.' I'd start walking out of the room, and they would say, 'OK, let's talk.' So we did some things for them, but later we had a hard time getting them to account for some of the equipment. We would buy them vehicles, then check back and find out that some police officials had given away vehicles as a retirement gift. Eventually, we were able to get the vehicles returned."

While the Foreign Service has embraced the promotion of good governance as a major part of its mission, several officers expressed discomfort with the term "transformational diplomacy," saying that it could be interpreted as an effort to change countries in the U.S. image. Both the Bush and Obama administrations said that was a misunderstanding of the concept.

Development, foreign aid and USAID

Much of what transformational diplomacy – or making the world more secure and prosperous – is about has to do with development, and there are officers in the Foreign Service who are experts in that area. They work for the U.S. Agency for International Development

(USAID) whose "mission is to advance economic growth, democracy and human progress in developing countries," with the "ultimate goal" of "creating conditions where U.S. assistance is no longer needed."[5] USAID, whose total staff in Washington and overseas is more than 8,000,[6] has long suffered from chronic underfunding, though its budget has increased significantly in recent years.

USAID has been under the secretary of state's authority since it was founded in 1961, but it was Rice who decided that the assistance Washington provides to other countries should be more directly linked to its foreign policy priorities. What does that mean? It depends on whom you ask. According to critics, it means politicizing foreign aid – rewarding governments that cooperate with the United States and punishing those that do not, instead of helping countries based purely on their humanitarian needs.

Rice's argument was that "America must get more out of our foreign assistance institutions" and a better return on its investments. While there is much suffering in the world, she said that U.S. taxpayer dollars must be used not only to improve people's lives but also to advance the U.S. national interest by bringing about stability and good governance, and to prevent conflict. "The resources we commit must empower developing countries to strengthen security, to consolidate democracy, to increase trade and investment," Rice said when first announcing the changes in 2006. "America's foreign assistance must promote responsible sovereignty, not permanent dependency."[7]

Anne-Marie Slaughter, Clinton's former policy-planning director, said it is "critical to be able to explain that we help strengthen health care systems in other countries, for example, because that will protect against viruses circulating around the world, it will decrease the number of refugees, it will strengthen these countries' economies, or whatever" the case may be. "We have to be able to show how what we are doing connects back to our central mission," Slaughter told me. "The job of the U.S. government is to advance the interests of the United States, and that means, when we do foreign assistance, it does have to fit into the big picture."

USAID's importance and budget have grown since 2009,[8] when Clinton set out to elevate development as an equal pillar of national security, alongside defense and diplomacy, and vowed to make it the world's premier development agency. In addition to the State Department and USAID, another agency that provides non-military assistance is the Millennium Challenge Corporation, which was founded in 2004 to help fight global poverty and has a different model for rewarding funds. A country must meet 17 criteria related to good governance and transparency before it is determined eligible to receive aid. The country has to identify and justify its priority areas, and it also leads the implementation of the projects being funded.[9]

In 2011, the U.S. foreign aid budget across the three agencies was about $35 billion, which was less than 1 percent of the total federal budget.[10] In an attempt to be more transparent about how exactly the U.S. taxpayers' money is being spent, USAID built an interactive website showing the amount each country receives. At the top of the list is usually Israel, for which $3 billion was appropriated in 2011, followed by Afghanistan with $2.6 billion and Pakistan with $1.8 billion.[11] The top 12 recipients of U.S. aid in 2012 are in the table below.

USAID started another online project called "Dollars to Results," based on "visual presentations" linking investments to impact on the ground. For example, it documented that in Ghana in 2011, $27.5 million in U.S. aid helped fight malaria by paying to spray 185,000 houses with an insecticide to kill mosquitoes that spread the disease, as well as by training 25,000 people in treatment and prevention, and by distributing more than 2 million insecticide-treated nets and 725,000 rapid diagnostic tests.[12]

Top 12 Recipients of U.S. Foreign Aid for FY2012
(in millions of dollars)

Israel	3,075
Afghanistan	2,327
Pakistan	2,102
Iraq	1,683
Egypt	1,557
Jordan	676
Kenya	652
Nigeria	625
Ethiopia	580
Tanzania	531
South Africa	500
West Bank & Gaza	496

Source: U.S. Agency for International Development

USAID provides a large part of its grants as contracts to U.S. companies and organizations – in fact, many in Washington refer to it as a contracting agency, because its limited financial resources have made it difficult to hire more full-time staff. It has been criticized for awarding lucrative contracts to companies with connections to the administration in office, whether Republican or Democratic. For example, watchdog groups accused the Bush administration of favoring the Bechtel Corporation, the largest U.S. construction and engineering company, for post-war reconstruction projects in Iraq, after only a handful of selected firms were allowed to bid.[13] Bechtel received contracts worth over $2 billion, according to company documents.[14] In 2007, government auditors uncovered mismanagement of funds, for which they blamed both Bechtel and USAID.[15] In 2011, congressional Republicans accused the Obama administration of favoritism when USAID awarded a $3.4 million grant to support civil society in Cuba to a human rights group linked to the Cuban American National Foundation. The critics said the group had insufficient experience and was chosen only because of the foundation's warm ties with the administration.[16]

Although Foreign Service officers from the State Department have more of an advisory and lobbying role in transformational diplomacy, while their USAID colleagues manage programs and oversee specific projects, their work is complementary and often interchangeable. "The best ambassadors and deputy chiefs of mission really value what we do, because they see us as a resource in their toolkit for promoting U.S. foreign policy objectives," said Andrew Sisson, who joined USAID in 1983 and was its mission director in Pakistan when I visited in early 2012. "We believe that stabilization and economic and social development are very much in the U.S. interest."

In countries where USAID has a limited presence or none at all, State Department employees perform both the advisory and implementing duties. The pursuit of good governance and better living conditions in developing countries includes organizing free elections, training government workers, creating independent media, building and reforming democratic institutions, infrastructure, education and health care systems, as I noted in Chapter 1.

Promoting democracy and human rights

Hans Wechsel, the former restaurant manager who helped overturn the Belgian law claiming universal jurisdiction over crimes against humanity that we discussed in Chapter 4, had a very different challenge when he arrived at his next post in Abu Dhabi in 2004. He was the first regional director for the Arabian Peninsula of the Middle East Partnership Initiative (MEPI), which the Bush administration had created two years earlier to help build and strengthen civil society, and to support the region's democratic aspirations.[17]

Wechsel's main task was to find local organizations in eight countries – Bahrain, Jordan, Kuwait, Oman, Qatar, Saudi Arabia, Yemen and the United Arab Emirates – and award them grants for projects promoting the U.S. agenda. "The way a society is governed is important to whether extremism develops or not," Wechsel said. "So we try to get to the roots of terrorism by addressing not only political rights, but also economic opportunity, education, women's rights, because these are all linked."

In 2005, 26-year-old Yemeni Tawakkul Karman co-founded a group called Women Journalists Without Chains to promote human rights and press freedom. With great ambitions but almost no funds, Karman was not able to make a big difference at the beginning – until Wechsel and his team met her and gave her organization $50,000 for a pilot project to seek freedoms, rights and protections for journalists in non-democratic Yemen. "I don't want to overstate the case, but she was this woman who had never done a program before, with this small, non-consequential organization, so we did launch her as an activist with capacity," Wechsel said. "Eventually, her impact became greater, and she has never looked back."

That capacity increased so much that Karman emerged as the public face of Yemen's uprising when the country joined the Arab Spring pro-democracy movement in 2011, with massive protests against the rule of former President Ali Abdullah Saleh, who had been in power longer than Karman had been alive. She was even called "the mother of the revolution."[18]

That same year, the 32-year-old mother of three became the youngest person and first Arab woman to receive the Nobel Peace Prize, which she shared with two Liberian women, President Ellen Johnson Sirleaf and peace activist Leymah Gbowee. "In the most trying circumstances, both before and during the Arab Spring, Tawakkul Karman has played a leading part in the struggle for women's rights and for democracy and peace in Yemen," the Nobel Committee said in its announcement.[19]

Three weeks later, Karman met with Hillary Clinton at the State Department.[20] But not long after thanking and hugging Clinton, she accused the U.S. of propping up Saleh's regime. "In Yemen, it has been nine months that people have been camped in the squares," she told the Yemeni press. "Until now, we didn't see that Obama came to value the sacrifice of the Yemeni people. Instead, the American administration is giving guarantees to Saleh."[21]

For years, Washington has had to play a careful balancing act between its support for democracy and the benefits it gets from some of the autocratic regimes in the Middle East. Saudi Arabia, for example, has one of the most conservative monarchies in the region, but in May 2012, the Obama administration said that Saudi intelligence had helped foil a plot to smuggle a bomb onto a U.S.-bound plane.[22] While the administration did not approve of many of Saleh's policies in Yemen, it valued the counterterrorism cooperation it received from his government. In late 2011, after he was severely burned during a rebel attack and underwent treatment abroad, Saleh agreed to a deal brokered by Yemen's Gulf Arab neighbors to hand power over to his vice president, Abdrabuh Mansur Hadi, which Saleh did in February 2012[23] – and the struggle for democracy continues.

Among the other projects Wechsel's office funded in Yemen were seminars and other training on democracy, human rights and the rule of law for imams and preachers, many of whom not only preside over worship services but are community leaders and scholars. Another grant focused on the growing importance of public opinion and its impact on legislation and political decisions.

Projects in Kuwait helped non-governmental organizations promote electoral reform and trained women how to lobby for gender equality and economic independence, and how to become entrepreneurs. In Bahrain, the Middle East Partnership Initiative sponsored a documentary about domestic violence and other negative implications of strict Islamic Sharia law for women and children.[24] And in Saudi Arabia, an essay contest asked young people to answer the question: "How can I turn my passion and enthusiasm into actions that will make Saudi Arabia a country that I'm proud of in the next 10 years?"[25]

While transformational U.S. diplomacy in most of the Middle East targets civil society, the private sector and academia – many of the authorities there are hardly thrilled about democracy – in other countries, the Foreign Service works directly with governments. Some of the most successful such efforts took place in Central and Eastern Europe in the 1990s, and still continue in some of those nations.

"Countries weak in government effectiveness, rule of law and control of corruption have a 30 to 45 percent higher risk of civil war, and significantly higher risk of extreme criminal violence than other developing countries," according to USAID. "In fiscal year 2011, we expanded political participation by training more than 70,000 domestic election observers and officials, and providing voter education reaching more than 2 million people," the agency said.[26] That same year, it "assisted more than 130 civil society organizations" around the world and "supported more than 150 independent and democratic trade or labor unions to promote international labor standards in nine countries."[27]

When Tracey Jacobson, the ambassador to Kosovo whom we met in Chapter 2, assumed the ambassadorial post in Turkmenistan in 2003, religious freedom in the former Soviet republic did not exist. "According to the Turkmen law at the time, you had to have at least 500 registered members of your religious organization to be legal," she said. "In practice, that meant only state-controlled Islam and the Russian Orthodox Church were legal, and any others were illegal and subject to sometimes quite brutal harassment. Even the Catholics weren't registered."

During her first meeting with then-president Saparmurat Niyazov, Jacobson warned him that his country "was looking at U.S. sanctions under the International Freedom of Religion Act," and told him she would like to "work with his government to avoid these sanctions. Within six months, they changed the law to require only five members in order to register a religious group," Jacobson recalled. "I'm not saying religion became completely free, but it became significantly better."

Maintaining peace and stability

The development work in Africa is usually viewed as the most challenging, but it is also the most rewarding, American diplomats said. As I mentioned in Chapter 1, Marc Wall and his colleagues created counterterrorism, anti-corruption and other programs for the government of Chad when he was ambassador there in the mid-2000s.

"We did what we could to encourage better democratic government in Chad," Wall said. "They started producing oil when I was there, and we helped them to ensure transparency in the management of their oil revenues, and to make sure that the money would be spent in ways that would actually benefit the poor. These were part of the conditions for international financing. This is a country that is as violence-prone and conflict-prone as there is in the world – and sure enough, we were caught in the throes of a number of civil war attempts. We had to evacuate the embassy at one point. But it was an exciting time."

Internal and regional stability was also threatened by the influx of refugees fleeing the genocide in neighboring Darfur, in western Sudan. "Many of them were taking exile in Chad, and we had close interactions with them and were very involved in the Darfur diplomacy at the time," Wall said. Several celebrities involved in raising awareness about the Darfur conflict came through Chad while he was there, including actors George Clooney, Angelina Jolie and Mia Farrow, Wall added.

Anjalina Sen, whom we also met at the beginning of Chapter 1, dealt with refugees from East Asia for two years while serving in Bangkok, beginning in 2010. The process of designating displaced people as refugees and resettling them is rather long, she explained.

"We have several bars to meet before we can even consider sending them to the U.S.," she said. "The U.N. High Commissioner for Refugees (UNHCR) has the international mandate, and individuals enter the process as persons of concern. Then they become asylum-seekers, go through refugee status determination, and then get the refugee designation. However, that doesn't mean they are refugees under U.S. law quite yet – for that to happen, UNHCR has to formally refer a person for resettlement, and then the Department of Homeland Security has to make a decision on admissibility to the United States."

All through that lengthy and uncertain process, those displaced people need protection and assistance, and that was where Sen and her colleagues came in. "We were in a situation where no one is willing to speak for these people but us," she said in reference to American diplomats, who help meet the refugees' urgent needs, ensure their safety and offer them hope.

According to UNHCR, there were more than 42 million "forcibly displaced people" worldwide in 2011, nearly 26 million of whom were under the U.N. agency's protection.[28] Data from the Department of Health and Human Services shows that the U.S. admitted over 56,000 refugees that year, and 32,000 of them came from the region for which Sen was responsible.[29]

"We don't get out and tell the story very much," she said. "We do humanitarian work, but we don't benefit from it necessarily." In addition to the humanitarian reasons, Washington spends significant resources to help refugees – regardless of whether they end up in the United States – because large refugee camps full of desperate people with no desirable prospects could ignite violence and cause regional instability.

Another long-term project that seemingly has little to do with security is the Lower Mekong Initiative, which Hillary Clinton launched at the annual summit of the Association of Southeast Asian Nations (ASEAN) in 2009. The Mekong River runs through southwest China, Burma, Laos, Thailand, Cambodia and Vietnam.

The initiative "involves USAID, the U.S. Geological Survey, the U.S. Army Corps of Engineers and the National Park Service," said the Quadrennial Diplomacy and Development Review.[30] It helps "the region manage one of its most important resources in ways that will improve regional stability and security" by providing better economic and business opportunities to the people in those nations. It aims to "expand cooperation on issues that affect the daily lives of the people across the region – from protecting the environment to managing water resources to improving infrastructure, education, and public health," Clinton said in Cambodia in July 2012.[31]

The impact of climate change on global stability is sometimes underestimated, but it is very real, diplomats said. It "will likely constrain our own economic well-being and may result in conflicts over resources, migrant and refugee flows, drought and famine, and catastrophic natural disasters," according to the QDDR.

Providing essential services and economic opportunity

In 2005, a powerful 7.6-magnitude earthquake struck eastern Pakistan, killing about 75,000 people – 18,000 of them were children who never returned home from school.[32] In fact, 6,000 schools were completely destroyed. In the years since, dozens of those schools, as well as health facilities, have been rebuilt by USAID.[33] In 2010, when deadly floods caused massive damage in Pakistan, the agency provided clean water to more than 2 million victims.[34]

The first sign of a functioning government is its ability to meet its people's basic needs, such as food, water, safety, health care, education and employment. Natural disasters test authorities everywhere, but they hit governments in developing countries particularly hard. U.S. assistance becomes news in such cases, as it did after the Pakistan earthquake and floods, and following the 2010 Haiti earthquake. But American diplomats provide hands-on help to those nations every day of the year. In 2010 alone, USAID improved access to drinking water for 2.8 million people, and to sanitation facilities for 2.9 million.[35] It has numerous programs on food security, nutrition, child survival and eradicating diseases. So the United States continues to do things *for* other countries. At the same time, however, in line with Condoleezza Rice's goal of doing things *with* others and promoting "responsible sovereignty, not permanent dependency," it also focuses on building and improving countries' capacity to provide essential services on their own.

James Miller, the Middle East watcher at the embassy in Paris whom we met in Chapter 4, took on an unusual task for a diplomat after he arrived in Iraq in 2007. He ran a pilot project that helped Iraqis deliver kerosene, which is widely used for cooking in the country, without profiteering or stealing. "We set up a group of experts at the embassy – on pipelines, on how kerosene should and shouldn't be transported – and we identified our counterparts in the Iraqi government and advised them," Miller said. "We essentially created an incubation cell for transparent, effective governance."

In Nigeria, which struggles to feed its people despite its vast oil reserves, USAID sponsored a public-private project called "Markets," aimed at transforming the country's agricultural sector, beginning with rice farms. Up to that point, nearly half of the 5 million tons of rice consumed annually were imported.[36] Fertile land was plentiful in the large West African nation, but Nigeria lacked a strategy to make agriculture profitable. Most farmers lived on less than $2 a day. "We were producing rice with bad quality, and many people didn't want to buy it," rice farmer Vitalis Tarnongo said in a video posted on USAID's website.[37]

The agency's team first found out what rice-processing companies wanted to buy, and once those requirements were determined, it trained the farmers how to produce quality rice. "For the first time, we've been able to grow rice and process it into a product that can compete with imports on both price and quality," Tim Prewitt, the project's director, said in that same video. Next, Prewitt's team persuaded banks to extend credit to the farmers, which resulted in a significant investor interest in rice production. Farmers' income increased 400 percent in just a few years. The same strategy was applied to the production of corn, sesame, cassava, and even to the fish-processing industry. More than 500,000 Nigerians have been trained by the "Markets" project.

One of the areas where the U.S. government is most active and generous around the world is health. In fact, according to the QDDR, "the Department of Health and Human Services and its Centers for Disease Control and Prevention strengthen public health systems in more than 50 countries." In total, U.S. government "health investments are at work" in almost 80 countries, the document said. Kristie Kenney, the ambassador to Thailand whom we met in Chapter 2, said there are more than 600 people at her embassy "who work on global health issues." In the 24 countries where USAID has been most heavily involved in reducing maternal mortality, those rates have declined between 40 and 65 percent, according to the agency.[38] In Ethiopia, it financed a government program to train more than 30,000 health workers, with the goal of reducing maternal, neonatal and child mortality. Through the President's Emergency Program for AIDS Relief (PEPFAR), which was established by the Bush administration in 2003, USAID has provided treatment to nearly 4 million people and counseling and testing to more than 40 million.

"I recently visited one of the 1,427 health huts in Senegal," USAID Administrator Rajiv Shah said at the National Press Club in Washington in June 2010. "In these huts, volunteers who are selected by their communities and trained by USAID and by the Senegalese Health Ministry are offering life-saving – basic but life-saving – interventions to women or children who have health needs, or they are referring them into the proper health system. By training local health workers and hiring local staff for project management, the program lowers overall costs while saving more lives. And it builds local capacity so that one day our aid will no longer be necessary."[39]

Shortly before Cameron Munter left his ambassadorial post in Islamabad, he launched the Pakistan Gender Coalition, a national network of civil society groups, academic institutions and media organizations dedicated to promoting gender equality. The coalition was formed thanks to the embassy's $40 million five-year USAID Gender Equity Program, which "aims to expand women's access to justice and human rights," as well as to "combat gender-based violence, and strengthen the capacity of Pakistani organizations that advocate for gender equity," the embassy said.[40] Such an effort is about much more than women's rights, on which both Clinton and Rice worked hard during their time at the State Department. It is about the well-being of entire families – their safety, food, clean water, their children's education and even employment.

Providing economic opportunity is another vital part of good governance, made even more important by the demographic reality in many developing countries, where young people are the majority of the population. Keeping them employed is a key condition for maintaining stability, as I mentioned earlier, and that is a formidable challenge. U.S. diplomats try to address it by promoting economic growth and open markets. "USAID assistance has resulted in tremendous growth in credit to the private sector worldwide, as well as increased access to credit by hundreds of thousands of small and medium enterprises that would not otherwise have been able to obtain financing for investment," the agency said.[41]

For Laird Treiber, the economic counselor in Ankara we met in Chapter 4, one of his most exciting assignments in the Foreign Service was his second tour in Saudi Arabia in the late 2000s because of the economic reforms the Saudis undertook at the time. The kingdom's decision to diversify its oil-dependent economy actually dates back to 1998, when the price of oil plummeted to under $10 a barrel. Despite some modest efforts, true reforms did not begin until the rise to power of King Abdullah in 2005.

Those reforms included "opening previously off-limits sectors of the economy, such as mining and utilities, to private investment, strengthening regulation of the capital markets," joining the WTO and partially privatizing big state companies in the telecommunications and other sectors, according to Reuters news agency.[42] While the country has a long way to go, the reforms have created new job opportunities for young Saudis, Treiber said. "Finding a way for the female population to be educated and employed is nothing short of incredible," he added.

As often happens in diplomacy and development, a project aiming for one result ends up having a secondary or even tertiary impact. The English language programs we discussed in Chapter 6 are much more than a public diplomacy effort. English proficiency often provides people in non-English-speaking countries with better employment opportunities, as well as higher chances for professional development.

Some exchange programs also have a "side effect," said Bruce Wharton, the former deputy assistant secretary for African affairs whom we met in Chapter 6. "We brought about 120 young people from Africa to the White House in 2010," he said. "We took the first lady to a group of young African leaders we assembled in South Africa in 2011, and we had 75 young entrepreneurs who spent three years in the United States. Some of the participants in these youth programs have been called in and questioned by their governments. Why are the Americans meeting with you and not with us? What did you talk about? So in sort of a roundabout way, our own focus on young Africans has encouraged African governments to be more responsive to their young people."

Chapter 9

Expeditionary Diplomacy

Whenever Howard Keegan visited a street market or just walked around downtown, he was mobbed by shoppers, store owners and local reporters peppering him with questions and complaining about the difficulties of their daily lives. Having direct access to someone to complain to was a novelty for the citizens of Kirkuk, an ethnically diverse city of about 800,000 Kurds, Arabs, Turkmen and others in northeastern Iraq.

As his name suggests, Keegan is not an Iraqi – he led a U.S. provincial reconstruction team in Kirkuk from 2007 until 2009. Because interaction between constituents and the authorities was not "commonplace in Iraq," he said he started bringing local officials along on this neighborhood walks. "I wanted to introduce the people to their representatives," he said. "I tried to get officials to go out once or twice a week to answer people's questions."

As the top U.S. official in Kirkuk Province, Keegan's most pressing task was quelling the ethnic violence raging at the time. His group was one of more than 30 civil-military reconstruction teams created to help stabilize and rebuild Iraq amid a ruthless insurgency. They were closed down when the American military withdrew from Iraq at the end of 2011, though three of them became U.S. consulates, including the one in Kirkuk. The U.S. teams were led by State Department officials, with military deputies, and also had representatives from USAID, the departments of Justice and Agriculture, and sometimes other agencies.

Stability in the oil-rich Kirkuk Province was vital to the central government in Baghdad, and ethnic reconciliation there was seen as hugely important for improving the security situation across Iraq. Keegan said he began his tenure by "reuniting the provincial government," which was crippled by a boycott of Arabs and Turkmen, in protest of what they called the dictatorial style of the Kurdish majority. There was – and still is – long-running animosity in particular between Arabs and Kurds, who were repressed by Saddam Hussein's regime and finally felt empowered by free elections.

"I told the Provincial Council that I wouldn't recognize them or attend a single council meeting unless I saw them unified," said Keegan, who had major influence on the province's daily functioning under the U.S. occupation. Nine months of "intense negotiations" led to a formal agreement between Kurd and Arab council members, with Arabs getting more government posts, including the deputy governorship.

The Arabs, however, were still missing from the very next council meeting. "Despite their assurance of attendance, they stood me up," Keegan said. "I called all Arab members in and told them that they would be placed on the coalition's list of hostile individuals if they didn't retake their seats. That scared them into doing the right thing, and the following week they all came. Getting the chip off their shoulder was very productive, and we subsequently enjoyed a very good rapport and productive relations."

Although sharp disagreements on the council remained, Keegan said he viewed his team as "an honest broker between the different ethnic groups" and considered "establishing a relationship of trust with the local leadership as critical" to his efforts.

But the Iraqis were skeptical at the beginning. One of the first questions the provincial governor asked Keegan when he arrived in Kirkuk was "When are you leaving?" – a reference to the one-year assignments the Americans had in Iraq, which sometimes ended up being even shorter. "I could see what they needed was continuity," Keegan recalled. "I said that, to accomplish what was needed, I would stay an extra year, and I stood by that decision. I went over there to do a job, not to get a paycheck. So we developed a solid relationship with the governor, and that opened the doors for us to work on a longer-term developmental reconstruction plan."

The plan's reconciliation efforts included not only political actions, but simple things like "building parks where people of all ages and ethnic groups could come together," Keegan said. In other areas, "our rule-of-law program was effective – bringing the judicial system back to its feet and getting it to function" – through training and logistical support, he added. "We built over 100 schools throughout the province and worked to improve the curriculum. We also built state-of-the-art health clinics, but the Iraqis weren't in a position to sustain them. We had limited success in trying to improve health care and pushing doctors to go out to underrepresented areas. Our USAID agricultural projects didn't always pan out well, because we were in the middle of a drought. We didn't make as many strides on the economic side as we had hoped for, because it's hard to create jobs in a drought in an agrarian area."

A gruff and stout former Marine, Keegan eventually refused to wear body armor during his walks around the city – to the horror of his security detail – to make a statement that the security situation had improved, so the people he met could feel more comfortable. Kirkuk was actually supposed to be only a three-month assignment for Keegan – he filled a staffing gap created by an officer who had left prematurely – after which he was scheduled to head up another team in the northern city of Mosul. However, he "got along extremely well with the local government and the U.S. military," so the State Department and the Pentagon "realized the relationships I had established were too valuable to lose by transferring me to Mosul," he said.

A year into Keegan's tour, *Stars and Stripes*, the Armed Forces' newspaper, published a fairly positive article about his team, which included more than 100 members at its peak, he said. While "stark challenges still remain," the paper wrote, "both Iraqis and team members say efforts by the [team] have helped the province make strides in easing ethnic tensions and coming to a political agreement."[1]

Rebuilding Iraq and Afghanistan

The civilian efforts to rebuild Iraq and Afghanistan, with the help of the U.S. military while it was fighting wars in the two countries, became known as *expeditionary diplomacy*. As I noted in Chapter 1, American diplomats had done similar work under comparable conditions in Vietnam in the 1960s and 1970s, though there were major differences, including the nature of the enemy and each country's geographical, historical and cultural circumstances. Service in Pakistan since 2001 is also considered part of expeditionary diplomacy, but with some significant caveats, as we will see later in the chapter.

The concept of provincial reconstruction teams originated in Afghanistan in 2002. Those units, however, were quite different from the ones created later in Iraq, in terms of both personnel and mission. They were led by and staffed mostly with military members, with single representatives from the departments of State and Agriculture and USAID. Unlike the long-term goals and relatively large programs that were the priority in Iraq, most teams in Afghanistan were "responsible for building small, quick-impact development projects using local contractors," the U.S. Institute of Peace wrote in a 2007 report.[2] Of the 27 provincial teams that still operated in the country in 2012, 12 were U.S.-led, according to the embassy in Kabul.[3] However, as the planned 2014 transfer of responsibility for the country's security to the Afghan government drew nearer, the reconstruction teams focused more on governance and longer-term rebuilding. "We are trying to link the district-level government with the provincial-level government, and if we can do that, then people can start working their issues," Lieutenant Colonel James Blashford of the U.S. Army said in a video produced by the team in Khost, in eastern Afghanistan.[4]

The more politically and socially advanced Iraqi society – however held back it may have been by Saddam Hussein's regime – provided the provincial teams there with more opportunities for actual reconstruction, rather than creating institutions from scratch, though that happened, too.

In addition to the schools, hospitals and parks Keegan's team helped build in Kirkuk, he and his colleagues worked on water and electricity projects, as well as in the areas of transportation, industry, government capacity building and commerce. "Our office was in the Provincial Council building, so we would convoy out with the military from our base in the morning," Keegan said. "Our budget was in the millions of dollars per year, and we had a proportionate distribution among the different ethnic groups in all districts to keep things fair."

The deadly ethnic violence Keegan lived with in Kirkuk was also familiar to Cameron Munter, the former ambassador to Pakistan and Serbia, who led the first provincial reconstruction team in Iraq – in Mosul, capital of the Nineveh Province – during the first half of 2006. "Every time I left the base, I had nine gunners and three armored vehicles," Munter said. "The bad guys would either shoot at us or try to hit us with roadside bombs. What was much more frequent than that was the so-called indirect fire – the shelling of the base with either mortars or rockets. That happened at some points daily."

To say that Munter was not used to such working conditions would be an understatement – as he pointed out in Chapter 1, he had spent his entire 20-year Foreign Service career up to that point in Europe. He had never participated in anything like his challenge in Iraq, let alone lead such a monumental effort. But he had volunteered to go to Mosul, and there was no time to lose. He divided his team members into four groups: governance, economics, reconstruction and rule of law.

As Keegan's team did in Kirkuk, "we put the provincial government in touch with its constituents," Munter said. "Provincial officials had never left Mosul to visit people outside the city. We actually flew them, with our soldiers, to meet with their constituents in small towns." Department of Justice representatives "did seminars for judges to teach them the rules of conduct in court," he added. "We'd also send people to supervise the prison in Mosul. An officer from the Army Corps of Engineers managed the tender process by which reconstruction was done in the province."

Each work day began with a staff meeting, followed by some reporting and correspondence, after which Munter "tried to get people to leave the base and take care of their projects" around the province. "If it's our job to be at the cutting edge, it's no good to be sitting at our desks like bureaucrats," he said. "We sent people every day to inspect projects, talk to local mayors, take a trip around the province and find out what was going on. Very rarely, locals would come to visit me on the base, but it was hard to get in, and they didn't like to do that."

The world's largest embassies

What American diplomats have done in the provinces of Iraq and Afghanistan over the last decade is very different from the work at the embassies in those countries' capitals, which in turn differs from the routine at other U.S. missions. Those two embassies are currently the largest in the world, with more than 1,000 American employees each. They occupy huge and heavily fortified compounds resembling small towns.

"We have thousands of people living here," including local and third-country hires, as well as contractors, "and I'm essentially the town sheriff," said Mark Hunter, a Diplomatic Security agent who was the Baghdad embassy's chief security officer when I visited in early 2012. The embassy has a sophisticated threat-warning system, and announcements about possible incoming fire were made on average several times a day during my stay. "This technology has saved lives," Hunter said. "You get a warning, and it gives people the time they need to seek shelter."

That same technology has also proven life-saving in Kabul, where the embassy has been targeted several times, including in September 2011, when it was subjected to a 19-hour attack with rocket-propelled grenades. One rocket penetrated the embassy compound, but there were no casualties among the personnel, while nine of the Taliban insurgents were killed by NATO and Afghan forces. The nearby NATO headquarters was attacked at the same time.[5]

It is difficult to imagine working under such a threat every day, but U.S. diplomats try to go about their business nonetheless. For Doug Silliman, the political counselor in Baghdad whom we met in Chapter 4, a typical day started with a review of the U.S. and local press. "We have a morning gaggle with the senior staff, and a meeting with my deputies to let them know what the ambassador's priorities are," he said. "Then I try to get out and meet with people as much as possible – I focus on higher-level officials. Except on rare occasions, I don't really go out just to get information to send back in a cable. I spend much of my afternoons editing things that my section produces."

In terms of "explaining U.S. views to Iraqi officials" and "trying to get the government to do what we want them to do," Silliman said that is always a challenge in any country, but he did not find it any more difficult in Baghdad. "In fact, it might be easier, because I have such easy access to a broad range of officials," he said.

Contrary to some reports in the U.S. media, "our access has improved since the military left," Silliman added. "People have received me more warmly, because I'm wearing a suit, not a uniform. I've found myself invited to a lot more Iraqi homes and meetings, and I have better connections. I don't know how much of that is because the military has departed or because people have just loosened up."

Other diplomats have had a different experience. A June 2012 report of the Inspector-General for Iraq Reconstruction said the "turbulent domestic politics and power struggles" in Iraq that followed the withdrawal of U.S. troops made it "more difficult for the United States to partner with the government of Iraq."[6]

As violence continues to be a frequent occurrence in Iraq and Afghanistan, the most challenging aspect of conducting business is the difficulty of movement outside the embassy compound, several diplomats in both countries said. Since the military's withdrawal from Iraq, private State Department contractors have provided protection to embassy employees.

"You can't go anywhere without a lot of armed men," Silliman said. "The security people are very good and try to be unobtrusive, but there are a lot of them. The ambassador and I are going to the Foreign Ministry today, and we'll have a large security detail and several cars to take us to the Red Zone," he said in reference to the space outside the heavily protected international zone, which is also known as the Green Zone.

Also with the help of contractors, the State Department operates its own air service called Embassy Air, which I took from Erbil to Baghdad and back at the invitation of Ambassador James Jeffrey, whom we met in Chapter 4. Its fleet of about 40 small passenger planes is used to transport personnel between various Iraqi cities, as well as to Kuwait and Jordan. Commercial international flights out of Erbil are still preferable to using Baghdad's airport, because Erbil is much safer and its airport is in many ways better than most U.S. airports. My first visit there was during a 2006 trip with Condoleezza Rice.

A city of about 1.3 million people and capital of the autonomous Iraqi Kurdistan, Erbil is an oasis in the war-torn country. Although there were sporadic terrorist attacks there early on during the U.S. occupation, the situation at the time I visited was closer to normal than perhaps anywhere else in Iraq – not only in terms of security, but politically and economically as well.

While U.S. Consulate rules still required employees to be escorted when leaving the compound, many of them said those rules could be at least somewhat eased. Until a new consulate is built, the post consists of dozens of houses used either as offices or residential quarters – the site had been the base of a provincial reconstruction team until a few weeks before my visit.

Matt Ference, the public affairs officer in Erbil whom we first met in Chapter 2, noticed a big difference as soon as he arrived in 2011 from Karbala, a city in central Iraq where he previously served in a provincial reconstruction team.

"I think the basic reason that Erbil is different from the rest of our posts in Iraq is that the population of Iraqi Kurdistan and its government truly want us to be here," Ference said. "The positive developments in the Kurdistan Region after the 1991 Gulf war, and again after 2003, have happened under the umbrella of U.S. protection, and people here are eager for continued and deeper engagement. If anything, they want more U.S. presence, rather than less. That is not the case in the rest of Iraq, where feelings are mixed."

Civilian life in a war zone

Unless the weather makes flying impossible, Baghdad embassy employees and official visitors are taken from the airport to the embassy compound by helicopter. That 15-minute ride over the Tigris River was familiar to me from earlier trips with Rice and Colin Powell, but at the time the U.S. mission was located at Saddam Hussein's former Republican Palace. This was my first visit to the newly built and much talked about embassy – the largest in the world. Although the State Department publishes personnel numbers for the entire U.S. mission in a foreign country, most of the 1,235 government employees and 13,772 contractors posted to Iraq, as of June 2012, were based in Baghdad.[7]

At the helipad, I was met by Michael McClellan, the deputy public affairs officer, after which we took a very short ride to the residential buildings, across the street from the embassy. My apartment – one of hundreds of furnished units – was modern but simple, and a far cry from the trailers I had slept in on my previous visits.

I quickly plunged into the embassy routine: Meetings in one of the two office buildings or the ambassador's residence or the Green Bean café not far from the post office; meals in the so-called DFAC, the military acronym for dining facility, where the abundance of food made it very easy to put on more pounds than one could shed at the embassy gym; drinks at Baghdaddy's, the iconic bar that sometimes hosted concerts by Diplomatic Security agent Jim Combs.

These and other facilities were built because, for security reasons, employees were not allowed to visit outside establishments – except for a few officially approved ones. There was not much more to do on the compound, so people worked almost all the time, including on weekends.

The posts in Iraq, Afghanistan and Pakistan, as well as in a few other countries like Sudan, are designated as "unaccompanied," so employees are not permitted to bring their families along – unless spouses happen to have a job at the same post. Most married or partnered diplomats said that, next to the security situation, this was the hardest aspect of serving in a war zone.

Because there were not enough apartments for every person working for the embassies in Iraq and Afghanistan, contractors, military members and some visitors lived in trailers or similar units.

That was actually the only accommodation available at the old embassy in Baghdad, before the new one was opened in 2009. "The trailer next to mine was completely destroyed during my tour," said James Miller, who arrived in Baghdad in 2007 and ran the kerosene project I mentioned in Chapter 8. "People I worked closely with died – one was an Iraqi-American interpreter and the other was an Army major. We used to stay late at the office, and one of the reasons was, the less time you spent in your trailer, the less chance you had of being hit. We don't get or deserve the credit soldiers do because they are on the front lines, but we don't carry guns, either."

Most provincial reconstruction teams were housed by military bases and used trailers as living quarters, and sometimes even as offices. Matt Ference, a former Army infantryman, said he shared an office trailer with five other team members in Karbala, while his living trailer was divided into three rooms, each about 8 feet by 8 feet. "The bathroom trailer, with showers, was about a 50-foot walk," he said. "We had a gym, a cafeteria, a basketball court with a broken rim, and a volleyball court. The ground was gravel and dirt, and became very muddy when it rained."

While the base in Karbala had only about 100 U.S. troops, according to Ference, there were about 3,000 at the Mosul base, Cameron Munter said. Munter's team worked in a dedicated office building, but it still had no water, he said. "We worked from 8 a.m. straight until about 10 p.m., because there was nothing else to do. The Army didn't drink, so I tried to convince the civilians not to drink, either, which was good for everyone's health," he said. At the same time, "we were eating corn dogs and ice cream every night at the chow hall."

The State Department considers service in Pakistan as much of a hardship as Iraq and Afghanistan for administrative purposes – assignments there are also unaccompanied and merit danger pay and other benefits. For those in the Foreign Service who have been through Iraq and Afghanistan, however, Pakistan is a major step up. Since 2001, there has been no shortage of terrorist attacks in Islamabad – and especially in provincial cities like Karachi and Lahore, where U.S. consulates are located – but the country is not a permanent war zone. It is quite telling that some embassy employees in Islamabad do not even live on the embassy compound. They are also allowed to drive in the city, which is out of the question in Baghdad and Kabul.

The people problem

Cameron Munter was deputy chief of mission in Prague when he answered Rice's call to American diplomats to serve in Iraq in 2006. Among the positions that needed to be filled in the country at the time, 18 required senior Foreign Service officers at Munter's grade, but he was the only one to volunteer, even though he did not speak Arabic, he said. The rest of the jobs went to lower-ranking officers, in what the State Department calls stretch assignments.

Finding people to go to Iraq and Afghanistan has been one of the service's main problems since 2001 – it has been less difficult to staff posts in Pakistan for the reasons described above. As discussed in Chapters 1 and 3, the reluctance of many in the service to work in a war zone with hardly any training was perceived by some outside the State Department as disloyalty and disobedience.

Expeditionary diplomacy was not new for the Foreign Service, as mentioned earlier – when Doug Silliman joined "in the 1980s, there were a lot of people who had served in Vietnam and referred to it as a defining moment in their lives," he said. By the mid-2000s, however, virtually all those people had left the service, and the new generation had come in not expecting to do what was eventually required of it in Iraq and Afghanistan, dozens of diplomats said. They were not the only ones without such expectations – the State Department did not anticipate the need for wartime service, either, which is why it did not prepare its employees for that type of work, or select them based on expeditionary skills and abilities in the first place.

But there was another factor during the Bush administration that gave pause to many in the service regarding Iraq in particular, Munter said. "My personal sense was that those people weren't volunteering not because they were scared, but because they thought the Iraq war was a loser, and they needed to be persuaded that they could make a difference," he said.

In a 2007 survey by the American Foreign Service Association, 1,592 of its members said they would not volunteer for Iraq positions because of "disagreement with policy," while 2,037 cited security concerns. In addition, 1,182 said they had been or would go to Iraq because of "patriotism/duty," and for 1,347 "extra pay and benefits" was also a major reason. The survey was sent to 11,500 members, but only 4,300 chose to participate, and the State Department dismissed the results as not truly reflective of the service's motivation.[8]

In an attempt to avoid forced assignments, the department took two main steps. First, it changed the bidding and assignment system used to staff Foreign Service posts in order to fill all positions in Iraq, Afghanistan and Pakistan. No assignments were allowed elsewhere in the world until those highest-priority posts were fully staffed. Second, it offered additional incentives for service in those posts, such as extra pay and vacation time, as well as promotions and priority for volunteers in bidding for their next assignments. That attracted some people for the wrong reasons, State Department officials said.

Another wrong reason, they said, was career advancement or, worse yet, saving a dying career. "I don't think that draws the right people," said a senior official who has served in Iraq twice. "You can't be worried about money or getting a promotion. It's hard getting up in the morning and facing that crap, unless you think you are making a difference. If you are counting the days until your assignment in Paris or your promotion, I don't think you can do it."

Whether someone went to Iraq or Afghanistan for the right or wrong reasons, many officers said some people had no place being there. "I've never met so many people with psychological problems, who were there because they wanted to get away from something," Munter said, not necessarily referring to members of his provincial reconstruction team in Mosul or even just Foreign Service officers.

Several officers criticized the contractor hiring process – for an open position, the team leader would get an e-mail message from Washington with several résumés and would have to pick one of the candidates. There was no proper vetting process to verify that everything on a résumé was true, they said.

Although Keegan tried to interview applicants over the phone, that did not work out most of the time because of the time difference and other issues, he said. "I wouldn't hire contract mercenaries, because they only cared about the money," which was about $250,000 a year, Keegan said. He pointed out that he had a rigorous trial period once new team members arrived in Kirkuk. He ended up firing or otherwise removing all categories of employees – from the State Department, other agencies and contractors. "I even returned soldiers to their command," Keegan said. In some cases, the dismissed team members found jobs in other provincial teams or at the embassy in Baghdad, he added.

Frank Ricciardone, the ambassador to Turkey whom we met in Chapter 2, served as deputy ambassador to Afghanistan for a year beginning in the summer of 2009. He said the one-year assignments in Iraq, Afghanistan and Pakistan – a third of a typical Foreign Service tour because of their "unaccompanied" designation – "made it especially tough to build and sustain continuity and teamwork" at those posts. During the one year, employees are entitled to about 60 vacation days, though some do not use all their time off.

Ricciardone linked some of the personnel problems to the recruitment process before 2009, which "had been skewed to urgent production of large numbers of people to serve at our extreme high-stress posts." Even though that attracted "some of our finest and highly motivated talent, a few people wound up arriving in Afghanistan with serious performance, personal and disciplinary problems," he said. "These ranged down to the kinds of 'notorious or scandalous behavior' that constitutes regulatory grounds for dismissal even from ordinary posts. The handful of such serious problem cases had a disproportionately severe impact" in Afghanistan, as well as in Iraq and Pakistan.

By 2009, it was clear that the State Department had to "carefully select, screen and fully prepare the right individuals" to serve in those posts, Ricciardone said. "We humanely but urgently had to weed out those seriously undisciplined or afflicted people already serving there, whose personal problems were damaging larger mission morale and cohesion, and in some cases endangering themselves or others," he added. "We couldn't afford the more customary conflict-avoidance approach of just waiting out the non-performers, and passing them on to their next assignments."

Munter, Keegan and Ricciardone all stressed that they did not mean to diminish the sacrifices of the many capable and hardworking people who served with them in a very precarious environment.

It is also worth noting that it has been less difficult to staff unaccompanied posts since 2009 for two main reasons. First, most of the Foreign Service realized that at least one such assignment is unavoidable if one wants to get promoted, though promotions are not guaranteed. Second, the change of administrations resolved the issues some officers had with the Iraq war during the Bush years.

Improvising in a 'non-permissive environment'

By most accounts, Howard Keegan was one of the most effective provincial reconstruction team leaders in Iraq. As mentioned earlier, those positions were meant for senior Foreign Service officers. But Keegan was neither senior nor a Foreign Service officer – he was an Information Management specialist, and though he had been in the service since 1985, he had not yet been promoted to the senior ranks when he was selected to go to Iraq.

After Kirkuk, he returned to working in his specialty in Mexico City, where he managed all communications for the embassy and the 10 U.S. consulates in Mexico, including telephone, computer and radio systems.

The fact that Keegan was not formally trained as a diplomat was by no means a disadvantage, he said. He and others pointed out that some trained diplomats had less success in Iraq than Keegan did. "Not everybody responds well to stress or adapts to what the military calls a non-permissive environment," he said. "It's hard for some people to get out of their comfort zone." What helped him, Keegan said, was his previous six-year service in the Middle East, his military experience and his common-sense approach to the challenges in Iraq. "We needed people who were good under pressure, didn't scare easily, wanted to make a difference and knew how to respectfully deal with humans from a different culture," he said.

Beyond that, improvising was essential, given the minimal preparation even seasoned diplomats had for wartime service, many officers said. James Miller said he "had a week of basic familiarization" before going to Baghdad in 2007, including "medical-response training, how to recognize explosives and how to shoot." Diplomats are not armed, but they are given a "two-hour orientation to firearms," as Matt Ference put it, in case they need to use a weapon for self-protection. Once in Iraq, "we had to improvise, and hope that the Foreign Service selection process brings in people who have versatility and adaptability," he added.

Both Munter and Keegan said they did not receive substantive instructions from the State Department in terms of the U.S. objectives in their respective provinces beyond the overall goal of stabilizing Iraq. That may not have been very helpful, but it gave them the freedom to set their own agenda, which we discussed earlier in the chapter. Munter said he told the department, "You are not giving me much guidance, so let me tell you what my job is." In the end, "I enjoyed building a team from very disparate elements and making an impact on that province," he said.

Kristofor Graf, one of Keegan's deputies in Kirkuk, said the team leader decided what the team did every day, and the section at the embassy in Baghdad in charge of provincial reconstruction had little influence. In fact, several officers said disagreements with the embassy were quite common, because each group did not fully understand what the other one did.

"I spent a lot of time in Mosul defending my people from taskings from Baghdad," Munter said. "They would say, 'The commanding general needs a briefer next week, so here are the slides you need to make.' No, if you want to make the slides, go ahead, but we are busy training people to build dams."

Because of the difficulty of finding enough volunteers for Iraq and Afghanistan, some entry-level officers had a rare chance of serving in positions that were more important and exciting than the average Foreign Service job. Those were usually either former military members or older people with previous professional experience, rather than recent college graduates. "They had much more responsibility than they would normally have at that point in their careers, and they rose to the challenge," Munter said of the officers on his team in Mosul.

Kris Graf, a former Navy pilot who joined the service in 2007, was on his second Foreign Service tour in Kirkuk, having first served in India. I met him in 2012 in Bangkok, where he was a consular officer. He said he had a "great experience" in Iraq that no other Foreign Service post would have given him.

Mike Guinan, the former lawyer from the public affairs section in Islamabad whom we met in Chapter 6, also spent his second tour in Iraq, on an Italian-led provincial reconstruction team. In fact, he enjoys serving in hardship posts so much that he chose Kabul as his next assignment after Pakistan. "I'm doing them all in a row," said Guinan, who has also served in Egypt and South Sudan. "I'm interested in places where the stakes are high."

First-tour officers are no longer allowed in Iraq, Afghanistan and Pakistan – "it was decided that it was not a good introductory experience," said Mark Pekala, a former director of the Entry-Level Division in the State Department's Office of Career Development. "It's not a good indication as to how the rest of the world works diplomatically. Our embassies in Baghdad and Kabul are not like any other embassy in the world," said Pekala, who became ambassador to Latvia in 2012.

More than 20 percent of the service has already gone through Iraq, Afghanistan or Pakistan at least once, the State Department said. Many officers have not volunteered not because they fail to recognize the importance of those posts, but because they think they can make more significant contributions elsewhere.

David Hodge, the public affairs counselor in Bangkok whom I first met in Mozambique in 2003 where he was the political counselor, said he "never got a hard push to go to Iraq or Afghanistan" from the department. "What in the world am I going to accomplish on a one-year tour? No language, no regional experience," Hodge said. "I'd go to check the box, and the money would be nice, too," Hodge said. "There are certain jobs I could do – I could run the Fulbright Program in Afghanistan and would probably do a decent job, but would I be good at doing other things? I doubt it."

Walter Douglas, the public affairs counselor in New Delhi whom we met in Chapter 6, said he would be "of little value to the State Department" working at a provincial reconstruction team. "They could find someone [outside the Foreign Service] to do that, but there is no one else [in other agencies or the private sector] who could do my job," said Douglas, who has served in Pakistan. "The department has to decide what it wants to use its diplomats for. As long as we are out there talking with village elders about digging wells, we are being taken away from our core function, and there aren't enough of us to spread around. There is a limit to what we can do."

Bonding with the military

Like most members of the U.S. military, Lieutenant General Robert Caslen had not worked closely with the Foreign Service until the Iraq war. He was aware of the two institutions' different cultures, as well as their varied approaches to Iraq's reconstruction – for example, while soldiers tried to fix problems quickly, diplomats were more interested in lasting solutions, even if it took longer to find them.

But as commander of the Army's 25th Infantry Division in northern Iraq in 2008 and 2009, having previously served two tours in Afghanistan, Caslen developed a much better and more nuanced understanding of the Foreign Service while working with several provincial reconstruction teams. "Military people tend to be very structured and orderly, and State Department people are not necessarily like that," he said. "But these wars are not structured and orderly. They are very complex and require interagency and intellectual solutions."

The U.S. Armed Forces and the Foreign Service had not had the bonding experience they shared in Iraq and Afghanistan since the Vietnam War, and dozens of diplomats and several military officials said it was predominantly positive.

James Miller said the mutual respect grew every year, and Cameron Munter said the interaction in his provincial reconstruction team was "great and quite friendly – both in terms of work and after hours."

Caslen said the diplomats he encountered in the provinces and at the embassy in Baghdad, where I met him in 2012, were not afraid to "get their hands dirty," and he admired them. "I love working with them," he said. "It's a different culture, but it's refreshing and educational. It's good for us military dinosaurs to work with somebody who knows how to operate in complex environments."

In spite of the disagreements and frustrations that are inevitable under such extreme circumstances, diplomats and soldiers said they learned a lot about each other – and about themselves – and gained greater mutual appreciation. The military officers said they were impressed by how much the Foreign Service could achieve with a fraction of the resources the military had, and the diplomats realized they could never measure up to the military in a war zone.

"We defined our contribution as whether we were doing everything the military was doing, but that's the wrong question," said Bill Burns, the deputy secretary of state. "We can't match the military – we don't have the resources or the people. The experience of the last decade reminded us what our value added is and gave people a clearer sense of purpose. What the military values are our language ability and knowing how to navigate foreign settings." The downsizing of the embassy in Baghdad that started in 2012 and is set to continue is "not a sign of the State Department abdicating its role, but of doing what's best for American interests," Burns said.

Howard Keegan said that reconstruction projects could not be successful without a good partnership with the military. "We had a very forward-leaning relationship with the Army," he said. "We were in tune and spoke with one voice for the U.S. government," he added, which was not always the case in other parts of Iraq, as other officers pointed out.

Munter said the military commanders took rank very seriously – at the time, his was equal to a one-star general – and lower-ranking Foreign Service officers on stretch assignments in senior posts may have been treated differently.

After the American troops left Iraq at the end of 2011, Caslen was the highest-ranking U.S. military officer in the country as chief of the embassy's Office of Security Cooperation. Although those offices are best known for managing weapons sales to the host country, in partnership with the political-military section, they do much more, Caslen said.

"Frankly, equipping the Iraqis is just giving them the toys. What you do with the toys is the most important part. So we do training on the equipment and also have maintenance programs for them," he said. "Then we help them build a professional security force through military education – we develop the curriculum and train the instructors. The Iraqis also have security cooperation through regional engagement, so we bring them into exercises with other countries." The United States decided to invest in a professional Iraqi force because of the stabilizing role it could play in the Middle East, especially with Iraq "sitting between Syria and Iran," said Caslen, whose previous foreign deployments include tours in Haiti, Honduras and the 1991 Gulf War.

Success and failure

While Caslen ran the Iraqi military training program, Michele Sison managed a similar effort for the country's police force, judicial system and prisons. "It's a very ambitious program spanning all that rule-of-law continuum – cops, courts, corrections. All those make up a $500 million program," said Sison, a former ambassador to Lebanon and the United Arab Emirates. During Saddam Hussein's rule, "the police were seen as a tool of oppression against the Iraqi people," she said. "The police force and Ministry of the Interior were rebuilt after 2003 under a number of Department of Defense programs, but there is still a lot to be done to strengthen an accountable civilian police force, and to guarantee that policing is done in a democratic, humane and professional fashion."

Although Sison, who became ambassador to Sri Lanka in the summer of 2012, is probably one of the biggest optimists I have met in the Foreign Service, the future of her program in Baghdad seemed rather bleak. The $8 billion U.S. effort to train, staff and equip Iraqi police forces since 2003 was overseen by the Pentagon until October 2011, when the State Department assumed responsibility for it.

Within weeks, the department was criticized by the Special Inspector-General for Iraq Reconstruction for "poor planning," in which Sison had not been involved – "including the absence of a current assessment of Iraqi police force capabilities, high security costs and the lack of a written commitment from the government of Iraq for the program."

A capability assessment was done, but that did not solve the other two problems. In particular, "the decision to embark on a major program absent Iraqi buy-in has been costly," the inspector-general said in a July 2012 report.[9] "A major lesson learned from Iraq is that host-country buy-in to proposed programs is essential to the long-term success of relief and reconstruction activities."

With the Ministry of the Interior's rejection of some of the planned training that was supposed to be the centerpiece of the Police Development Program, it became clear that the project's original objectives would not be met. In addition, the embassy's security office "deemed it unsafe for advisers to travel to Iraqi-controlled facilities in Baghdad on a frequent basis," which limited most of the training to the U.S.-controlled Baghdad Police College Annex, the report said. So in mid-2012, the State Department decided to reduce significantly the program's scope and size. The number of in-country advisers – mostly U.S. government employees and contractors sent to Iraq to support the project – was lowered to 36 from the

85 who were there when I met Sison a few months earlier. The department also decided to refocus its training on five technical areas requested by the Ministry of the Interior, and to close the Police College Annex.

The inspector-general's report did not mince words. The annex's "closure amounts to a de facto waste of the estimated $108 million" invested in its construction, it said. In its response to the report, the State Department disagreed that the money was wasted, saying the facility will continue to be used by the Iraqis to support its criminal justice system. "We always intended to transfer the property to the Iraqi government, although this is an accelerated timeline," Patrick Kennedy, the undersecretary of state for management whom we met in Chapter 3, said at a congressional hearing in June 2012.[10]

As the cost of the wars in Iraq and Afghanistan exceeded $3 trillion even by the most conservative estimates,[11] U.S. government waste became the subject of numerous reports and books.

Another report, issued by the congressionally mandated Commission on Wartime Contracting in Iraq and Afghanistan in August 2011, said that "at least $31 billion, and possibly as much as $60 billion, has been lost to contract waste and fraud in America's contingency operations" in those two countries.[12] "An ill-conceived project, no matter how well-managed, is wasteful if it does not fit the cultural, political and economic norms of the society it is meant to serve, or if it cannot be supported and maintained," the commission said. It cited three main reasons for the waste: "poor planning and oversight by the U.S. government," "poor performance on the part of contractors," and "criminal behavior and blatant corruption."

The State Department is by no means the only federal agency to have made mistakes in Iraq and Afghanistan, but as the Quadrennial Diplomacy and Development Review recognizes, it is vital that the department reduces its dependence on contractors and improve its contracting practices. That process should start with turning to experts in other government agencies before using contractors, the document said. "State will use private contractors for non-governmental functions when other agencies lack appropriate skills or are otherwise unwilling or unable to provide the services needed in an effective manner," it added.[13]

Most Foreign Service members who have served in Iraq or Afghanistan have witnessed or heard about waste and corruption. Howard Keegan said a civilian with the U.S. Army Corps of Engineers in Kirkuk Province who worked on a water project ran a scam – "he changed the design standards, and instead of a 6-inch pump, he had a 4-inch pump, so it was cheaper, and the contractor pocketed the rest of the money," Keegan said. The case prompted an FBI investigation, and the engineer, Joselito Domingo, was eventually arrested and convicted of bribery.[14] He was sentenced to 39 months in prison, a two-year supervised release and a $70,000 fine. As of July 2012, the work of the special inspector-general had led to "90 indictments, 72 convictions, and more than $177 million in fines, forfeitures, recoveries, restitution and other monetary results," the inspector-general's office said.[15]

U.S. diplomats readily acknowledge the State Department's – and their own – mistakes in Iraq and Afghanistan, but most of them say the failures should not overshadow the success that has been achieved, however limited it may be.

While the different ethnic groups in Kirkuk have not got along swimmingly since Keegan left in 2009, the foundation he and his team laid for political reconciliation has helped the province's overall development and attracted foreign investors' interest. In Baghdad, Doug Silliman said the embassy "played a major role in getting the Iraqi Sunni group back into the parliament and government" in late 2011 and early 2012, following a boycott.

In Erbil, Matt Ference and his colleague at the consulate, Melinda Crowley, took me to visit a school built with U.S. assistance, which paid for half of the $1.6 million project. "It has become one of the most popular schools in the Iraqi Kurdistan Region, and I've met lots of parents interested in sending their children there," Ference said. "We are also using the school to host other educational programs, including teaching disadvantaged and vulnerable women English and computer skills, so they can find jobs in Erbil's booming economy." The Mar Qardakh school, where many of the students from kindergarten through grade 12 are Christians but other religious groups are welcome as well, is more modern than some U.S. schools.[16] "A true picture of the work done in Iraq would recognize that there have been both successes and failures," Ference said.

Ronald Neumann, the former ambassador to Afghanistan we met in Chapter 2 who also served in Iraq and was a young infantryman during the Vietnam War, said that expeditionary diplomacy of sorts was done in the period between that war and the recent conflicts. He referred to service in Bosnia and Kosovo in the 1990s, and to some extent in Libya following the 2011 ouster of Muammar Qaddafi. "The State Department needs to continue building the skills to do this work, although probably on a smaller scale," Neumann said. "We had to learn a lot by trial and error in Afghanistan. We need to learn from the past, not forget it and then not screw up the next challenge."

For some Foreign Service officers, the wars in Iraq and Afghanistan have been a distraction from the already complex and vital work of American diplomacy. For others, the conflicts have provided an opportunity to improve the service's skill set and capabilities, because the lessons learned from the experience can be applied elsewhere, not necessarily in war zones. In other words, expeditionary diplomacy – the challenge to the modern service's identity discussed in Chapter 1 – has long-term implications and should not be viewed as a momentary or isolated occurrence.

Still, the expenditure of more than $3 trillion is hard for some diplomats to come to terms with, given the difficulty of securing resources for peacetime diplomacy. One officer, who has served in Afghanistan and asked not to be named, said he was "personally offended" by the wars' price tag. "Frankly, I'm not convinced that what we've been doing in Iraq and Afghanistan is in the best interest of the United States," he said. "The intentions were right, for the most part. But to be where we are in both countries, particularly Afghanistan, one has to ask, purely from a return-on-investment standpoint, what we've gained. What has our investment accomplished? What could we have done with a fraction of that money in the last decade in the United States to look after our own citizens?"

PART FOUR

LOOKING IN THE MIRROR

Chapter 10

Teaching Diplomacy

When Hans Wechsel, the former restaurant manager whose work on the Middle East Partnership Initiative (MEPI) we discussed in Chapter 8, was selected for that position in 2004, he had little idea what exactly he would do or how he would do it. He knew this much: He was supposed to open the program's Arabian Peninsula office in Abu Dhabi, monitor the implementation of local projects awarded by the State Department to U.S. organizations, and find local non-governmental groups in eight Middle Eastern countries worthy of U.S. grants to help strengthen civil society and support the region's democratic aspirations.

However, Wechsel had never done anything like this before. After joining the Foreign Service with no background in international affairs, he was a consular and economic reporting officer in Ghana. Then he worked as a political officer in Belgium, where he helped overturn the Belgian law claiming universal jurisdiction over crimes against humanity, about which I wrote in Chapter 4.

Wechsel received no training before going to Abu Dhabi – not even basic Arabic language instruction. His superiors in Washington provided "no guidelines" beyond "vague ideas about how this was supposed to work," he said. In fact, he got the impression that they "hadn't really figured it out themselves, because they hadn't had a regional MEPI office before." They did know what kind of person they were looking for: "Somebody for whom the challenge wasn't too daunting, and who liked figuring things out, building something from scratch, setting up an office and creating a vision," Wechsel said.

"When I got there, I had nothing," he recalled. "I didn't even have a computer. I walked into the office space they had set up, and it was just some desks – that was it. So I had to start literally by procuring office supplies and getting a computer. Eventually, I had a deputy, an office manager, and I hired four local employees." Ironically, Wechsel's restaurant management experience proved much more helpful in establishing the new office than his previous two Foreign Service tours, he said.

In terms of grant-making, he quickly educated himself and started thinking strategically about how the process already set up by Washington could be improved to better achieve the U.S. goals of transforming the region through strengthening civil society. So he replaced the annual requests for grant proposals the State Department had put in place with a rolling process. "I realized we needed to be more proactive, and go out and find organizations, not just rely on them to find us," he said.

The U.S. embassies in the eight countries Wechsel's office covered – Bahrain, Jordan, Kuwait, Oman, Qatar, Saudi Arabia, Yemen and the United Arab Emirates – were the most natural resource. "We decided to tap into their contacts," he said. "We told political officers who were responsible for the annual human rights reports, 'Imagine if you could lend support to these people, instead of just writing about them or about press freedom or the status of women. You could actually help.' In some countries like Qatar, there were only a handful of registered non-governmental organizations, which is very limiting, so we took a different approach of finding out from the embassy who the main players were, even if it was just a single activist or a university professor." During Wechsel's three years in Abu Dhabi, his office's budget more than quadrupled, exceeding $2 million by the end of his tour.

Thrown in a pool, learning how to swim

Wechsel's experience is very common in the Foreign Service – officers learn on the job almost everything they need to know, and they often have to figure things out on their own. Many of them compared it to being thrown in a pool and learning how to swim. So the importance of self-education cannot be overstated. While a certain amount of on-the-job training is inevitable in this line of work, the State Department's philosophy until a few years ago was that classroom sessions were no use in teaching people how to be diplomats.

"This was a culture that didn't value training," said Grant Green, undersecretary of state for management during Colin Powell's tenure who has held several civilian and military leadership positions in the federal government. "People saw no advantage in it. To them it was a waste of time, with no relationship to better assignments or promotions." That philosophy was particularly perplexing for people with military backgrounds who are used to mandatory training at every level, such as Powell and Green, and it affected negatively some entry-level diplomats coming from the military.

One of them was Kris Graf, the former Navy pilot we met in Chapter 9, who joined the Foreign Service in 2007. Even though by then the State Department was taking into account advanced degrees and previous experience when assigning grades to incoming officers, "they eliminated half of my military time," because it was spent in training, Graf said. That resulted in a lower grade, which meant a lower salary and a slower promotion to a mid-level officer. "I was a flight instructor in the Navy, so there was a lot of flight training and weapons training. That's what you do in the military – you train all the time. But they said it was not professional experience."

The United States has had official representatives abroad since the 19th century, but the beginning of the professional Foreign Service dates back only to 1924, with the enactment of the Rogers Act, legislation introduced by John Jacob Rogers, a Republican congressman from Massachusetts. There have been diplomatic training facilities – many of them short-lived – since the early 20th century, including the Consular School of Application and the Foreign Service Officers' Training School. The longest-lasting and current facility, the Foreign Service Institute, was established in 1947.[1] For decades, the institute focused on three main areas: The A-100 class for new officers, which I mentioned in Chapters 1 and 2; foreign language instruction; and consular and other technical training. There was also a seminar for those promoted to the senior Foreign Service, as well as one for retiring officers. What the curriculum lacked were the mandatory tradecraft courses – political, economic, etc. – that have become a staple of the institute's programs in recent years.

American diplomats pride themselves on having better language skills overall than their counterparts from other countries – about 70 languages are taught at the institute. Even so, language proficiency in the Foreign Service is not at the level it should be, dozens of officers said. Many overseas positions do not require language skills, even when having such skills would be beneficial, as was the case with Wechsel's job in Abu Dhabi. Moreover, officers have sometimes received waivers for "language-designated" positions, because they were urgently needed at their new posts. A perfect recent example of that is service in Iraq, Afghanistan and Pakistan, where the demand for officers has been much greater than the number of those speaking the respective languages.

Joy Sakurai, a mid-level officer who began her mandatory consular tour in Islamabad in 2006, said her biggest challenge was "not speaking any of the Pakistani local languages," because she received no training. "I conducted visa interviews either via a staff interpreter or in English. If I had had language training, or even a brief area studies class, I would have had a better understanding of Pakistani culture," she told me in 2011 in Tokyo, where she was a cultural affairs officer. "Interpreting situations and the reality of people's lives, and making a clear judgment on those applicants, without a cultural background is tough."

Frank Ricciardone, the former ambassador to Egypt who is a fluent Arabic speaker, said his language skills were useful not only in his dealings with officials in Cairo – actually, many of them spoke English – but also in his interactions with ordinary Egyptians and the media. "The first time you go there and speak in Arabic – not just classroom Arabic, but taxicab Arabic – it's like a dog riding a bicycle," Ricciardone said. "No one notices that the dog rides in a wobbly way. They don't notice the errors and the circumlocutions. It's the same in any of these hard languages. Even if you are at the 2,000-word-of-vocabulary level and some basic grammar, they think you are a genius, because nobody can master their language. They also see that you really made an effort to get to know them. That effort tends to demonstrate modesty and respect, which can help to disarm or disabuse foreigners predisposed to think we are arrogant and bossy."

Not surprisingly, public diplomacy officers in the Foreign Service love working for an ambassador who speaks the local language, because that makes their work easier and more effective. The Foreign Service Institute has designated Arabic, along with Chinese, Japanese and Korean, a "super hard language," and offers a two-year program, with half of it spent at the institute, and half in the respective country or region. Officers studying "hard languages," such as Russian and Hungarian, receive one-year training, while those studying Western languages like Spanish and German get six months.

The 'luxury' of professional development

The attention Colin Powell paid to taking care of his employees extended to training as well. He told me the "concept of professional development, particularly with respect to leadership and management," did not exist in the Foreign Service until he became secretary of state in 2001. "There were many people in senior positions who didn't have not only leadership skills but training, either," he said. They did not know "basic things," he added: "How to take care of people, how to accomplish a mission, how to reward or punish people and have accountability. That's what leaders do – they solve problems. They don't sit around writing papers."

Nancy Powell, the ambassador to India and former director-general of the Foreign Service whom we met in Chapter 2, said she did not receive "any leadership training" until she became a deputy chief of mission. "I had been in the Foreign Service for 14 years," she said. "I had learned by watching an enormous number of people. I'd say to myself: 'I'm going to do this, but oh my God, I'll never, ever do that.'"

Colin Powell's efforts to increase the Foreign Service Institute's budget, expand its curriculum and embed training in the State Department's career development system were broadened by his successors, Condoleezza Rice and Hillary Clinton. In her 2006 speech on transformational diplomacy I cited in Chapter 8, Rice described training as essential to the service's ability to fulfill its mission. "We will train our diplomats not only as expert analysts of policy but as first-rate administrators of programs, capable of helping foreign citizens to strengthen the rule of law, to start businesses, to improve health and to reform education," she said.[2]

Mike Hammer, the assistant secretary of state for public affairs, said the ever-increasing demands of modern diplomacy, along with the new skill sets required to achieve the Foreign Service's ambitious mission, make high-quality training more urgent than ever. "Diplomacy in the 21st century has so many dimensions that you can't just learn it on your own or through osmosis," he said.

Today, the Foreign Service Institute has more than 600 courses in its curriculum, including over 100 in leadership and management, and about a dozen in each of the five career tracks discussed in Chapter 2. Some 100,000 people from the State Department and over 40 other government agencies enroll in at least one class every year.[3]

"We won't be a luxury that [the service] can't afford anymore," Ruth Whiteside, the institute's director whom we met in Chapter 2, said in reference to diplomats' inability in the past to take time off work for training. "One of our goals has been to try to keep demonstrating the value added of training – it isn't just a nice thing to do, but it makes people more productive, better-skilled diplomats and stronger leaders." Whiteside also noted the institute's emphasis on distance-learning to help employees improve their skills without having to return to Washington from halfway around the world. "Classroom time should be spent on more complex subjects, not just imparting basic information," she said. "If people can get that for five hours online and then arrive with that under their belt, you save classroom time for higher-quality training."

Many officers said that, despite the Foreign Service Institute's significant success in the last several years, it still has a long way to go. They cited a tendency to use material in the classroom that has little or outdated resemblance to the real world as one of the areas in need of improvement. That is often a result of using instructors who have not practiced what they teach in a long time, or have never been in the Foreign Service, or are not in the top tier among their peers, the officers said – after all, the best diplomats are needed much more in the field than in a classroom. Some of the institute's instructors are State Department employees and some are outside lecturers.

I was allowed to audit classes there over several weeks in early 2012 – the first time someone who does not work for the federal government has been granted such access – and my impressions were similar to the observations above.

The A-100 class, whose duration has fluctuated between five and seven weeks in the last few years, also came in for some criticism from diplomats. The most frequent comment was that new officers are thrown into the system with only very basic knowledge of the State Department's operations in Washington and around the world. "Entry-level officers often don't really know what's going on around them," said Eric Watnik, the public affairs counselor in Singapore whom we met in Chapter 7. "It would be useful for them to know in more depth, before they go to their first post, what we do in Washington, and what we do overseas. For example, they should know what people at the State Department read from the cable traffic coming from posts, and what they expect from the officers who write those cables at embassies. It's surprising to me when somebody in the consular section doesn't know what the public affairs section does."

Whiteside said the purpose of A-100 is not to teach new officers how to be diplomats – in fact, she described it as an orientation, rather than training. It tries to familiarize officers with the part of the bureaucracy they need to know about immediately, so they can get paid, enroll in the necessary language classes, move their families to Washington and beyond, and prepare for their first tour. The class also tries to give them a sense of the Foreign Service lifestyle, including living conditions, safety, schooling and spousal employment. The actual training begins once A-100 is over and officers know what their first assignment will be, Whiteside said. "Most of them will be here for close to a year between A-100 and various tradecraft and language courses," she said.

Hundreds of officers at all grade levels said the biggest benefit of A-100 was the opportunity to build relationships with their classmates, which are among the most lasting ones throughout their careers.

Although A-100 teaches cable-writing – and there is further emphasis on it in the political and economic tradecraft courses – some entry-level officers are still not sufficiently prepared when they arrive at their posts, said Louis Mazel, deputy chief of mission in Singapore. Mazel joined the Foreign Service in 1984 and has spent most of his career in Africa. "What they should do," he said in reference to the Foreign Service Institute, "is go out to posts in the field and ask, 'How do you use your entry-level officers? What do they do? Are they prepared?' Then, whether it's on the management or the political and economic side, draw from the field and design the course. New officers should learn the art of effective note-taking, then learn how to translate that into cable-writing, and then practice being a note-taker for a senior-level discussion between a U.S. official and a foreign minister. We do a lot of mock training in the consular course, and I think we should do it in A-100 and other classes – writing, note-taking, briefing. Entry-level officers are frequently called upon to brief more senior officials."

Hillary Clinton praised the institute's efforts but also acknowledged the difficulty of training American diplomats in the 21st century, given the limited resources and expanding demands in a fast-changing world. The Foreign Service "must be a constantly learning organization," she told me. "There is no doubt that we cannot rest on our laurels," she said. "People have to keep pushing themselves."

Susan Johnson, the president of the American Foreign Service Association whom we met in Chapter 2, said the association "wants to shift the focus from training to professional formation and education for diplomatic practice," because "both areas need serious and sustained attention and work."

How exactly does one teach diplomacy?

Before George – not his real name – joined the Foreign Service, he had no idea the service even existed. Based on information about the different career tracks provided on the State Department website, he decided that the management track would be most suitable for him. Any hopes for a glamorous life George may have had vanished not long after he took up his first assignment as a general services officer at the embassy in a small impoverished country. Among his responsibilities were all facilities used by the embassy, including residential buildings, which were a far cry from modern Western homes.

Being in charge of assigning houses and maintaining them turned out to be a much more serious challenge than the living conditions. The "constant, incessant complaining" by embassy employees – from the State Department and other agencies – showed George "the worst in people," he said. "Everybody knew we were strapped for resources, they knew the construction and housing standards were low, and the skills of the locals working at the embassy were not up to par, but they still expected to live like they do in Washington. We all sacrifice a lot to serve in foreign countries, but there is a culture of entitlement in the Foreign Service."

Bombarded with never-ending demands from his "clients," as he called them, George began to worry about his sanity. "I seriously thought, 'What am I going to do? I can't do this for 20 years,'" he recalled. "We get free housing and utilities, as well as many other benefits in the Foreign Service, but there is a lot less thankfulness for what we are given than there should be."

Another officer at a hardship post said he admired management officers who have to deal with the issues George faced. Normally very nice people "become beasts when you are in charge of their housing," the officer said, suggesting that the stress and pressure of serving in dangerous places may be part of the reason. "We have management colleagues here who won't socialize with anybody, because they don't want five people jumping on them saying, 'Hey, my toilet isn't working,' or 'I don't like the color of my wall.' You can't get away from it. These guys have it tough."

It is hardly surprising that George did not expect to be essentially working in customer service as a diplomat, but as we saw in earlier chapters, the diversity of positions in the Foreign Service requires a wider variety of skills than perhaps any other profession. Moreover, even though officers have their career tracks, they are expected to take assignments outside their specialty and broaden their experience in order to get promoted. Even if that were not the case, they often branch out for non-professional reasons, such as living conditions and family needs. If an officer has a baby, he or she would naturally prefer to go to a country with decent health care, and the only position the officer might be able to get there could well be outside his or her career track.

At the same time, some people may spend their entire careers in one specialty, as is the case with many senior public diplomacy officers, including Walter Douglas, whom we met in Chapter 6. If we add to that the State Department's tendency in recent years to hire a vastly diverse pool of diplomats and ask them to perform more nontraditional duties that challenge their identity, as Mike Hammer put it in Chapter 1, the task of properly training today's Foreign Service becomes truly overwhelming.

So how should the department go about it? As discussed earlier, what it does now is A-100, language instruction, introductory and advanced tradecraft courses – often not mandatory – on-the-job training and mentoring. A few officers attend academic institutions, such as the National Defense University, each year, but they usually do it while waiting for their next chosen position to open up.

In addition to the suggestions from officers for improving existing classes listed earlier in the chapter, other ideas included designing an in-depth overview course on the substance of U.S. diplomacy, which could be mandatory for promotion to the service's mid-levels. Although some substance, such as specific foreign policy issues and case studies, is covered in current classes, it is not clear how those often disjointed examples fit into the big picture of the U.S. national interest and global affairs, several officers said.

Such a course, as well as others, could also focus on strategic thinking, they added, which is now mostly left to officers to master on their own. In fact, many diplomats said strategic thinking is not encouraged – at least not until they rise to the most senior policy positions, which many of them never do. "It gets beaten out of you, and it takes a certain kind of person to fight that," said Yuri Kim, the political counselor in Ankara whom we met in Chapter 1. "The best officers have a strategic vision, but also the guts to smash concrete to get things done," she said. "That's the kind of Foreign Service officer I want to be. Do you want every officer to be like that? No, but every once in a while, you want that kind of trailblazing leader."

James Jeffrey, the former ambassador to Iraq and Turkey whom we met in Chapter 4, said the Foreign Service's paramount role should be "to provide expertise and advice to the country's top political leadership needed to formulate U.S. foreign policy and to carry it out in the field." However, he added, "for various politically correct reasons, we do not formally acknowledge or institutionalize this seemingly self-evident truth. Thus, career patterns, training, promotions and assignments cannot flow from and support that reality."

Among those reasons, Jeffrey suggested, is the risk of "slighting the work" of management and consular officers. As a result, the Foreign Service Institute's curriculum does not do a good job at preparing officers to "shape and execute policy at the highest levels," he said.

Turning potential into success

In the late summer of 1986, four years after joining the Foreign Service, Bill Burns began his first assignment outside the State Department – in the Middle East office of the National Security Council (NSC) in the Reagan White House.

A couple of months later, that office was shaken by a huge scandal that became known as Iran-Contra. A more senior staff member on detail from the military, Lieutenant Colonel Oliver North, had devised a plan to sell weapons to Iran and use the money to fund illegally Nicaraguan anti-communist rebels known as Contras. The plan had been approved by Reagan's national security adviser at the time, John Poindexter – no evidence has been found suggesting that the president himself authorized it[4] – and other staff members had helped to implement it. Within months, most on the NSC staff, including Poindexter, were replaced.

Burns, who had no idea about Iran-Contra until it was publicly exposed, was one of the few to survive. "I was so junior, I don't think anybody took any notice," he said. At the end of 1987, Colin Powell became national security adviser, and the following year he put Burns in charge of the Middle East office. "I thought more senior people should do it, but Powell said, 'I wouldn't ask you if I didn't think you could do it.' It was dumb luck. I was 32," Burns recalled. "In the Foreign Service, how well you do depends a lot on who you work for and what you work on. I was really lucky, but I know people who weren't so lucky."

Having bosses who entrusted Burns with significant responsibilities helped him get promoted to the senior Foreign Service in 10 years, which is half the time it takes the average officer. But there is another factor when it comes to having a long and fulfilling career, he noted. "To become a good professional, you have to do it right, so you are well prepared for your next job," he said. "If you want to build a good foundation, not only does that create more career options, but it's also going to be more interesting. So develop a foothold in more than one region."

Burns did just that – at the end of his first decade in the service, he decided to add Russia to his Middle East expertise. During Burns' training in preparation for his assignment as political counselor in Moscow, Tom Pickering, the ambassador there at the time, asked Burns to cut his studies short and come to Russia earlier to be deputy chief of mission. As much as Burns respected and admired Pickering, he declined the offer. "I wasn't ready," he said. "I wanted to do it right." He later went to Moscow as political counselor, as planned, and returned there as ambassador in 2005.

Burns' bosses gave him various opportunities, because they recognized his potential early on – whether it was Powell at the National Security Council or James Baker, President George H. W. Bush's secretary of state, on whose policy-planning staff Burns worked after leaving the White House. In general, however, identifying promising young Foreign Service officers and nurturing them to become strong leaders and top-notch diplomats has been a weakness of the service, many officers said.

"Here the Foreign Service could learn from the military," Condoleezza Rice told me. "The military identifies early on people who they think are going to make it to the higher ranks and gives them a series of experiences that make sure they are ready. They actually do career planning with their people." Cameron Munter, the former ambassador to Pakistan and Serbia, agreed. Top military leaders "look at the captain and major levels and pick the winners," he said. "Maybe someone wants to go drive tanks, but he has to go spend a year in Tennessee instead to learn about logistics – not because they need a guy to learn about logistics, but because they need a leader with the specific training necessary for future jobs the service needs. We don't do anything of the sort."

Burns also urged senior officers to "pay more attention to the mid-levels" in particular, where assignments should be taken more seriously, because those are the formative years for most diplomats. "We need to make a conscious effort to put the right people in the right places," he said. Such an approach would be useful in the senior levels, too, Burns added. For example, when selecting a career ambassador to a certain country, "we ask, 'Who do we want to send there?' What we should do is take a step back and say, 'Who are the 20 people who are up and coming, talented but not ambassadors yet, whom we want to get a chief of mission office?,'" Burns said. Then plan ahead and decide where each of those officers would go. "Too often, we do it the other way around," he said.

James Jeffrey said "the way you prepare" young officers for high-level positions is to hire them as staff assistants and "have them follow you around and watch what you do" every day. "If you've picked correctly, their minds work a mile a minute," he said. "Typically, they have to move you around and coordinate security and flights and various other things. But at the same time, the other half of their brain – they have so much excess capacity, they are like powerful computers – is monitoring what you do and critiquing it."

Munter suggested that some officers might see anointing certain colleagues early on as favoritism, and might even sue the State Department for discrimination, but he said there is a "subtle way to do it." The bigger problem, he added, is that, to the best of his knowledge, "no one has sat down and thought about where the Foreign Service will be in 10 years, and what kind of people we want. Do we want people like Bill Burns or Pat Kennedy?" he said in reference to the undersecretary of state for management, whom we met in Chapter 3. While Burns is viewed as more of a strategic thinker and capable policy adviser, Kennedy is considered more operational and a master of the bureaucracy. "What is it these people have? We need to think about whether people like them should be groomed for certain jobs," Munter said.

Because formal training and professional development in the Foreign Service remains a challenge, personal mentoring by senior officers has taken on increasing importance. Deputy chiefs of mission usually play the role of informal mentors, though at large embassies that becomes difficult, and section chiefs take on that task. In fact, as part of officers' annual performance evaluations, they are required to hold counseling sessions with their supervisors throughout the year and document the results. However, mentoring or counseling cannot be a substitute for professional training, many officers said. Sometimes, career-making advice a senior officer gives a less experienced colleague may be considered career suicide by another longtime diplomat. Assessing an officer's skills and abilities can be quite subjective. At the embassy in Sudan in 2004, I met a political officer whom the acting ambassador told me was the best he had ever met in the service. A couple of weeks later in Beijing, I mentioned that political officer to the deputy chief of mission, for whom the officer in question had worked previously. He said the officer was among the worst he knew.

Why leadership skills matter

As soon as Brad – not his real name – arrived at his second post in the Foreign Service, the deputy chief of mission sat him down and gave him an unusual warning. "This may be a challenging year, but I know you will make it through," he said, according to Brad.

The reason for that remark was Brad's new boss and political section chief, whose name he declined to share. The boss "lacked interpersonal skills, was very dysfunctional as a leader and instilled fear in everybody," Brad said. "I had never written a cable in my life, and after the first thing I wrote for him, his reaction was, 'This is a bunch of shit!' He was slamming doors, throwing things. I took the [introductory] political-economic course [at the Foreign Service Institute], which was helpful, but there is no way that can really prepare you to do the work."

Although Brad said he had "a fabulous boss" during his second year at that same post, the passion and candor with which he spoke about the "horrible boss" sounded extraordinary coming from a Foreign Service officer – albeit one who asked to remain anonymous. "He made that experience the most horrible time of my life," said Brad, whose wife and children were also affected by his problems at work. "I was literally sick. I didn't want to go to work every day. I even thought about quitting. How somebody like him can stay in the service for 20 years without being kicked out is amazing. I don't know how he made it that far." The officer in question, whose reputation preceded him, as the deputy chief of mission's warning made clear, was not promoted to the senior Foreign Service, which automatically ended his career, Brad said.

Almost every organization has its horrible boss stories, but not many have been told publicly about the Foreign Service, because diplomats are concerned that telling them might reflect negatively on the entire service – even though the bad bosses are fewer than the good ones. Even so, Brad's story is a reminder that leadership training and professional development are not just fancy phrases, but an urgent necessity. Eliot Cohen, the former State Department counselor under Rice, said that effective leadership in the service remains a challenge despite the efforts made since Powell's tenure. "If you come across good leaders, they just happened to be born that way," he said. "The institution doesn't do enough to develop good leadership, as far as I can tell. There are leaders like Bill Burns, but that's because of whatever magic was in his DNA."

Another reason why many officers neglect to reveal negative experiences is that the service's rotational system naturally limits the time a bad supervisor has to torment employees, so they just suck it up and hope for a better boss after the old one leaves or at their next post. Still, the low morale that results from such cases invariably affects the work of the respective sections or even missions.

A mid-level officer who spent his mandatory consular tour in India said he witnessed that first-hand. Even though it was just months after September 11, 2001, and the rules for granting and denying U.S. visas to foreigners were being tightened by the day, the consular section chief put enormous pressure on his employees to approve certain applications the interviewing officers thought should be rejected, the officer said. "There were a number of officers who were very concerned about it. I told him it was my decision, and if he wanted to overturn it, he'd have to put his name down and take responsibility," the mid-level officer said of his former boss.

Along with bad bosses, there are, of course, underperforming employees in the Foreign Service, but unlike in the private sector, it is very difficult to fire someone or even to remove them from a particular post, many officers said. "In the business world, you get rid of someone who is not performing by firing them, but here you have to wait them out," said Charles Rivkin, the ambassador to France whom we met in Chapter 2. If the employee in question does not improve, one way to deal with the situation is to "focus on someone else" in the same section who is good, Rivkin said. Munter said he tried to dismiss an employee at one of his European posts for poor performance, but she complained to the Foreign Service Grievance Board, which sided with her.

Kristie Kenney, the ambassador to Thailand whom we also met in Chapter 2, had a less unpleasant experience with a first-tour officer at one of her previous posts who actually recognized her own deficiencies. "She needed more coaching and mentoring, and we provided that," Kenney said. "Her immediate boss brought it to me very quickly, and we gave her every opportunity to learn and get extra help. But in the end, it wasn't enough. We all recognized it wasn't a great fit. It was entry level, so the system took care of it – she didn't get tenured and had to leave the service." Kenney said, however, that such cases should not be blamed on the Foreign Service entrance exam. "You can't have a perfect test," and sometimes people who do not have what it takes still get in, she said. "But also people change along the way. Living overseas can be different from what people expect, or they may not be doing what they thought they would do at work, or perhaps their families are unhappy. Things happen."

Chapter 11

Navigating the Bureaucracy

Kerry O'Connor, the former Foreign Service officer we met in Chapter 1 who converted to the Civil Service, made a surprising discovery when she joined the State Department in 2001. There was no manual or database with information about how management officers and others at overseas posts could accomplish basic tasks, such as leasing a house or fixing a broken sink. "You got thrown into these situations with no playbook," O'Connor said. "I was at the mercy of the quality of the employee who came before me, and I had to figure things out."

When she became a general services officer in Morocco in 2004, she encountered more bureaucratic practices that made little sense in the 21st century. She found herself thinking, "Why do we still have carbon-copy work orders? Why do I have to fill out forms in triplicate so somebody can get a sink fixed? Why does every single embassy around the world have its own way of doing things?"

In her next position as a management analyst in Washington, O'Connor decided to follow her "intellectual curiosity" and began studying private-sector innovation jams. "My goal was to be a catalyst, so that our learning curve isn't always so steep, and we streamline our processes," she said. "I wanted to apply principles of behavioral economics and get things done. The last thing we need our diplomats doing is administrative overhead. They literally need to hit the ground running when they get to a new post." So with help from her superiors and other colleagues, and "thanks to social media inside our firewall," O'Connor started creating an electronic database. "It's like a playbook where you can go and find out how we lease a house or do procurement," she said. "We also have process maps." Although e-diplomacy – using the web, as well as information and communication technologies, for diplomacy purposes – was already being deployed by the State Department, O'Connor's efforts helped to make knowledge management a significant part of it.

Less than two weeks after Hillary Clinton became secretary of state in January 2009, she held her first town hall meeting with State Department employees. O'Connor was one of the hundreds in the auditorium. She was happy to hear Clinton promise to start within two days a discussion forum on the department's internal website about how to improve operations in Washington and overseas. "Each of us must do our part internally to assure that we are efficient, effective and productive," the secretary said. "I want your best ideas, your best assessment of the impact of the suggestions you are making, and your best sense of the potential implementation challenges."[1]

As O'Connor listened to Clinton, she thought, "I wonder who will run this board." Her enthusiasm about the idea was evident from the suggestions she began making immediately to her boss – for example, she recommended that the e-diplomacy office, which already had software and designers, build the new platform. The only outstanding issue was the forum's governance. "What are people allowed to talk about? We decided that they are allowed to talk about the *how* of foreign policy, but not the *what* or the *why*," she said, noting that there are other online communities on the department's intranet where policy can be discussed. "So the Sounding Board was born," with O'Connor in charge of it.

'Better, faster, cheaper and friendlier'

Patrick Kennedy, the undersecretary of state for management whom we met in Chapter 3, joined the Foreign Service in 1973. There have been many changes to the way the service does business since then, but the biggest has to do with the enormous advances in technology, he said. "Back then, if you were in a former British colony in West Africa and wanted to call a country next door that had been a French colony, you had to book a call to London," he recalled. "Then they would connect you to Paris, from where you'd be connected back to Africa. So to talk to someone a couple of hundred miles away, you had to go around thousands of miles."

Another significant change, Kennedy said, is increasing the demands on U.S. diplomats – both on the exams before they join the Foreign Service and once they start working. "Standards for generalists and specialists are higher," he said. Technology and automation have made certain parts of the State Department bureaucracy more efficient, but when Kennedy became undersecretary in 2007, he realized that there were still policies and practices hindering the system's effectiveness and productivity. Some of those problems – from budgeting to assignments to promotions, as well as the issues O'Connor raised above – directly affected the Foreign Service's capabilities in the pursuit of its ambitious mission, Kennedy said. He added that, while the service has made greater demands on diplomats, they have their own expectations in terms of the work environment and quality of life.

So, even though he did not understand social media as well as the younger generation of diplomats, Kennedy embraced Clinton's decision to create the Sounding Board and was thrilled by her interest in management reforms and her determination to make a difference. The board's function, he said, is to help make the State Department's operations "better, faster, cheaper," and to have a bureaucracy that is "warmer and friendlier."

O'Connor said that Kennedy often sends her messages about comments he reads on the Sounding Board, and sometimes even proactively provides answers to questions employees pose. As I mentioned in Chapter 10, he knows the system inside and out, and he "sees this as an opportunity to educate people," O'Connor said. The board has proved very popular and had more than 52,000 active users when I visited her in early 2012. She also explained some of the rules for posting comments.

"The ideas on the board have to be germane," she said in her office, just a few doors down from Clinton's suite at the State Department. "They can't be individually specific but broadly applicable." O'Connor moderated the board herself, with the help of just one colleague, Molly Moran. "We don't edit ideas," she added. "If it's full of typos, we leave it as it is, though it's compared against pre-published guidelines. It's our way of letting people know that this is their authentic voice. I try to provide human interaction to help get them a little bit more information, so they can redirect their line of inquiry in a productive way. Some people said I should automate responses, and I can't do that. We get enough automated stuff in our lives. I want them to know that there is a live body here that actually cares about what they write."

When an idea is posted on the board, O'Connor determines its importance and feasibility and moves it to the next appropriate level, such as "community review" or "in the works" or "already at State." Among the most popular topics, she said, are the use of iPads and other new technologies that might present a security risk, managers who mistreat their subordinates, the annual employee evaluations and mental health. Seeking psychological help in the Foreign Service has threatened employees' security clearance in the past, she noted. In fact, when the board first started, "people were afraid for their security clearance" and wanted to post anonymously regarding mental health issues. But now they discuss such issues without fear of losing their clearance, O'Connor said.

The Sounding Board is not only a forum where employees bring attention to problems and propose solutions, but an opportunity to give them information they cannot find anywhere else, and to clear up misperceptions, O'Connor said. For example, Foreign Service members are sometimes confused about the exact nature of the diplomatic immunities and other privileges they have overseas, she said, because they do not fully understand the Vienna Conventions on Consular and Diplomatic Relations.

"There are different levels of privileges for different types of employees," but when Foreign Service specialists receive less than what generalists – or officers – are entitled to overseas, such as sales tax exemption, "some see it as discrimination," O'Connor said. "It's international law – there is nothing we can do about it." There is also a difference between the immunities at an embassy and a consulate, she explained. "If you are a Foreign Service officer in an embassy, you have full diplomatic immunity whatever you do in your personal and professional capacity. However, anyone in a consulate has immunity for what they do in their professional but not personal life."

As I noted in Chapter 1, one of the aspects to the humanizing of diplomacy that has occurred in recent years has to do with making the State Department bureaucracy friendlier, more accessible and transparent to employees. The Sounding Board is one of the steps that have been taken toward that goal, and we will discuss others later in the chapter, as well as in Chapter 12. Those efforts, however, have by no means resolved all problems.

In fact, the expanding bureaucracy has become a problem in itself. Aneta Stefanova, the Bulgarian employee of the embassy in Sofia whom we met in Chapter 2, said that it has been "frustrating" to watch the "shift of priorities for our American colleagues as the State Department grows into a mammoth bureaucracy." As a result, "the inspired and hard-working diplomats whose job it is to soak up the local culture and life, gaining a deep understanding of the host nation's issues to better inform U.S. policies, have been replaced by increasingly harried bureaucrats," Stefanova said. "They have precious little time to think and analyze because of the stupefying amount of administration they – and we – contend with, which many of us have taken to calling 'e-hell.'"

The administrative burden, which takes up much of diplomats' time, is partly responsible for the perception that "embassy people are out of touch" with their host society, said Philip Frayne, a public diplomacy officer whom I first met in Cairo in 2003. "We tend to spend most of our time in capitals and travel in westernized elite circles, but we are not as isolated as people might think," he said. "We do get out of capitals, and we do speak to ordinary people."

Inefficiencies and inertia linger

Justin – not his real name – had a hard time getting ready for his first assignment in the Foreign Service a few years ago. The problem was that, for weeks, he was unable to reach the Human Resources officer in charge of his paperwork, known as official "permanent change of station" orders. "You can't do anything without orders," he said, including booking a plane ticket, applying for a diplomatic visa from the host country or getting a housing assignment at the new post, among other essential tasks. Not knowing what else to do as his scheduled departure drew closer, Justin kept e-mailing the officer in question. "No response," he said. "Just silence."

Finally, after more e-mail messages and phone calls, the officer surfaced and wrote Justin's orders almost at the last minute. The stress was huge, unnecessary and completely avoidable, and not the way someone new to the Foreign Service should be treated, Justin said.

To his utter astonishment, the same story repeated itself when he was trying to move to his second post two years later. Desperate and frustrated, this time he sought help from his career development officer, who worked in a different Human Resources office and had nothing to do with the officer responsible for the orders. "It's bad enough that nobody tells you what you need to do and you have to figure things out," but even when you do, you are still dependent on other people – and not just for orders, but for many other bureaucratic requirements, Justin said. That second time, he actually felt a need to visit his assignment officer in person when he was back in Washington. "Her office looked like a bomb went off," he recalled. "There were papers everywhere. It took her 15 minutes to find my file, literally just moving piles of paper all over her desk."

I met Justin as he prepared for yet another assignment. Although his new position was language-designated, the time he had before he was expected to report at his next post was not enough to take the full training required. So he had applied for a waiver that would allow him to shorten his language instruction. With only three months left at his previous post, Justin still had not heard back – that was the job of another Human Resources office, not the assignment officer. As a result, he had no idea how long he and his family would have to stay in Washington before heading overseas again. "I don't know what other classes I might have to take, either," he said. "You always have to push, and many people don't even answer e-mails and phone calls. I don't know what happens if you don't push."

Hundreds of Foreign Service members complained about various practices in the State Department's Bureau of Human Resources, though not about every single one of its activities. One of the most frequent complaints was that new employees do not receive enough help as they make their first attempts at navigating the huge bureaucracy. Several officers had stories similar to Justin's, though none of them wanted to be quoted. They said that among the people less responsive to their inquiries and requests are Civil Service employees who have been in their jobs for many years, which might explain their complacency and lack of enthusiasm. Whatever the reasons for Justin's assignment officer's behavior – whether understaffing or personal problems or just laziness – such poor performance affects real people's lives and the posts waiting for them, he said. Others in the service had issues with its bidding and assignment system, as well as with evaluations and promotions, as we will see later in the chapter.

Several senior Foreign Service officers who have worked in the Bureau of Human Resources – including Nancy Powell, who headed the bureau as the service's director-general before becoming ambassador to India, and Patrick Kennedy, who oversees the bureau as undersecretary for management – said that measures have been taken to improve performance. "Both Nancy and I have tried to explain to the people in Human Resources that their clients are the State Department's best assets, and we need to communicate better with them," Kennedy said. "I think they have been working harder to be friendlier and more efficient."

While those appeals have not eradicated all inefficiencies and inertia, Justin said that his old assignment officer no longer works in the department – it was not clear what exactly happened to her and if it had anything to do with her performance. "From what I understand, there have been some reshuffles in the way they handle getting orders," Justin said. "The process seems to move more smoothly now. After the wait for my language waiver, I had no issues getting my orders this time around."

Looking at the big picture and the department's culture in general, several officers noted a seeming anomaly: While there are numerous rules and bureaucratic procedures that create the impression of a complex structure, employees who know how to work the system often break those rules.

Kris Graf, the entry-level officer and former Navy pilot whom we met in Chapter 9, said it disturbs him when colleagues say, "I don't like this rule, so I'll find a way around it." Coming from the military, "if I'm told that I'm not eligible to bid on a certain position, I'd say fine," he added. "But then I find out that someone else with my circumstances bid on it and got the job. Why? That stuff bothers me. It makes the system unfair. In the military, if someone tells you that's the rule, you live with it. That said, having been in the Foreign Service for five years now, I can see some of the benefits to that sometimes. Once you know the system, you have more leeway to push things the way you want to happen. But when you first start out, you are at a disadvantage, because you have no real idea what's going on."

Top State Department managers highly value flexibility in the system – political appointees in particular, including secretaries of state, have tried to give senior positions to Foreign Service officers whose formal grade was lower than the one required for those positions. As I noted in Chapter 9, "stretch assignments" are allowed in the service, but "double stretches" are very difficult to pull off, especially up to the senior Foreign Service by mid-level officers.

Condoleezza Rice said she faced a "firestorm" in 2005, when she appointed two mid-level officers who had worked for her at the National Security Council, Kurt Volker and Matthew Bryza, to the senior positions of deputy assistant secretaries in the European bureau. "If you are going to sit around and make people go through every level, even though they are ready for [higher] positions, then you are going to lose a lot of very good people," Rice said. "The complications of promoting very early on are a problem. In other professions, early promotion is not the norm, but it's not considered outside of the possible realm, either. We promote people to tenure early at Stanford, and people have no problem with it – I was promoted early." Rice was first hired by Stanford University in 1981 and returned there after leaving the State Department in 2009.

William Harrop, the former career ambassador we met in Chapter 2, said a better basis for comparison than private academic institutions when it comes to promotions might be the U.S. Army. There, "short of extraordinary battlefield circumstances, a double promotion would flout normal procedures," Harrop said. Rice's "appointment of mid-level officers with whom she had worked to very senior positions in the department was viewed as cronyism by the Foreign Service. This may not have been a judicious introduction by a new leader to an unfamiliar institution."

The opaqueness of making assignments

One of the most anticipated internal documents the State Department puts out, along with the promotion list, is the bid list with available Foreign Service positions. It comes out twice a year – once for the main summer rotation cycle, and a shorter version for the winter cycle. Then it is updated periodically, as positions are added or removed. The importance of the bid list and the lobbying that takes place over the following months cannot be overstated. Every three years, on average, U.S. diplomats have to decide where in the world they should go next – which position might offer a rewarding experience and possibly a promotion, but also which post might meet the needs of the entire family.

So it is hardly surprising that Foreign Service members take this career-shaping and potentially life-changing process very seriously. Yet many of them do not fully understand it. Who exactly decides who goes where? Can Human Resources overrule the post's choice? Is the direct supervisor of the future employee the one who has the biggest say? What if he or she is rotating out and will not actually supervise the incoming officer?

The question that puzzles most officers is this: On what criteria are decisions based? There is no clear answer, and the process is opaque and subjective, hundreds of officers said. Some decision-makers prefer previous experience in the respective region, they said, while others would rather take someone who has performed superbly in another region. Some like – or at least do not mind – being approached by bidding officers, while others hate that. Some value "corridor reputation," while others care little for it.

These uncertainties are particularly hard on officers in the early part of their careers, said Sumreen Mirza, the former political officer in Baghdad whom we first met in Chapter 2. "I don't have a solution, so I have a hard time criticizing the process, but it's just opaque, because lobbying happens on all levels and in different places," she said. "You must be qualified for the job, but who you know, and who they know, also matters."

Nancy Powell said she made a deliberate effort to increase transparency in the assignment system when she was director-general of the Foreign Service, and several officers said that helped but there is much more to be desired. "She tried to do away with what a lot of people perceived as backroom negotiations," Mark Pekala, the ambassador to Latvia whom we met in Chapter 10, said of Powell. "She publicized more explicitly the actual procedures, arcane as they might be. There is transparency that did not exist in the past."

Actually, Powell said that there was no transparent bid list at all when she joined the Foreign Service in 1977. Today, even ambassadorial positions are "advertised," she added. "There is a note that goes out for almost all of them – those that are going to be for career people – and it says, 'Here is a list of anticipated openings for 2013 at the chief-of-mission level, and if you are interested, you need to let the [respective] bureau know.'"

Personal connections are corridor reputation usually play a role in selecting candidates from the bid lists at most levels, though few managers will hire someone just because they know him or her, without proper qualifications, several officers said. Entry-level officers do not officially bid on positions – rather, they are "directed" after submitting their preferences, which means they are unable to lobby.

In November 1997, Mike Hammer, whom we first met in Chapter 1, did advance work on President Clinton's visit to Vancouver for the annual Asia-Pacific Economic Cooperation (APEC) summit. Once the president's party arrived, Glyn Davies, a Foreign Service officer who was the executive secretary of the National Security Council (NSC) at the time, approached Hammer with a special task. Clinton "wanted to go out to dinner with a group of friends," and Davies wondered if Hammer, who had been in the city for about 10 days and was familiar with a few restaurants and knew some of the local consulate employees, could help. Even though Hammer was a political officer with nine years of experience in the Foreign Service, he had no problem making a dinner reservation. "I had in essence a 30-minute bus ride to make arrangements, but I did manage to find a restaurant close by, and everybody ended up having a good evening out," he recalled.

About a year later, Hammer bid on a position in the NSC's Europe office and also sent his résumé directly to Davies. "Glyn came back and said, 'I don't necessarily see a match for the Europe job, but there is a vacancy in our press shop at the NSC.' I was pretty stunned," Hammer said. He ended up getting the press job – the first time he did press work in his career, which eventually led to Hammer's appointment as the first NSC spokesman in the Obama White House, and later as assistant secretary of state for public affairs. He said he does not believe any of that would have happened had he not arranged that dinner for Clinton in Vancouver. "If someone comes to you, and you are able to do little things right, you might be given bigger opportunities," he said. "People don't necessarily focus on whether you are the best note-taker or cable-writer, but if you have a good head on your shoulders, and you can solve problems, then perhaps you'll be given other opportunities."

'Skewed' but consequential evaluations

Early to mid-spring is not a favorite time of year for local embassy employees. "You can really tell the evaluation season is upon our American colleagues when we suddenly start feeling the tension in the office, when the officers turn competitors rather than colleagues, and when your usually friendly supervisor suddenly finds fault with an insignificant issue at work," said Aneta Stefanova.

The Foreign Service's evaluation and promotion system received more complaints from the officers interviewed for this book than any other single issue. The most frequently cited problem with the evaluation reports, on which promotions are based, was their tendency to be overly positive and consequently not a true reflection of officers' performance.

"The evaluation process is very skewed," one officer said. "People spend an enormous amount of time writing these things, and half of the time they are not even true." Stefanova said that, in nearly two decades, she has "rarely seen or heard of anyone receiving a bad review, regardless of how they have performed." She suggested that the process may have been "devised to protect the State Department from litigation." Still, "it's not fair to put an equation mark between those who perform at their best and those who are worse than average," she said. "A 360-degree review might be an improvement on the current system."

Many senior managers and officers who have sat on promotion boards remember unusually flattering or even comical evaluations. Louis Mazel, the deputy chief of mission in Singapore whom we met in Chapter 10, recalled an evaluation report written by a lower-level manager about an employee. "I remember that person wrote in the area for improvement, 'So and so is so good, she doesn't know how good she is.' I said, 'No, everyone has something they could work on,' so I sent it back" for revision, Mazel said.

Tracey Jacobson, the ambassador to Kosovo who was previously deputy director of the Foreign Service Institute, chaired a promotion board in the summer of 2011 and read hundreds of evaluation reports. "The one comment that stuck in my mind was, 'There are many stars in the Foreign Service, but this one is a supernova.' What does that mean? Are they about to collapse into a black hole? But that's not the norm" in performance reviews, Jacobson said. It is true, however, that "success has many fathers, and sometimes several people claim credit for the same thing, because policy successes require a team effort," she added.

Performance reviews are supposed to be written each year by an officer's immediate supervisor, with the officer's input. About a decade ago, many reports were said to have been written – or at least drafted – by the employee, but that has changed.

A more likely scenario today is for the boss to ask the employee for a list of his or her accomplishments and write the review, on which the officer has the right to comment in a dedicated section, and even to disagree with the content, Jacobson said. "You should own your evaluation," she said. "You should provide your boss with robust input, read it and sign it. You are also supposed to have documented counseling throughout the year. When it comes time for me to write your evaluation, I can't remember everything, but if we have sessions and write down what's going on, it's much easier. People used to just make up counseling dates. These days, people take this more seriously."

An officer's evaluation reports are the only thing that matters when it comes to promotion, said Nancy Powell. "Corridor reputation may be important in the assignment process, but not so much in promotion," she said. "You can't say, 'I know John did this, but it's not in his file.' You can't promote John on the basis of knowing something that's not documented, and you can't keep him from being promoted. You can't say, 'I know John really screwed up, but his boss didn't put it in here.' You've got to do it based on what's in the reports."

How exactly does one get promoted?

Many officers said that the Foreign Service's promotion criteria have traditionally been so vague and subjective that they often have little idea what exactly they need to do to earn a higher grade. Promotions are based on published "precepts" divided into six skill categories: leadership, managerial, interpersonal, communication and foreign language, intellectual and substantive knowledge. In each category, there are subcategories, such as innovation, team-building and crisis management.² All that, however, still does not bring enough specificity and transparency to the process, many officers said. A frequent comment on the subject I heard was, "I've been surprised not to get promoted, and I've also been surprised to get promoted."

Beth Payne, the former consular officer in Baghdad whom we met in Chapter 7, said there are very different perceptions of what a successful career in the service should be. "It's frustrating for some people, because they are not getting the rewards they thought they would get, even though they thought they did everything right," she said. "And I thought I did everything wrong. I did what I liked, but I did it well and was promoted. So do what you like to do well, and you'll succeed."

Kurt Volker, one of the two controversial Rice appointees as deputy assistant secretary I mentioned earlier, said he was still a mid-level officer at the time of that appointment because he had taken assignments "outside the mainstream, instead of ticking the boxes designed by the personnel system," and had not been promoted as quickly as other officers. Both Volker and Matthew Bryza, the other appointee mentioned earlier, were promoted to the senior Foreign Service while in the European bureau. Volker later became ambassador to NATO, and Bryza ambassador to Azerbaijan. Both have now left the service.

For years, common wisdom said that the key to rapid promotion was more time spent in Washington, particularly as a staff assistant, but that is now less likely to happen absent experience in a hardship post. In fact, I met at least one officer who was recently promoted to the senior Foreign Service without having ever served in Washington or at an unaccompanied post.

If you ask Joan Wadelton, an economic officer who joined the Foreign Service in 1980, opaqueness and subjectivity are by no means the promotion system's biggest problem. She said she has proof that employees in Human Resources changed the results on several of her promotion boards' score sheets, which prevented her from being promoted to the senior ranks in favor of those employees' "friends." She has obtained copies of the sheets in question, showing apparent alterations of the hand-written numbers, which have been posted on a blog called "Whirled View."³

The State Department has dismissed Wadelton's claim and rejected her accusation of wrongdoing. The Foreign Service Grievance Board, however, ordered that several of her promotion boards be reconstituted – Human Resources "insists that those boards ranked me at the bottom every time," she said. "Copies of documents from the boards show severe irregularities, including signatures of people who don't recall sitting on those boards," she added.

The department has denied her access to the original score sheets, Wadelton said, and she filed a lawsuit in federal district court to gain such access, which was still pending as of August 2012. The department has also rejected a request from the Office of the Special Counsel, an independent federal investigative and prosecutorial agency, to interview members of Wadelton's promotion boards, she said.[4]

"I have proof of wrongdoing – criminal matters, in fact – and have pursued it very vigorously," said Wadelton, who was one of the first diplomats to serve in Iraq after the U.S. invasion. During Colin Powell's tenure, she helped create the State Department's Congressional Liaison Office while working for Joe Biden, who at the time was a Democratic senator from Delaware.

The Foreign Service has an up-or-out system, and in December 2011, Wadelton was fired for failing to get promoted before she "TICed out," in State Department speak – TIC stands for "time in class." Although she has spent hundreds of thousands of dollars on legal fees, she said she has no intention of giving up her fight.

The up-or-out system's current rules have received some criticism, because they force out relatively young but capable officers. "People leave the service too early, because the system only allows for very few to reach the highest grades," said George Shultz, President Reagan's secretary of state. "They are in their early 50s, on top of their game, and now they go. We should hold on to people a little longer." Condoleezza Rice agreed. "A lot of people leave early because the promotional flow is just too slow," she said. Shultz's and Rice's comments had nothing to do with Wadelton's case.

Susan Johnson, the president of the American Foreign Service Association whom we first met in Chapter 2, said that "either people are being pushed out too soon" or "succession planning – growing the leaders we need – is not happening as it should" in the service. "The up-or-out system, as currently structured and implemented, needs serious study to test its original assumptions, its record, and whether it is the best use of taxpayer investment in the nation's diplomatic service," she said. "It is not clear that it is very effective or efficient in driving out deadwood or non-performers, but it does drive out a considerable amount of talent, knowledge and experience that the institution has invested in developing over decades. It's a cumbersome, expensive and not very effective way to deal with poor performers. Clearer standards of professional behavior and performance and better management would probably do more and cost much less. In addition, some believe that up-or-out generates competition against colleagues, instead of pushing individuals to work together to meet a higher performance standard, and undermines effective teamwork in the process."

Lack of continuity and institutional memory

Eliot Cohen, the former State Department counselor under Rice whom we met in Chapter 1, is first and foremost a teacher and military scholar. So he was surprised to discover that the Foreign Service, and the department in general, did not have the institutional memory that befits one of the oldest U.S. federal agencies – or an effective mechanism to build such memory.

"We at State have no lessons-learned operation, no system for collecting oral histories, no operational narratives of the kind produced in such abundance by our military counterparts," Cohen said in a 2008 speech in Washington. "We do not have studies of success and, so much more importantly, failure that Department of State professionals should chew over in the classroom, so that they do not repeat them in the field."

One of the biggest consequences of the memory deficit is the lack of continuity at many overseas posts when officers rotate out and fail to pass on to their successors the information and contacts they have built during their tours, many diplomats said. The reason for that is the absence of overlap between officers. "What I would love is for successors to overlap with [incumbents] by a week, or even a month," said Charles Rivkin, the ambassador to France whom we met in Chapter 2. "Knowledge is one thing, but relationships are even more important."

Patrick Kennedy said the department has tried to address the lack of overlap, but a solution has proved difficult to find. "The problem we have had in the past – and probably can never fix – is the shortfall of personnel, though we are getting more resources," he said. "The other problem we face is a very human one. Americans love their kids and usually believe that the most important thing they can give their children after food and safety is a good education. Therefore, everybody wants to move in the summer, and they also want to get a little bit of home leave, and maybe a little bit of training. That means they have to leave post in June, right after school is out, get their training, so they can arrive at their new post before Labor Day to make sure their kids get into school on time. I don't know how to deal with that. We've thought about it a lot. We thought about trying to stagger, but people don't want to change."

Modern technology has provided significant help in passing information on, Kennedy said. "It's very easy for successors to communicate with their predecessors and ask them questions," he added. "Because of computerization, we have much better biographical data and other information on foreign leaders, and on who the movers and shakers are in a country, than we had before." But he conceded that technology "doesn't really answer the major issue about how to avoid the summer gaps."

This issue has also been discussed on the Sounding Board, said Kerry O'Connor, and some employees think there is not sufficient "up-to-date technology to organize and pass on information to successors." Bill Burns, the deputy secretary of state, said it is "the responsibility of the outgoing officer, even if they don't overlap, to ensure a greater sense of continuity, and that's what the leadership at a post is supposed to do."

Burns agreed that the Foreign Service relies heavily on improvisation, saying that it "perversely prides itself on its ability to adapt quickly to different circumstances, and we are not particularly systematic about how we go about doing that." The department has tried to improve, and the increase in resources under Hillary Clinton has helped to think more seriously about building institutional memory, Burns said. "We need to be more systematic," he added. Eliot Cohen said that changes to the State Department's "culture and practices" are necessary to succeed. Otherwise, the department "will become nothing more than an innkeeper for the U.S. government abroad, and a modest provider of diplomatic services in a world shrunk by e-mail, easy international travel and teleconferencing."

In fact, instant communications have already diminished the authority of some Foreign Service officers, said Kurt Volker. "In the age of the Blackberry, power has been concentrated higher and higher up in administrations, stripping ambassadors, office directors and deputy assistant secretaries of authorities they used to wield," he said. "Meanwhile, officers in the field have been used increasingly to fill gaps, implement programs and staff crisis zones. Is that what we want?" That brings the more fundamental question of what kind of Foreign Service the United States should have, and how American diplomats should be selected and trained, which we discussed in Chapter 10.

"The law that defines the current Foreign Service was passed in 1980 – before the fall of the Berlin Wall, the Internet, globalization,

9/11, Iraq and Afghanistan, China's rise and the Arab Spring," Volker said in reference to the Foreign Service Act. "We have adapted by pushing the people we have into new roles, without really thinking through what we are doing, and what we as a country need. But are we hiring the right people to do this? Is there a long-term cost to pay when Foreign Service officers are neither expected nor challenged to become top foreign policy strategists and thinkers, figuring we can just bring in political appointees for that?"

Volker suggested that the current expectation that every officer be able to perform a variety of duties in different specialties requires rethinking. "We may need to sort out several roles, and hire and reward accordingly – for example, managers for management, legal practitioners for consular roles, policy types for policy and strategy, former military and NGO field workers for program roles, journalists and PR types for public diplomacy," he said. "As talented as Foreign Service officers are, the consistent result is less than the sum of its parts. We ought to do something about that."

Chapter 12

The Foreign Service Way of Life

Carol Hazzard was a 20-year-old secretary at the University of Buffalo in 1969, but the life she dreamed of was far removed from the monotony of upstate New York. "My only goal was to travel and see the world," she recalled.

One night, her mother asked her to go to the corner grocery store for some milk, and on her way there, she ran into her former high-school basketball coach, who was working as a flight attendant for the now-defunct Eastern Airlines. Hazzard thought such a job would help her realize her dream of traveling. But the former coach was not enthusiastic about recommending her new profession to others. Instead, she advised Hazzard that she could see the world while continuing to work as a secretary. "She told me the best job I could wish for was with the State Department, working at American embassies overseas," Hazzard said.

After a long application process, she joined the Foreign Service in 1973, and with only three weeks of training, began working as a secretary at the U.S. Embassy in Paris. Hazzard has witnessed the glitz and glamour associated with the world of diplomacy – her office at the embassy in Rome, a former royal palace where she worked in the late 1990s, used to be the Italian queen's drawing room, said Hazzard, who met Pope John Paul II during that tour. But she has also lived in conditions she did not expect to experience.

Hazzard was one of four Foreign Service members sent to open the U.S. Embassy in Guinea-Bissau in 1976, a couple of years after the tiny West African country gained independence from Portugal. The water and electricity both went out for hours every day, and the embassy had no generator of its own, Hazzard said. "The most important diplomatic notes to the Ministry of Foreign Affairs I typed on my manual typewriter requisitioned bread and eggs," she added.

In Haiti, where she moved in 2011, "many people still live without water and electricity," so "we run on generators pretty much all day long, because there is very little city power," she said. "We also have our own water supply – the embassy brings trucks to fill the water tanks."

In 2007, Hazzard retired from the State Department, but life in Florida was not her cup of tea, and she decided to get back in the game. She volunteered for temporary assignments and was happy to go to some of the most challenging posts in Africa, such as the Democratic Republic of the Congo. In 2011, she rejoined the Foreign Service as a full-time employee and had no qualms about working in Haiti. After all these years, she has chosen to remain what the State Department now calls an office-management specialist, rather than become a Foreign Service officer.

Hazzard has served in nearly 80 countries – both on regular assignments and as a "rover," filling positions at various missions for several weeks or months. In fact, I first met her at one of her roving posts, in Slovakia, in 2003. "I've been to some interesting and some bizarre places, and I always enjoyed the bizarre ones more," she said. "My brothers and sisters don't understand why I've spent over 30 years traveling. The first 15 years they thought I was a bit odd, but now they enjoy my stories and take me for what I am." Whether she wants to or not, Hazzard will have to retire – this time permanently – at the end of 2014, when she reaches the mandatory retirement age of 65. She has decided to stay in Haiti until then, even though her tour will exceed a normal two-year assignment in the impoverished country by 20 months.

"I'm exactly where I'm supposed to be – places like this make me more compassionate, and I have no complaints," she told me. "I just pray that I'll get the Foreign Service out of my system when it's time to retire. But I'll be the biggest fan of the service until they put me six feet under. I always wanted to be a recruiter – I wanted to shout from the roof, 'People, you are missing a great opportunity!'"

Behind the glamour: Carjacked, kidnapped or killed

If you have come this far in the book, you know that modern diplomacy is not all glamour. While American diplomats still spend time in the company of kings, queens, presidents and prime ministers, and remain some of the most sought-after people in foreign capitals, they also contend with security threats, severe pollution and disease in dozens of overseas posts. Hundreds of Foreign Service members said they could not imagine doing anything else for a living, but they added that being constantly on the move and far from home means giving up much of what most Americans take for granted. Many of them also said they were torn between a desire to serve and an adventurous spirit, on one hand, and trying to raise a family, on the other.

Indeed, as we saw in the previous chapters, the posting histories of many in the Foreign Service reveal remarkable journeys that have enriched them both professionally and personally in ways no other job can. Those experiences have challenged their own previous perceptions of diplomacy. Anjalina Sen, the former refugee officer in Bangkok whom we first met in Chapter 1, said she wore flip-flops much more often than suits during that tour, because she was "in refugee camps most of the time." Louis Mazel, the deputy chief of mission in Singapore whom we met in Chapter 10, said that he took a train from Senegal to his first Foreign Service post in the African country of Mali in 1984. The train "broke down twice" before reaching the capital Bamako. "The toilets were unusable an hour into the journey, and cockroaches came out in the middle of the night and crawled all over me," Mazel said.

Natural disasters have not only inconvenienced and wounded American diplomats but also killed them. As I mentioned in Chapter 1, David Lindwall's house in Haiti collapsed after the 2010 earthquake, and he is alive today only because he was not home at the time. His colleague Victoria DeLong, however, was not that lucky – she died when the powerful quake destroyed her house. DeLong, who was the cultural affairs officer at the embassy in Port-au-Prince, spent 27 of her 57 years in the Foreign Service.[1]

U.S. diplomats have also put their own safety at risk to help others. After the 2011 earthquake and tsunami in Japan, which led to a nuclear plant disaster, the embassy faced the arduous task of helping to find thousands of Americans who were reported missing. Hundreds of Foreign Service members from around the world volunteered to fly to Tokyo immediately to assist their colleagues at the embassy, said James Zumwalt, the deputy chief of mission at the time, whom we met in Chapter 1. While other Western embassies shut down and evacuated their staff, worried about exposing employees to harmful radiation, 140 U.S. diplomats posted to other countries came to Tokyo despite the potential risks, Zumwalt said.

One of those officers was Edward McKeon, minister-counselor for consular affairs in Mexico City. "Of course, I was concerned about the risks," said McKeon, who had served in Japan three times since joining the Foreign Service in 1975 and retired later in 2011. "I had actually had an earlier bout with cancer, but a quick call to my doctors cleared me to travel. Some of my best memories involved living and working in Japan. I adopted my younger son in Japan. It was gratifying to be able to use my experience to go back and help when I was needed."

Ian Hillman was a consular officer in Nigeria when he heard about the Japan earthquake and tsunami – they had affected an area that was part of a consular district he covered in his previous position at the consulate in the northern city of Sapporo. "I believed I could make a useful contribution," Hillman said. "I became a consular officer out of a desire to assist Americans in need overseas. I remember taking several phone calls from U.S. citizens in Japan, asking if our embassy would be closing, like many other embassies were doing at the time. I assured them we were open for business."

Violent crime is another reality of life in the Foreign Service. During my travels researching this book, I heard many stories about carjackings, kidnappings, robberies, and diplomats being held at gunpoint over the years. Several of them have actually been murdered. On New Year's Day in 2008, John Granville, a 33-year-old USAID officer, was fatally shot in Sudan while returning from a holiday party at the British Embassy.[2] In 2002, Laurence Foley, 60, also with USAID, was gunned down in front of his home in Jordan.[3] In 1968, John Gordon Mein, 54, became the first U.S. ambassador to be assassinated while in office when he was shot by rebels in Guatemala.[4]

Philip Frayne, the former press officer in Cairo whom we met in Chapter 11, said he was driving to a meeting in Yemen in 1993 in an embassy vehicle when he was carjacked by "three guys with Kalashnikovs" pointed at him. "I asked them in Arabic if I could get my bag from the back seat, but by then they were already in the car and driving away," Frayne recalled. "About six months later, someone from the embassy security office saw the car in the parking lot of the presidential palace – the diplomatic license plates hadn't been changed. I don't think it was taken by the president's men, but it was probably taken by tribesmen and later traded or confiscated by the presidential forces." Frayne said his boss in Yemen, Haynes Mahoney, was kidnapped for a week.

Laura Clerici, the retired officer we met in Chapter 7, said she was "ambushed by bandits" in Guatemala in the late 1970s while driving with three colleagues and six children. "When they saw that the guy from the defense attaché's office had a handgun, they started shooting at us," Clerici said. "Fortunately, all they wanted was our money, but when we got back, I absolutely fell apart." Still, work in such places gave "richness to my life that would have never happened, no matter what I had done in Washington," she said. "I've had one of the most exciting lives anybody could possibly want."

Fighting a 'bunker mentality'

It was lunchtime on April 18, 1983, and the cafeteria of the U.S. Embassy in Beirut was buzzing with customers. At about 1 p.m., a powerful blast tore apart the front of the seven-story building. The bomb, hidden in a van reported stolen from the embassy 10 months earlier, killed 63 employees, including 17 Americans.[5] It was the first time a U.S. embassy had become a terrorist target, and it forever changed the way the Diplomatic Security Service, the State Department's law-enforcement division, operates around the world.

"The bombings of the embassy in West Beirut in 1983 and of the embassy annex in East Beirut in 1984 were a major catalyst for creating the Bureau of Diplomatic Security," said John Murphy, a former special agent for nearly 29 years who was in charge of Colin Powell's protective detail when he was secretary of state. The annex was a former apartment building rented by the embassy after the first bombing. Also in 1983, terrorists attacked the U.S. Marine barracks in Beirut, as well as the embassy in Kuwait.

The increased attention to security still was not enough. On August 7, 1998, terrorists linked to al-Qaida attacked the embassies in Kenya and Tanzania. As I mentioned in Chapter 3, more than 200 people were killed, including 12 Americans.[6] More than 5,000 were wounded. Madeleine Albright said that was her worst day as secretary of state. "It wasn't that we didn't see it coming," said a former senior security official in Washington. "Our directions were to prevent bombings, and that was an absolute priority. But with well over 200 facilities around the world, we could only do so much with the budget and time constraints we had." New embassies were being built to higher security standards even before 1998, "but you can't change every building overnight," the former official said. "It's a massive and very expensive undertaking."

After the Africa embassy bombings, and especially since September 11, 2001, the State Department has been struggling to prevent the heightened security at its overseas facilities from hurting its diplomatic mission. But a visit to a U.S. embassy or consulate anywhere in the world today means entering what both Americans and foreigners describe as a fortress – a far cry from the welcoming buildings of the past, where millions had their first contact with the United States. The Foreign Service has accepted that the days when anyone could walk up the steps of an embassy unescorted are long gone. But some officers said certain screening procedures seem excessive and unnecessary. "I've seen walls go up literally and figuratively," an officer in Europe said. "Our security is ever stricter [with] all those restrictions on what we can do and who we can bring in and what they have to go through."

Several officers said the new practice of building embassies and other missions on the outskirts of cities, rather than in their centers, not only makes them less accessible to local populations, but also keeps the Americans away from the host country's officials and citizens. They said the hassle of traveling for as long as an hour to attend a meeting forces them to spend most of their time in the office, losing touch with their constituents. "We get into a bunker mentality," the officer in Europe said. "Trying to make ourselves better understood requires understanding of how other people look at us."

However, other officers said that some of their colleagues' bunker mentality has little to do with the embassy's location. "Part of effectively representing the United States means understanding the culture where we are living," another officer in Europe said. "I've been surprised how many people are content with just staying in their communities." Whatever the reason for not getting out of the office – whether a long drive to a meeting or too many administrative tasks or lack of interest in socializing – I found that some diplomats lack in-depth knowledge about their host country and society.

Francis Taylor, who was assistant secretary of state for diplomatic security during Powell's tenure, said there is always "tension between security and public access" at posts. "Balance is a challenge every day in this business," he said. "We want to be able to operate in an environment where our people can be safe and reach out to the constituency they have to work with in order to promote American foreign policy. But our embassies are not impenetrable. There are procedures that allow private citizens to get in. They just can't do what they did 30 years ago, when they walked up to the front door unescorted, because of the nature of the threats we are facing." Taylor said his colleagues in Diplomatic Security "worry about it every day" because they are "paid to be paranoid."

More than any previous attacks before or since, the Africa embassy bombings had a traumatic effect on thousands of American diplomats around the globe. Those incidents – and the additional uncertainties of the post-September 11 world – have taught them that they are potential targets not only at work, but also in residential compounds, schools and at social gatherings. "The day they brought the bodies home in 1998, I was leaving for Israel," said

Deborah Schwartz, who was the economic counselor at the embassy in Mexico City when I met her in 2003. "I was standing in the lobby of my mother's building waiting for a taxi to go to the airport, and my mother was crying. I had to promise her that I wouldn't come back in a body bag."

'How do you ask another person to put their life on hold?'

Victoria Nuland, the State Department spokesperson and former ambassador to NATO, was not necessarily looking for love when she joined the Foreign Service in 1984 at age 23, but she found it anyway – fairly quickly and not too far away. While working on the China desk in Washington, she started dating a young speechwriter for Secretary of State George Shultz named Robert Kagan, who had been a foreign policy adviser to a Republican member of Congress.

When they got married three years later, the inevitable question arose: What would Kagan do while his diplomat wife served abroad? He did not think that joining the Foreign Service himself would be the best solution, and he really wanted to write. So that was what he did. "He wrote his first book, on Nicaragua, in the spare bedroom of our Moscow apartment," recalled Nuland, who was a political officer in Russia from 1991 until 1993. "The KGB used to rifle his office regularly – we could tell by the lingering stench of cigarettes and body odor. They couldn't fathom that he was really just a writer." Kagan's role as the "trailing spouse" of a Foreign Service officer was not to the liking of his mentors back home, and they "lamented to his parents that such a promising career was wasted," Nuland said.

When her Moscow tour ended, they decided to go back to Washington and start a family, so they ended up staying there for six years. During that time, Kagan co-founded a now-defunct think tank called Project for the New American Century, which focused on studying and promoting American leadership in the world. Nuland became deputy chief of mission at NATO in 1999, and Kagan followed her to Brussels, where he helped to take care of their two children and began writing another book. That book, "Of Paradise and Power," was his first bestseller and established him as a leading thinker and writer on foreign affairs. "He reminded me that he wrote it as a direct result of coming to Europe with me," Nuland said. "More broadly, he credits Foreign Service spousehood with deepening his global education."

Rising quickly up the promotion ladder in the Foreign Service – Nuland became a senior officer in 15 years – and raising a family and keeping a spouse happy is a rare combination. She attributed it to "lots of luck, great mentors and a heavy dose of bending the service to be more modern" and accommodating. "I married a very flexible, portable guy who was willing to make huge sacrifices in his own career to make mine possible, and who had generous bosses," Nuland said. Kagan was a senior associate at the Carnegie Endowment for International Peace for 13 years, and Carnegie President Jessica Matthews "kept him on and let him live in Brussels," Nuland said. When she returned to NATO as ambassador in 2005, Kagan helped to open Carnegie's Brussels office.

Most Foreign Service members interviewed for this book said that, whatever they give up to serve their country, they knew at least partially what they were getting into when they joined. It is their partners who make the biggest sacrifices, they said. "How do you ask another person to put their life on hold and follow you?" was a question several officers posed. Many diplomats have not been as lucky as Nuland and others whose spouses have portable professions, such as teachers or journalists. At a town hall meeting with about two dozen spouses the embassy in Tokyo organized for me during my first research visit there in 2003, several of them said the Foreign Service lifestyle destroyed their careers – among them were architects and lawyers.

The State Department has tried to create more positions for spouses at foreign posts, but most of them are secretarial and lack opportunities for advancement in pay and grade level, which means that new hires have to start from the beginning every time. Spouses are eligible for language training at the Foreign Service Institute, but basic language proficiency does not make it too much easier to find a fulfilling job in a new country. The labor laws in many countries only add to the difficulties.

Adrianne Treiber, wife of Laird Treiber, the economic counselor in Ankara whom we first met in Chapter 4, said there were "a limited number of jobs and huge competition" at the embassy. An oncology nurse by training, she worked as a part-time secretary whenever there were gaps to fill in various embassy sections. "The opportunities in the local economy in Turkey are also pretty limited, because they wouldn't employ an American when they have a Turkish candidate with the same skill set," she said.

Anjalina Sen was in a long-term relationship when she joined the Foreign Service in 2007, but her first tour was in China, and her boyfriend was able to come only as a tourist on short-term single-entry visas, she said. Employment was out of the question. "We had different ideas about what we wanted our lives to look like," and the relationship ended, Sen said. "Many of us join the service as double-income families, but then all of a sudden we drop to a single income – and it's often the lower income. In most cases, we have partners who are just as educated and motivated, and we are asking them to sit out on their career for lengthy periods of time. That's the aspect of the Foreign Service life that's very difficult."

To solve the problem, some spouses also join the service, only to find out that it is not that easy for "tandem couples" to secure jobs at the same post. When I visited Kristie Kenney, the ambassador to Thailand, in early 2012, her husband, William Brownfield, was assistant secretary of state for international narcotics and law enforcement affairs in Washington. "When he was in Venezuela, I was in Ecuador for half of his tour and Manila for the other half," Kenney said. The more senior you get in the service, the more difficult it gets to stay together, she said. Kenney and Brownfield did serve together in several countries, including Argentina and Switzerland, earlier in their careers, and "spent a lot of time in Washington," she added.

At unaccompanied posts, being a tandem couple is of course the only way to have a spouse present. Heidi Ramsay was a second-tour officer when I met her in Baghdad soon after visiting Kenney in Bangkok, and the main reason she was there was that she and her husband, a Diplomatic Security agent, could be at the same post – that embassy was certainly big enough for both of them.

Raising a family on the go

Ramsay and her husband may have been together in Iraq, but their children were thousands of miles away – they have two kids each from previous marriages, and "all of them are with their other parents back in the U.S.," she told me in Baghdad. "We Skype pretty regularly. In two weeks, we'll be going back and taking all four kids on a Disney cruise to Mexico." A former insurance executive who also has years of military experience under her belt, Ramsay said she was "much more ambitious" in her "younger days," but having two sons with special needs "has somewhat tempered" her career advancement. "There is a lot to weigh as a family, and a lot to factor in – two careers, four children, schooling for special-needs kids – and I considered all that before I came into the Foreign Service."

The spouses or partners of Foreign Service members often have a say in making the initial decision to join, but children almost never do. Growing up in the service produces mixed results, many diplomats said. Living in different countries is culturally enriching and creates a worldview that a child would not acquire in the United States. But being uprooted every couple of years deprives children of a sense of belonging and makes it difficult for them to maintain friendships, they said.

Several parents said one of the most important lessons their children have learned is how much suffering there is in the world, and how lucky they are to have been born in the United States. "My daughter's feeling about the kids in the U.S. was that they didn't realize how much they have and are very materialistic," said Hilary Olsin-Windecker, the public affairs counselor at the embassy in Israel whom I met in Abu Dhabi in 2003.

On that same round-the-world trip, I also met Stephen McFarland, the deputy chief of mission in Venezuela at the time whom I mentioned in Chapter 2. His son Chris, then a 10th-grader, said that "being a Foreign Service child means being a better-rounded American, because most Americans are geographically incompetent." A schoolmate of his, 11th-grader Allison Arias, daughter of another officer in Caracas, said: "I've become more patriotic because I'm away from my country."

All interviewed parents said their children's well-being is a major factor in deciding what assignments to take. Although Victoria Nuland's husband has given up a lot to follow her overseas, she has had to make some sacrifices, too, she said. "I've spent almost two-thirds of my career in Washington to accommodate Bob and the kids, including turning down the first two ambassadorships I was offered in the late 1990s, because they didn't work for the family," said Nuland, who has also taken leave without pay. "In the last four years, I've taken myself out of the ambassadorial sweepstakes again, including for some very interesting posts, because the kids wanted to attend high school in the U.S. I love the job – it's all I've ever wanted to do – but I love my husband and kids more. We've always made all our decisions together."

Eric Watnik, the public affairs counselor in Singapore whom we met in Chapter 7, said he had been married for barely two years when he went to Iraq by himself in 2004. During his assignment as deputy chief of mission in the Marshall Islands, in the northern Pacific, at the end of the last decade, his wife and newborn son were back home "for more than six months in a two-year tour," said Watnik, who has also served in Colombia, Bolivia and Chile. So when it was time to bid again, he added, "I gave my wife the bid list and said, 'You tell me where we are going next.' I was tracking other jobs that might have furthered my career, but I let them go, because my wife wanted Singapore. She was pregnant with our second son at the time, and she wanted to have good hospitals, safe food and good schools. Singapore is a First World post, but not necessarily one that will advance my career."

When I met Cynthia Haley, who said in Chapter 1 that she had "negotiated with foreign ministers" and "watched people's luggage," in early 2012, she was the head of the State Department's passport agency in El Paso, Texas. There was a good reason for this posting. Her previous posts were in Bolivia and the Mexican city of Ciudad Juárez, which has gained notoriety in recent years for its violent crime linked to drug-trafficking. When it came to raising children, the quality of life in El Paso, and the schools in particular, offered a much better alternative, Haley said. "The kids are 13 and 14, and this is the first time they can ride bikes to their friends' houses or play at a park without an adult hovering over them," she added.

Just before Haley and her family arrived in Juárez in 2005, the wife and children of one of the Diplomatic Security agents at the U.S. Consulate "had been two cars back from a shootout," she said.

During Haley's first year, her children went to school in El Paso, commuting every day from Juárez, which is just across the U.S.-Mexico border. Initially, a consulate bus took several employees' kids to El Paso, but later that service ended and Haley had to drive them herself, with the commute exceeding an hour each way. "So I put my children in a bilingual school in Juárez, but it wasn't really bilingual – none of the teachers was a native English speaker, and the kids were right at that grade level where they needed to learn English from native speakers," she said. "Overall, the schools in Juárez were not really up to the standards I wanted, so my husband started homeschooling the children."

Overseas posts have family liaison offices that help newcomers to get settled, offering advice on schooling and child care, among other family matters. Some Foreign Service children flourish, while others find it difficult to adjust to the distinctive environment and people in every new country. There are also medical practitioners at posts – doctors at big posts and nurses at smaller ones.

The State Department has become more flexible and accommodating when it comes to the needs of Foreign Service families, said Victoria Nuland. "In 1998, when I asked for my second maternity leave in 18 months, the Human Resources folks looked at me like I had two heads – and then said yes," she recalled. "Now it's routine for mothers and fathers to be granted generous leave without pay or telecommuting options for each kid, or if a parent or partner needs them."

Advances for gay diplomats

In 1984, Jan Krc was a 27-year-old officer who had just completed his first Foreign Service tour in Belgrade, when the security office at the U.S. Information Agency (USIA) in Washington, where Krc was on staff, summoned him for what turned into a nine-hour interrogation, he said.

The office had received information that Krc was gay, he was told, and "pressured" him to sign a statement that he had engaged in sexual relations with other men. His next assignment in South Africa was canceled, and his security clearance was limited to Washington, which ended his Foreign Service career, and he became a Civil Service employee. The reason he was not simply fired, he said, was the lack of wrongdoing – officers were not required to report relations with locals unless they became serious, with long-term prospects.

Having had his dream of serving around the world crushed, the Czech-born Krc decided to fight for his rights before the Foreign Service Grievance Board. "None of this would have happened to a straight officer," he said of the way he was treated. "You couldn't have any intimate relations with the locals in communist countries, but Yugoslavia was not in the Soviet bloc. It was an obvious discrimination case, but as in most such cases, the department wasn't foolish enough to say they were doing this because I was gay. At the same time, USIA had a director of security who briefed incoming officers, saying homosexuals didn't belong in the Foreign Service."

After a two-year investigation, which proved very costly because "people were literally dragged from overseas for questioning," the Grievance Board ruled that Krc should be reinstated, he said. However, the security office invoked a rule allowing it not to abide by the board's decision if it would "endanger national security," Krc said. "They even took it to federal court, claiming that I had higher susceptibility to hostile intelligence approaches."

After nearly a decade in the courts, including an initial win and subsequent losses on appeal, a "clever lawyer noticed a paragraph in the Foreign Service Act," Krc said. The paragraph stated that an officer separated from the service could not reapply, unless his separation has been ruled unlawful by the Grievance Board, which was the case with Krc. So he passed the exams again and rejoined the service in 1993 – his previous promotion while he was in Belgrade was not honored, and "they even made me sit through A-100 again," he said, adding that the Clinton administration ended discrimination against gays.

In June 2012, as public affairs counselor at the embassy in Austria, Krc recorded a video about the importance of gay rights, on the occasion of what gays and lesbians celebrate as "pride month," which was posted on the embassy website and YouTube. A lot has changed since he first joined the Foreign Service in 1982. "Now we have gay junior officers arriving with their partners, and they expect to be treated like any other couple, and they are," he said in reference to the benefits Hillary Clinton gave to same-sex partners, which we discussed in Chapter 3. "They have diplomatic passports and are eligible for jobs at the embassy – not that the jobs that are left for the spouses are so great."

While life for gay diplomats and their partners has improved dramatically in the last few years, not all issues have been resolved, said about two dozen gay officers in Washington and several overseas posts. The biggest hurdle to truly equal rights in the Foreign Service, they said, remains the federal law defining marriage as a union between a man and a woman, known as the Defense of Marriage Act (DOMA). Clayton Bond, whom we met in Chapter 2, said the law does not allow same-sex couples with children to have one family insurance policy. Bond and his diplomat husband hoped to adopt, and "if that effort is successful, we would still have to have two policies, which would be more expensive," he said. "This is not right. So there is still quite a bit that needs to be done for equal rights, but it requires the repeal of DOMA."

American partners of gay diplomats who are not in the service themselves are at least formally recognized by the State Department, which issues them diplomatic passports – whether their host countries give them diplomatic visas is another issue. That is not the case, however, with partners who are not U.S. citizens. Because of DOMA, they are not eligible to apply for citizenship – a right still reserved only for heterosexual foreign spouses.

Kenneth Kero was a political-military officer at the embassy in Berlin in 2006 when he met a German film editor and photographer named David Mentz. Two years later, they got married, and even changed both their last names to Kero-Mentz. But that made no difference when they had to move to Ken's next post in Sri Lanka, where homosexuality is illegal, he said. David was refused a long-term visa and had to go as a tourist. It took months of fighting with the government to resolve the issue.

There was also a problem at the embassy. Even though David had access to the compound and "the ambassador treated him very well," the security office told the couple that, if something were to happen to David, the embassy would do nothing to help him, "because he was not an American and did not have a U.S. diplomatic passport," Ken said. Being "treated badly" by both the Sri Lankan government and the U.S. Embassy, coupled with the impossibility of having a job, made David "deeply unhappy," which strained their relationship, Ken said. David even contemplated going back to Germany, but in the end, he decided to stay with his husband.

However, Ken cut his tour in Sri Lanka short, and they moved to Washington after two years. David's extended presence in the United States would have been a problem just a year earlier, but thanks to Hillary Clinton, the State Department found a way to grant foreign same-sex partners long-term visitor visas, Ken said. Before then, the only way for partners to accompany gay diplomats during domestic assignments was to enroll as students at U.S. universities or to independently find jobs at American companies, which could sponsor them for work visas.

Ken, who has also served in Brazil and Iraq, said he would be very careful on what posts he bids when it is time to go overseas again. "It will have to be a First World post, because I don't think David can manage another developing country, especially one where homosexuality remains criminalized," Ken said.

In the summer of 2012, Ken took up a position at the State Department that could not even exist just a few years earlier, working on human rights for lesbian, gay, bisexual and transgender (LGBT) people around the world. He was also elected president of the organization of LGBT American diplomats, Gays and Lesbians in Foreign Affairs Agencies (GLIFAA).[7] For its hundreds of members, what Hillary Clinton did in her speech in Geneva in December 2011, which I mentioned in Chapter 3, was nothing short of a miracle – Jan Krc actually called it "mind-blowing."

Clinton urged other countries to "be on the right side of history" and "galvanize more support for the human rights of the LGBT community" worldwide. "Being LGBT does not make you less human," she said.[8]

Single in the Foreign Service: 'It's a little death every time'

Foreign Service members who are single and have no children are sometimes envied by their colleagues for having no additional responsibilities. But several of them said that being in a foreign country and having no one to go home to at night has difficulties of its own.

Of course, there are also single parents, whose career sacrifices are even bigger than those made by married or partnered officers. Paul Fitzgerald, the consul-general in Tokyo, is a single father whose children's needs always came first when choosing assignments – and unaccompanied posts were not an option. However, as soon as he "sent the younger of two kids off to college" in 2009, he volunteered to lead a provincial reconstruction team in Iraq, he said. One of Fitzgerald's colleagues in Tokyo, the embassy's chief press officer, Karen Kelley, is a single mother whom I first met in Manila in 2003. One of her assignments after the Philippines was as a public diplomacy adviser at U.S. Pacific Command in Honolulu – not necessarily a career-advancing post, but great for her two boys.

Carol Hazzard said she first got married during her second tour in the service, but the marriage did not last long, and she chose to remain single for the next 29 years. "It was an easier way to travel and see the world," she said. Hazzard, who has no children, is now married to a man she met in Cyprus not long before her first – and short-lived – retirement from the Foreign Service. Her husband, however, is not with her in Haiti. "He said he couldn't take the misery," she told me.

Laura Clerici was also single during most of her 33-year career, but she said she had no regrets. "You have to make up your mind what's important. I decided early on I wasn't going to get married. I've lost two brothers and my parents, and I was not in the U.S. for any of their deaths. But I felt called to public service, so I don't begrudge any of it," said Clerici, who has served in countries as diverse as Indonesia, Britain, Poland, Honduras, Russia and Spain. "Most people in the Foreign Service are ambitious and capable, and if you want to advance, you have to make a lot of sacrifices."

For gay officers, serious relationships were almost impossible in the old days, Jan Krc said. "Basically, it was kind of like the priesthood," he said. "I joined knowing that, apart from something on the side like a one-night stand, I really could not have any expectations for a relationship, because the relationship couldn't travel with me. There was no way."

Naomi Walcott, the economic officer in Tokyo we met in Chapter 2, said she was surprised to find a husband in the Foreign Service – he also worked at the embassy in Japan when I met her in 2011. "When I joined, I assumed I would be single for the rest of my life," Walcott said. "From what people had told me, it didn't sound like a good dating scene at all. So it was one of the biggest surprises that I ended up meeting my spouse through this job. That was something I was concerned about. I thought that being single would come with the job – that I would sacrifice this particular part of my life."

Cameron Munter, the former ambassador to Pakistan and Serbia who retired from the service in September 2012, said it is a good idea for anyone starting a diplomatic career to make a decision at the very beginning about the importance of their personal life. Munter's wife was with him in Islamabad, but they were apart for about 18 months after the attack on the embassy in Belgrade and during Munter's subsequent tour in Baghdad.

"Don't come in to find the Foreign Service as a mirror to look at yourself," he advised new and future diplomats. "Look at yourself and then come into the service. If you are single, and you want to stay single, just be conscious of that. If you are single but want to get married or to have a partner, decide that. But if you let the Foreign Service make the choice for you, it will. Whatever you put on the altar the Foreign Service will take, and it won't thank you for it."

Being single in the service may provide more freedom when making career choices, but it also takes a toll, several officers said.

"The hardest thing is that you arrive in a new country alone," said Barbara Zigli, a public diplomacy officer whom I first met in Slovakia at the same time as Hazzard in 2003. "I can't take anybody with me who has the same memories. To have a social life, I have to create it. I have to make new friends. And then it all ends. After four years in Hong Kong in 2001, I cried on the way to the airport. I knew it was a whole life I was leaving behind once that plane took off. It's a little death every time. But I've never regretted joining the Foreign Service. It makes me feel alive."

Postscript

Now What?

When I set out to write this book, my main objective was not to judge, criticize or glorify the Foreign Service, but to tell its story. I thought that explaining what American diplomats do and why in plain English, humanizing their work, and making it interesting and even entertaining was a sufficiently challenging task. I wanted to provide as objective and accurate a picture of the service as possible, and leave the judging to the reader.

As you have no doubt noticed, there are elements of critique in the narrative, particularly in Part Four, which is titled "Looking In the Mirror" for a good reason. Most of that critique, however, comes from inside the service – U.S. diplomats offer their own views on what works and what doesn't, what might be improved and what is beyond repair.

So what are we supposed to do with all this information – both the stories and the critique?

Some might say that educating the reader about what diplomacy is today and what the Foreign Service does is enough. Indeed, education was part of my motivation in deciding to undertake this project. The work of American diplomats is too important to remain a mystery – the country's very security and prosperity depend on it. But the other part of my motivation was an attempt to provoke a public debate about diplomacy as a profession, and about what kind of Foreign Service the United States should have. After all, strong and effective U.S. diplomacy is in the interest of all Americans – and even the service's biggest fans would agree that it could do better.

A book is hardly enough to achieve such an ambitious goal, so I have decided to establish a nonprofit called Center on the Practice of Diplomacy. Its mission will be to demystify and humanize diplomacy in order to elevate its importance to U.S. national security in the public consciousness, and to serve as an incubator of ideas among practitioners about the future of their profession. The center will produce its own content on its website and in the media, and will host events around the country – and hopefully overseas – culminating in an annual conference in Washington.

If you'd like to get involved by making a donation or a grant to the effort to launch the center, or by helping to organize an event, please go to AmericasOtherArmy.com.

Now it's time to express my gratitude to those who helped me make this book a reality, beginning with the hundreds of Foreign Service members who shared their views and experiences with me. I was unable to quote everyone by name, but I thank them all for their cooperation, and for their service. Of course, the book would not have been possible without the willingness of the State Department to provide the unprecedented access it did over nine years – both in Washington and overseas. The Una Chapman Cox Foundation assisted with a travel grant during the initial research phase.

For the extraordinary opportunities they gave me while traveling with them around the world, I owe special thanks to *my* secretaries of state, as I call them – Hillary Clinton, Condoleezza Rice, Colin Powell and Madeleine Albright.

I'm also much indebted to the editors who gave me the assignment of accompanying these secretaries, including Julia Marozzi, formerly of the *Financial Times* in London, and former *Washington Times* editors David Jones and Barbara Slavin, who was also an invaluable consultant as I made my way through the huge amount of research and drafted each chapter.

For their help in the book's preparation, I'm profoundly thankful to my editors Darrell Delamaide and Markus Nottelmann, cover designer Jennifer Fleischmann, photographer Mary Calvert, as well as my research assistants Daniel Mahoney, Jane Xie, Daniel Fisher and Alexander Vagg.

I hope the book kept you good company, and I look forward to the day we meet.

Nicholas Kralev
Washington, D.C.
September 2012

References

Chapter 1

1. http://www.washingtonpost.com/wp-dyn/content/article/2011/02/21/AR2011022102801.html
2. http://www.whitehouse.gov/sites/default/files/rss_viewer/national_security_strategy.pdf
3. http://www.state.gov/documents/organization/153142.pdf
4. http://siadapp.dmdc.osd.mil/personnel/MILITARY/history/hst1112.pdf
5. http://siadapp.dmdc.osd.mil/personnel/CIVILIAN/fy2011/december 2010/december2010.pdf
6. http://www.gpo.gov/fdsys/pkg/BUDGET-2013-BUD/pdf/BUDGET-2013-BUD-18.pdf
7. http://comptroller.defense.gov/defbudget/fy2012/FY2012_Budget_Request_Overview_Book.pdf
8. http://www.gpo.gov/fdsys/pkg/BUDGET-2013-BUD/pdf/BUDGET-2013-BUD-7.pdf
9. http://www.imf.org/external/pubs/ft/weo/2012/01/weodata/index.aspx
10. http://www.defense.gov/speeches/speech.aspx?speechid=1199
11. http://www.defense.gov/speeches/speech.aspx?speechid=1211
12. http://www.gpo.gov/fdsys/pkg/BILLS-112hr5736ih/pdf/BILLS-112hr5736ih.pdf
13. http://www.state.gov/r/pa/prs/ps/2012/05/190757.htm
14. http://www.state.gov/s/partnerships/
15. http://bushlibrary.tamu.edu/research/pdfs/national_security_strategy_90.pdf
16. http://www.fas.org/spp/military/docops/national/1996stra.htm
17. http://pufone.org/blog/george-bush-nation-building-debate-2000-video/

Chapter 2

1. http://www.usdiplomacy.org/history/service/representative.php
2. http://www.diabetes.org/for-media/2012/state-dept-guidelines.html
3. http://news.bbc.co.uk/2/hi/south_asia/4021983.stm
4. http://mepi.state.gov/
5. http://www.glifaa.org/content/history
6. http://2010.census.gov/2010census/data/
7. http://www.nytimes.com/1988/12/07/us/bush-s-selections-for-united-

nations-cia-top-economic-posts-thomas- reeve.html
8. http://www.nytimes.com/1989/03/08/world/senate-backs-un-delegate.html
9. http://2001-2009.state.gov/secretary/rm/2009/01/115155.htm
10. http://history.state.gov/departmenthistory/people/principalofficers/career-ambassador
11. http://georgewbush-whitehouse.archives.gov/news/releases/2009/01/20090115.html
12. http://oig.state.gov/documents/organization/191912.pdf
13. http://oig.state.gov/documents/organization/156129.pdf
14. http://oig.state.gov/documents/organization/160374.pdf
15. http://transition.usaid.gov/policy/ads/400/fsa.pdf
16. http://www.foreignpolicy.com/articles/2003/07/01/rogue_state_department?page=full
17. http://www.foreignpolicy.com/articles/2003/07/01/foreign_disservice
18. http://articles.cnn.com/2003-10-09/us/robertson.state_1_pat-robertson-nuclear-device-nuclear-explosion
19. http://politicalticker.blogs.cnn.com/2011/11/07/perry-questions-intentions-of-american-diplomats/
20. http://georgewbush-whitehouse.archives.gov/news/releases/2009/01/20090115.html
21. http://www.afsa.org/FSJ/0612/files/assets/downloads/publication.pdf
22. http://2001-2009.state.gov/secretary/former/powell/remarks/2002/7330.htm

Chapter 3

1. Albright, Madeleine. "Madam Secretary." Miramax Books, 2003. Page 4.
2. http://www.gpo.gov/fdsys/pkg/BUDGET-1999-BUD/pdf/BUDGET-1999-BUD-7-3.pdf
3. http://www.pbs.org/newshour/bb/africa/embassy_bombing/map.html
4. http://2001-2009.state.gov/secretary/former/powell/travels/c13997.htm
5. http://obsdailyviews.blogspot.com/2012/02/madeleine-albright-on-iran-syria-and.html
6. http://2001-2009.state.gov/secretary/trvl/index.htm
7. http://www.state.gov/secretary/trvl/index.htm
8. http://www.commondreams.org/headlines04/0715-05.htm
9. http://www.washingtonpost.com/wp-dyn/content/article/2006/09/27/AR2006092700106.html
10. http://www.paloaltoonline.com/weekly/morgue/2005/2005_06_08.rickeys08ja.shtml
11. http://nicholaskralev.com/2010/03/01/political-punch-in-a-package-of-charm/
12. http://www.nytimes.com/2007/11/01/washington/01diplo.html
13. http://www.gao.gov/assets/600/591595.pdf
14. http://www.state.gov/secretary/rm/2009a/06/125083.htm
15. http://www.state.gov/secretary/rm/2011/12/178368.htm
16. http://www.state.gov/secretary/rm/2009a/02/119430.htm

17. http://www.hrw.org/news/2009/02/20/us-clinton-remarks-undermine-rights-reform-china

Chapter 4

1. http://2001-2009.state.gov/secretary/rm/2005/57602.htm
2. http://www.washingtonpost.com/wp-dyn/content/article/2005/11/01/AR2005110101644.html
3. http://2001-2009.state.gov/secretary/rm/2005/57643.htm
4. http://www.washingtontimes.com/news/2005/dec/8/20051208-113121-2797r/?page=all
5. http://news.bbc.co.uk/2/hi/americas/5321606.stm
6. http://wikileaks.org/cablegate.html
7. http://www.state.gov/documents/organization/112065.pdf
8. http://www.reuters.com/article/2012/07/03/us-pakistan-usa-nato-routes-idUSBRE8620V520120703
9. http://www.bbc.co.uk/news/world-asia-15901363
10. http://politicalticker.blogs.cnn.com/2011/05/03/sources-panetta-to-congress-pakistan-either-incompetent-or-involved/
11. http://www.washingtonpost.com/cia_contractor_raymond_davis_freed_after_blood_money_payment_/2010/08/19/AByVJ1d_page.html
12. http://www.nytimes.com/2011/03/17/world/asia/17pakistan.html?ref=global-home
13. http://www.nytimes.com/2012/06/06/world/asia/qaeda-deputy-killed-in-drone-strike-in-pakistan.html
14. http://www.whitehouse.gov/the-press-office/2012/06/05/press-briefing-press-secretary-jay-carney-secretary-education-arne-dunca
15. http://www.reuters.com/article/2011/04/21/us-pakistan-usa-aid-factbox-idUSTRE73K7F420110421
16. http://oig.state.gov/documents/organization/193863.pdf
17. http://www.reuters.com/article/2012/03/01/us-egypt-usa-ngos-idUSTRE8200H520120301
18. http://nicholaskralev.com/2010/02/27/the-new-statesman/
19. http://www.socialistinternational.org/
20. http://www.bbc.co.uk/news/world-europe-19017144
21. http://www.state.gov/documents/organization/153142.pdf
22. http://www.nytimes.com/2008/04/09/world/asia/09phils.html
23. http://articles.latimes.com/2003/mar/21/news/war-turkey21
24. http://www.state.gov/j/ct/rls/crt/2006/82738.htm
25. http://edition.cnn.com/2009/WORLD/meast/07/29/iraq.iranian.refugees/
26. http://articles.cnn.com/2012-02-18/middleeast/world_meast_iraq-camp-ashraf-relocation_1_iranian-opposition-group-iraqi-forces-iraqi-facility?_s=PM:MIDDLEEAST
27. http://www.nytimes.com/2003/04/01/world/belgium-rethinks-its-prosecutorial-zeal.html
28. http://2001-2009.state.gov/secretary/former/powell/remarks/2003/18810.htm
29. http://www.hrw.org/news/2003/08/01/belgium-universal-jurisdiction-law-repealed

30. http://www.nytimes.com/2003/06/14/world/belgium-resists-pressure-from-us-to-repeal-war-crimes-law.html
31. http://in.reuters.com/article/2012/07/04/kenya-iran-idINL6E8I46ST20120704

Chapter 5

1. http://www.whitehouse.gov/the-press-office/executive-order-national-export-initiative
2. http://www.trade.gov/press/press-releases/2012/jobs-supported-by-exports-031212.pdf
3. http://blogs.state.gov/index.php/site/entry/celebrating_economic_statecraft_day
4. http://www.state.gov/e/eb/rls/rm/2012/192236.htm
5. http://www.treasury.gov/press-center/press-releases/Pages/tg1623.aspx
6. http://www.state.gov/r/pa/prs/ps/2012/06/192408.htm
7. http://trade.gov/cs/about.asp
8. http://www.businessweek.com/ap/financialnews/D9RO8LQG0.htm
9. http://www.reuters.com/article/2011/12/20/aescorp-idUSL3E7NK6EU20111220
10. http://trade.gov/success/
11. http://www.cbsnews.com/8301-503543_162-20068872-503543.html
12. http://www.thenation.com/article/161057/wikileaks-haiti-let-them-live-3day
13. http://www.fas.usda.gov/ofso/overseas_post_directory/
14. http://www.fas.usda.gov/mos/em-markets/2010_1%20EMP_Success%20Stories.pdf
15. http://pakobserver.net/detailnews.asp?id=159068

Chapter 6

1. https://www.cia.gov/library/publications/the-world-factbook/geos/iv.html
2. http://www.bbc.co.uk/news/world-africa-12079552
3. http://www.nytimes.com/2011/05/22/world/africa/22ivory.html
4. http://corporate.discovery.com/our-company/map/
5. http://dosfan.lib.uic.edu/usia/usiahome/oldoview.htm
6. http://www.pewglobal.org/files/2012/06/Pew-Global-Attitudes-U.S.-Image-Report-FINAL-June-13-2012.pdf
7. http://www.youtube.com/watch?v=qKU7boFwLnU&feature=plcp
8. http://www.state.gov/r/pa/index.htm
9. http://www.bbg.gov/about-the-agency/board/
10. http://www.state.gov/documents/organization/181098.pdf
11. http://exchanges.state.gov/alumni/statealumni.html
12. http://www.nytimes.com/2012/05/05/us/politics/us-revises-foreign-student-job-program.html
13. http://video.msnbc.msn.com/rock-center/46741718#46741718
14. http://afp.google.com/article/ALeqM5jZ4MUOze82QJmr6Lv7C3

sbmc-K1w
15. http://www.thinktwicepakistan.com/portfolio/eighth-grader-stood-up-against-terrorism-for-education/
16. http://www.thinktwicepakistan.com/portfolio/drama-dhamak/
17. http://oig.state.gov/documents/organization/193863.pdf

Chapter 7

1. http://www.nctc.gov/site/groups/ai.html
2. http://www.america.gov/st/washfile-english/2006/May/20060525115413jmnamdeirfo.560177.html
3. http://news.bbc.co.uk/2/hi/middle_east/3712421.stm
4. http://www.washingtonpost.com/wp-dyn/articles/A21300-2004May12.html
5. http://articles.boston.com/2004-05-14/news/29210133_1_e-mails-show-berg-three-times-iraqi-police
6. http://adoption.state.gov/about_us/statistics.php
7. http://adoption.state.gov/
8. http://www.helpfinddavid.com/
9. Carman, Diane. "Travelers See Brits' Best, Yanks' Worst." Denver Post, July 2, 2003, Page B1.
10. https://house.resource.org/107/org.c-span.174085-1.raw.txt
11. https://house.resource.org/107/org.c-span.174085-1.raw.txt
12. http://nymag.com/nymetro/news/crimelaw/n_7909/
13. http://www.washingtontimes.com/news/2001/nov/15/20011115-031143-7857r/
14. http://globalresearch.ca/articles/COM403A.html
15. http://www.travel.state.gov/pdf/MultiYearTableI.pdf
16. http://www.fas.org/irp/news/2002/01/reidindictment.pdf
17. http://www.cbsnews.com/htdocs/pdf/Abdulmutallab_Indictment.pdf
18. http://www.washingtontimes.com/news/2010/jan/11/interagency-gaps-let-bomb-suspect-retain-visa/
19. http://www.whitehouse.gov/the-press-office/remarks-president-strengthening-intelligence-and-aviation-security
20. http://articles.timesofindia.indiatimes.com/2006-02-26/bangalore/27794487_1_visa-iisc-director-scientist
21. http://www.refuseandresist.org/article-print.php?aid=1019
22. http://www.iie.org/Research-and-Publications/Open-Doors/Data/International-Students/Enrollment-Trends/1948-2011
23. Jain, Piyush. "U.S. visa-seekers also look for some respect." Financial Times, September 13, 2006.
24. http://www.buffalo.edu/ubreporter/archives/vol35/vol35n2/articles/FSEC.html
25. http://www.travel.state.gov/pdf/FY2011NIVWorkloadbyVisaCategory.pdf
26. http://www.travel.state.gov/pdf/MultiYearTableI.pdf
27. http://travel.state.gov/visa/temp/wait/wait_4638.html
28. http://www.doi.gov/news/pressreleases/loader.cfm?csModule=

security/getfile&pageid=295021

29. http://tinet.ita.doc.gov/view/m-2011-I-001/table1.html
30. http://travel.state.gov/visa/temp/without/without_1990.html
31. http://www.cbc.ca/news/world/story/2011/01/12/haiti-anniversary-memorials.html
32. http://www.usatoday.com/news/world/2010-03-07-haiti_N.htm
33. http://foreignaffairs.house.gov/110/36725.pdf
34. http://travel.state.gov/passport/processing/processing_1740.html
35. http://travel.state.gov/passport/npic/agencies/agencies_913.html
36. http://www.foxnews.com/story/0,2933,330869,00.html
37. http://www.washingtonpost.com/wp-dyn/content/article/2008/06/05/AR2008060503469_pf.html
38. http://www.justice.gov/opa/pr/2003/May/03_crm_271.htm
39. http://www.justice.gov/opa/pr/2004/October/04_crm_715.htm
40. http://www.justice.gov/opa/pr/2003/June/03_crm_379.htm
41. http://federal-circuits.vlex.com/vid/usa-v-christ-matthew-35444680
42. http://www.state.gov/m/ds/rls/126748.htm

Chapter 8

1. http://www.law.georgetown.edu/journals/gjil/pdf/1_25_kauffman.pdf
2. http://2001-2009.state.gov/secretary/rm/2006/59306.htm
3. http://www.nytimes.com/2012/06/03/world/middleeast/crude-oil-output-is-soaring-in-iraq-easing-markets.html
4. http://adoption.state.gov/about_us/statistics.php
5. http://transition.usaid.gov/performance/afr/afr11.pdf?111811
6. http://transition.usaid.gov/careers/applicant.html
7. http://2001-2009.state.gov/secretary/rm/2006/59408.htm
8. http://transition.usaid.gov/performance/afr/afr11.pdf?111811
9. http://www.mcc.gov/pages/about
10. http://www.nytimes.com/interactive/2011/10/04/us/politics/us-foreign-aid-since-1977.html
11. http://foreignassistance.gov/CountryIntro.aspx
12. http://www.usaid.gov/results-and-data/progress-data/dollars-results-malaria-prevention-ghana-pilot
13. http://www.newyorker.com/archive/2003/05/05/030505ta_talk_mayer
14. http://www.bechtel.com/assets/files/projects/Accomplishments_and_Challenges.pdf
15. http://www.nytimes.com/2007/07/26/world/middleeast/26reconstruct.html
16. http://www.mcclatchydc.com/2011/12/19/133477/usaid-defends-34m-cuba-grant-program.html
17. http://mepi.state.gov/mepi/index.html
18. http://www.reuters.com/article/2011/10/07/us-nobel-peace-idUSTRE7963KM20111007
19. http://nobelpeaceprize.org/en_GB/laureates/laureates-2011/announce-2011/

20. http://www.state.gov/secretary/rm/2011/10/176354.htm
21. http://yemenpost.net/Detail123456789.aspx?ID=3&SubID=4252& MainCat=3
22. http://www.nytimes.com/2012/05/10/world/middleeast/years-of-us-saudi-teamwork-led-to-airline-plots-failure.html
23. http://www.bbc.co.uk/news/world-middle-east-17163321
24. http://www.arabianpeninsula.mepi.state.gov/b_11242010.html
25. http://www.arabianpeninsula.mepi.state.gov/s_05022009.html
26. http://www.usaid.gov/what-we-do/democracy-human-rights-and-governance/supporting-free-and-fair-elections
27. http://www.usaid.gov/what-we-do/democracy-human-rights-and-governance/supporting-vibrant-civil-society-independent-media
28. http://www.unhcr.org/4fd6f87f9.html
29. http://www.acf.hhs.gov/programs/orr/data/fy2011RA.htm
30. http://www.state.gov/documents/organization/153142.pdf
31. http://www.state.gov/secretary/rm/2012/07/195001.htm
32. http://news.bbc.co.uk/2/hi/south_asia/4801513.stm
33. http://transition.usaid.gov/pk/newsroom/news/earthquake/120613-earthquake.html
34. http://www.usaid.gov/what-we-do/water-and-sanitation
35. http://www.usaid.gov/what-we-do/water-and-sanitation/advancing-water-supply-sanitation-and-hygiene
36. http://www.nigeriamarkets.org/files/MARKETS%20Overview.pdf
37. http://www.usaid.gov/news-information/videos/markets
38. http://www.usaid.gov/what-we-do/global-health
39. http://transition.usaid.gov/press/speeches/2010/sp100618.html
40. http://islamabad.usembassy.gov/pr-coalition.html
41. http://www.usaid.gov/what-we-do/economic-growth-and-trade/supporting-private-enterprise
42. http://uk.reuters.com/article/2012/07/11/uk-saudi-economy-reform-idUKBRE86A0NT20120711

Chapter 9

1. http://www.stripes.com/news/kirkuk-reconstruction-team-sees-progress-but-fears-cutbacks-1.84081
2. http://web.archive.org/web/20080710055236/http://www.usip.org/pubs/specialreports/sr185.pdf
3. http://kabul.usembassy.gov/ipa.html
4. http://www.dvidshub.net/video/149467/prt-khost-package-long#.UA8m-jGe75Z
5. http://www.nytimes.com/2011/09/14/world/asia/14afghanistan.html
6. http://www.sigir.mil/files/audits/12-020.pdf
7. http://www.sigir.mil/files/audits/12-020.pdf
8. http://afp.google.com/article/ALeqM5hdTq2NlmOyHFT43YFJQocu VES37A
9. http://www.sigir.mil/files/audits/12-020.pdf
10. http://oversight.house.gov/wp-content/uploads/2012/06/6-28-12-NatSec-Kennedy.pdf

11. http://costsofwar.org/
12. http://www.wartimecontracting.gov/docs/CWC_FinalReport-lowres.pdf
13. http://www.state.gov/documents/organization/153142.pdf
14. http://www.fbi.gov/chicago/press-releases/2009/cg050409.htm

15. http://www.sigir.mil/files/quarterlyreports/July2012/Section5_-
_July_2012.pdf
16. http://www.marqardakhschool.org/

Chapter 10

1. http://history.state.gov/departmenthistory/people/principalofficers/
director-foreign-service-institute
2. http://2001-2009.state.gov/secretary/rm/2006/59306.htm
3. http://www.state.gov/m/fsi/
4. http://www.presidency.ucsb.edu/PS157/assignment%20files%20public
/TOWER%20EXCERPTS.htm

Chapter 11

1. http://www.state.gov/secretary/rm/2009a/02/116022.htm
2. http://fsitraining.state.gov/training/Training_Toolkit_for_FS/
Specialists_Toolkit/Foreign_Service_Promotion_Precepts.pdf
3. http://whirledview.typepad.com/files/joan-score-sheet-3.pdf
4. http://whirledview.typepad.com/files/osc-state-1.pdf

Chapter 12

1. http://www.washingtonpost.com/wp-
dyn/content/article/2010/01/15/AR2010011504026.html
2. http://www.nytimes.com/2008/01/02/world/africa/02sudan.html
3. http://news.bbc.co.uk/2/hi/middle_east/4796280.stm
4. http://www.time.com/time/magazine/article/0,9171,900329,00.html
5. http://www.pbs.org/wgbh/pages/frontline/shows/target/etc/cron.html
6. http://www.pbs.org/newshour/bb/africa/embassy_bombing/map.html
7. http://glifaa.org/
8. http://www.state.gov/secretary/rm/2011/12/178368.htm

Index

Made in the USA
Lexington, KY
09 March 2013